Object-Oriented Programming Using C++

COURSE
TECHNOLOGY

ONE MAIN STREET, CAMBRIDGE, MA 02142

an International Thomson Publishing company I(T)P®

Cambridge • Albany • Bonn • Boston • Cincinnati • London • Madrid • Melbourne • Mexico City
New York • Paris • San Francisco • Singapore • Tokyo • Toronto • Washington

Object-Oriented Programming Using C++

Joyce Farrell

McHenry County College

COURSE
TECHNOLOGY

ONE MAIN STREET, CAMBRIDGE, MA 02142

an International Thomson Publishing company I(T)P®

Cambridge • Albany • Bonn • Boston • Cincinnati • London • Madrid • Melbourne • Mexico City
New York • Paris • San Francisco • Singapore • Tokyo • Toronto • Washington

Object-Oriented Programming Using C++ is published by Course Technology.

Managing Editor	Kristen Duerr
Product Manager	Cheryl Ouellette
Editorial Assistant	Margarita Donovan
Developmental Editor	Mary-Terese Cozzola
Production Editor	Catherine G. DiMassa
Text Designer	Kim Munsell
Cover Designer	Douglas Goodman

© 1998 by Course Technology— I(T)P®

For more information contact:

Course Technology, Inc.
One Main Street
Cambridge, MA 02142

International Thomson Editores
Seneca, 53
Colonia Polanco
11560 Mexico D.F. Mexico

ITP Europe
Berkshire House 168-173
High Holborn
London WCIV 7AA
England

ITP GmbH
Königswinterer Strasse 418
53227 Bonn
Germany

ITP Asia
60 Albert Street, #15-01
Albert Complex
Singapore 189969

Nelson ITP, Australia
102 Dodds Street
South Melbourne, 3205
Victoria, Australia

ITP Japan
Hirakawacho Kyowa Building, 3F
2-2-1 Hirakawacho
Chiyoda-ku, Tokyo 102
Japan

ITP Nelson Canada
1120 Birchmount Road
Scarborough, Ontario
Canada M1K 5G4

ISBN 0-7600-5044-9

Printed in the United States of America

1 2 3 4 5 6 7 8 9 01 00 99 98

Preface

Object-Oriented Programming Using C++ is designed for a second programming course and assumes that students have a basic programming background. Basic C++ concepts are provided in the Overview, in which all the basic C++ knowledge the student should have is summarized. However, a student who has not programmed in C or C++ before will probably want to consult a more introductory text for a deeper understanding of the finer points of the language.

Organization and Coverage

Object-Oriented Programming Using C++ contains an Overview and 10 tutorials that present hands-on instruction. In these tutorials students learn to understand and appreciate the object-oriented approach. Each tutorial is divided into two lessons in which explanatory text is interspersed with step-by-step production of code. When students complete this book, they will have an understanding of object-oriented concepts as they apply to programming, and the ability to use these concepts to develop C++ programs.

Approach

Object-Oriented Programming Using C++ teaches object-oriented concepts using C++ as a tool to demonstrate these concepts. This book teaches programming concepts using a task-driven rather than a command-driven approach. By working through the tutorials, students learn how to apply concepts in a concrete fashion.

Features

Object-Oriented Programming Using C++ is an exceptional textbook because it also includes the following features:

- **Objectives**   A brief list of objectives appears at the beginning of each tutorial so the student has an overview of the main topics to be covered.
- **Tutorial Cases**   Each tutorial begins with a programming-related problem, followed by a demonstration of an application that solves the problem. Showing students the completed application before they learn how to create it is motivational and instructionally sound. By allowing the students to see the application, they can see that the concepts they are about to learn have a useful purpose. By allowing the students to examine the code they are about to create, they can see how an object-oriented solution to a problem can be implemented.
- **Lessons**   Each tutorial is divided into two lessons, A and B. Breaking each tutorial into two lessons provides a convenient point to stop, summarize, and review concepts in reasonably-sized units. Lessons or entire tutorials can be assigned to students based on whether the class meets once per week for a longer period of time, or two or three times per week for a shorter period.

- **Step-by-Step Methodology**   The unique Course Technology methodology keeps students on track. Students read about a concept, then enter code within the context of solving the problem posed in the tutorial case and using the concepts just presented.
- **TIPs**   provide additional information about a procedure or topic—for example, an alternative method of performing a procedure.
- **Summaries**   Following each lesson is a summary that recaps the programming concepts and commands covered in the lesson.
- **Questions and Exercises**   Each lesson concludes with meaningful questions that test students' understanding of what they learned in the lesson, and exercises that provide students with the opportunity to apply the concepts they have mastered.
- **Debugging Exercises**   Each lesson ends with debugging exercises—programs with a few syntax or logical errors. The student can find the errors and fix them, developing the crucial skills of reading others' programs, analyzing probable cause of errors, and solving problems.

The Supplements

- The author wrote the Instructor's Manual and it was quality assurance tested. It is available electronically on CD-ROM or through the Course Technology Faculty Online Companion on the World Wide Web. (Call your customer service representative for the URL and your password.) The Instructor's Manual contains the following items:
  - **Cases** that can be assigned as semester projects.
  - **Answers** to all of the questions and solutions to all of the exercises.
  - **Tutorial notes** that contain background information from the author about the Tutorial Case and the instructional progression of the tutorial.
- **Course Test Manager** provides a powerful testing and assessment package that enables instructors to create and print custom tests from a test bank of questions designed specifically for this book. The questions can be selected individually or at random, and it can print scrambled versions of the same test. In addition, instructors with access to a networked computer lab (LAN) can administer, grade, and track tests on-line.
- **Solution files** are included for every file students are asked to create or modify in the tutorials and exercises.
- **Student files** containing all of the data that students will use for the tutorials and exercises are provided through Course Technology's Online Companion, as well as on disk. A Readme file includes technical tips for lab management. See the inside front cover of this book and the "Read This Before You Begin" page before the Overview for more information on Student Files.

Acknowledgments

I would like to thank all of the people who helped make this book a reality, especially Mary-Terese Cozzola, my Development Editor. You have provided great service with patience and humor. Thanks also to Kristen Duerr, Managing Editor; Cathie DiMassa, Production Editor; and Brian McCooey and Seth Freeman, Quality Assurance testers.

I am grateful to the many reviewers who provided helpful and insightful comments during the development of this book, including Kevin Egypt, Durham Community Technical College; Stephen Kolars, San Antonio College; Randy Weinberg, St. Cloud State University; and Cathy Holloway, Tidewater Community College.

I would like to personally thank my husband Geoff, whose encouragement and support made this entire task possible. My children, Andrea and Audrey, endured my many hours at the keyboard, and patiently waited for their own phone calls while I was in conference with my developmental editor.

Joyce Farrell

Brief Contents

Contents

t u t o r i a l   6

OVERLOADING *221*

t u t o r i a l   7

INHERITANCE *261*

t u t o r i a l 8

ADVANCED INPUT AND OUTPUT 301

t u t o r i a l 9

TEMPLATES 331

t u t o r i a l   10

EXCEPTION HANDLING *359*

i n d e x *386*

Read This Before You Begin

To the Student

Student Data Flles

To complete the tutorials and exercises in your book, you will need data files. You can access these files on the World Wide Web at www.course.com and download them to your hard drive. Or, if you do not have access to the Web, your instructor can provide the files for you.

Using Your Own Computer

If you are going to work through this book using your own computer, you will need a C++ compiler. This text was written so that any C++ compiler can be used. The programs used in this book (except in Tutorial 10) were written on a Borland C++ compiler, version 3.0, and tested on Borland C++ 4.0 and 5.0, and Microsoft Visual C++, version 5.0. No special memory or hard disk requirements apply.

Older compilers may not support templates as discussed in Tutorial 10.

- **Student Data Files** Ask your instructor or lab manager for details on how to get Student Data Files. You will not be able to complete the tutorials or exercises in this book using your own computer until you have Student Data Files. The files may also be obtained electronically through the Internet. See the inside front cover of this book for more details.

Visit Our World Wide Web Site

Additional materials designed especially for you are available on the World Wide Web. Go to **www.course.com**.

To the Instructor

To complete the tutorials in this book, your students must use a set of student data files. These files are included in the Instructor's Resource Kit. They may also be obtained electronically through the Internet. See the inside front cover of this book for more details. Follow the instructions in the Readme file to copy the files to your server or standalone computer. You can view the Readme file using a text editor such as WordPad or Notepad.

Once the files are copied, you can make Student Disks for the students yourself, or tell students where to find the files so they can make their own Student Disks.

Course Technology Student Data Files

You are granted a license to copy the Student Data Files to any computer or computer network used by students who have purchased this book.

An Overview of Object-Oriented Programming and C++

The Task of Programming

Programming a computer involves writing instructions that enable a computer to carry out a single task or a group of tasks. Writing these sets of instructions, which are known as **programs** or **software**, requires using a computer programming language and resolving errors in the instructions so that they work correctly.

As with any language, learning a computer **programming language** requires learning both vocabulary and syntax. Just as humans speak a variety of languages, such as English and Japanese, programmers use many different programming languages, including BASIC, Pascal, COBOL, RPG, and **C++**.

tip

An **interpreter** is a program that translates instructions one line at a time; a **compiler** works by translating the entire program at once. C++ is a compiled language.

tip

Selecting data for testing is an art in itself. For example, imagine that you write a program to add two numbers, and test the program with the values 2 and 2. You cannot be sure that the program is free of logical errors just because the answer comes out 4. Perhaps you used the multiplication symbol rather than the addition symbol. You can confirm your program's accuracy by testing the program several times using a variety of data.

tip

All modern programming languages require that variable names be one word; that is, they cannot include any embedded spaces. Each programming language has other specific rules as to which characters are not allowed and how many characters may be used in the variable name.

The rules to any language make up its **syntax**. Writing in a programming language requires correct use of that language's syntax. In English, using incorrect syntax—that is, committing a **syntax error**—might make communication more difficult but usually will not prevent it altogether. If you ask, "Name yours what is?", most people will still be able to figure out what you mean. If you are vague or spell a word wrong when writing, most people will nevertheless understand your message. Computers are not nearly as smart as most humans, or as flexible. As a result, using correct syntax in a computer program is not just important—it's essential.

Most of today's programming languages follow syntax rules that are close enough to human language to make them accessible to anyone willing to learn and practice them. The statements you write in such a programming language must be subsequently translated into machine language, which is language that the computer can understand. A translator (called either a compiler or an interpreter) changes your written program statements into machine language and tells you whether you have committed any syntax errors. Therefore, syntax errors are not a big problem; you always have an opportunity to fix them before they can do any damage. For example, if you write a computer program in C++ but spell a word incorrectly or reverse the required order of two words, the compiler will inform you of such errors and will not let you run the program until you have corrected them.

Much more time-consuming to a programmer than syntax errors are logical errors. A **logical error** occurs when you use a statement that, although syntactically correct, doesn't do what you intended. For a program that is supposed to add two numbers and display the sum, logical errors arise when multiplication is used instead of addition, or when the sum is displayed before the arithmetic occurs. The language compiler will not tell you when you have committed a logical error; only running and testing your program will enable you to find any inappropriate statements. You **run** a program by issuing a command to execute the program statements. You **test** a program by using sample data to determine whether the program results are correct.

Programming Universals

All modern programming languages have several elements in common. For example, all programming languages provide methods for directing **output**—the information produced by a program—to a desired source such as a monitor screen, printer, or file. Similarly, all programming languages provide methods for sending **input**—the information produced by an outside source such as a keyboard, scanner, or file—into the computer program so that it can be manipulated.

tip
....

Ideally, variables have meaningful names, although no programming language actually requires that they meet this standard. A payroll program, for example, will be easier to read if a variable that is meant to hold your salary is called YourSalary, but it would be *legal* to call the variable ImHungry or JqxBr.

In addition, all programming languages provide for naming locations in computer memory. These locations are **variables** (or **attributes**). For example, if a person asks, "What is YourAge?", YourAge is considered a variable for two reasons: YourAge has different (varied) values for different people and any person can have a change in age. When writing a computer program, YourAge becomes the name of a position or location in computer memory; the *value at* that location or the *state of* that location may be 18 or 80, or it may be unknown.

A variable may have only one value at a time, but it is the ability of memory variables to *change* in value that makes computers and programming worthwhile. Because one memory location, or variable, can be used repeatedly with different values, program instructions can be written once and then used for thousands of problems. Thus, one set of payroll instructions at your company might produce every individual's paycheck and a variable for hourly wage might be reused for each employee.

In many computer languages, including C++, variables must be explicitly **declared**, or given a type and a name, before they can be used. The **type** determines what kind of values may be stored in a variable. Most computer languages allow at least two types: one for numbers and one for characters. **Numeric variables** hold values like *13* or *-6*. **Character variables** hold values like 'A' or '&'. Many languages include even more specialized types, such as **integer** (for storing whole numbers) or **floating point** (for storing numbers with decimal places). Some languages, including C++, also let you create your own types. The distinction between variable types is important because computers handle the various types of data differently; each type of variable requires a different amount of storage and answers to different rules for manipulation. When you declare a variable with a type, you aren't merely naming it, you are giving it a set of characteristics and allowable values.

Procedural Programming

For most of the history of computer programming, which now covers roughly 50 years, most programs were written procedurally. **Procedural programs** consist of a series of steps or procedures that take place one after the other. The programmer determines the exact conditions under which a procedure takes place, how often it takes place, and when the program stops.

Procedural programs are written in many programming languages, such as COBOL, BASIC, FORTRAN, and RPG. You can also write procedural programs in C++. Although each of these languages has a different syntax, they all share many elements.

Over the years, as programmers have sought better ways to accommodate the way people work best on computers, procedural programming techniques have evolved into object-oriented techniques.

Early Procedural Programs

When programming languages were first used, the programmer's job was to break down the task at hand into small, specific steps. Each step was then coded in an appropriate language.

Consider a program that creates customer bills for a small business. If you could write the program in English rather than a programming language, a simple version of the program might look something like:

```
Read in CustomerOrder from disk
Print CompanyName
Print CompanyAddress
Print CompanyCity, CompanyState, and CompanyZipCode
Print NameOfCustomer
Print CustomerAddress
Print CustomerCity, CustomerState, and CustomerZipCode
Determine PriceOfItemOrdered
Multiply PriceOfItemOrdered by QuantityOrdered giving BalanceDue
Print BalanceDue
```

The programmer creates every step needed to produce a bill. He or she also chooses descriptive variable names that are unique; CompanyCity is a different variable than CustomerCity, even though both may be located in the same city.

Three basic structures are used in procedural programming. In the first structure, a **sequence**, program steps happen one after another, without interruption. The order of some of the statements is important; you must determine the price of an item before you can multiply it by the quantity. For some other statements, however, order is unimportant. You can just as easily determine the price of the item and perform the multiplication before printing the company's or customer's name and address as after carrying out these tasks.

A second structure is the **loop**. When companies bill customers, they usually bill many customers at one time. The relevant program accesses a customer record from an input file, produces a bill, and continues to repeat the same steps until no more customers remain on the file.

```
Read in CustomerOrder from disk
While there are records on the disk
    Print CompanyName
    Print CompanyAddress
    Print CompanyCity, CompanyState, and CompanyZipCode
    Print NameOfCustomer
    Print CustomerAddress
    Print CustomerCity, CustomerState, and CustomerZipCode
    Get PriceOfItemOrdered
    Multiply PriceOfItemOrdered by QuantityOrdered giving BalanceDue
    Print BalanceDue
    Read in another CustomerOrder from disk
```

A usable loop structure must contain two very important parts. A test of a condition is required to determine whether some action should continue to take place: While there are records on the disk. In addition, an action must change the condition tested: Read in another CustomerOrder from disk. At some point, when you test the condition again, you'll find that you have reached the end of the records on the disk. It will then be time to move out of the loop and on to the next procedure in the program.

The third structure that may be included in procedural programs is **selection**, which you use to perform different tasks based on a condition. Perhaps you give a $5 discount to any customer who orders more than a dozen of an item.

```
Read in CustomerOrder from disk
While there are records on the disk
    Print CompanyName
    Print CompanyAddress
    Print CompanyCity, CompanyState, and CompanyZipCode
    Print NameOfCustomer
    Print CustomerAddress
    Print CustomerCity, CustomerState, and CustomerZipCode
    Get PriceOfItemOrdered
    Multiply PriceOfItemOrdered by QuantityOrdered giving BalanceDue
    If QuantityOrdered > 12 subtract $5 from BalanceDue
    Print BalanceDue
    Read in another CustomerOrder from disk
```

In this example, $5 is deducted from the BalanceDue if—and only if—the customer orders more than 12 items. The statement can also be constructed as follows:

```
If QuantityOrdered > 12 subtract $5 from BalanceDue
    else subtract $0 from BalanceDue
```

The actual program that produces bills for a company is far more detailed than this example. What if we're out of stock? What if the BalanceDue becomes negative after deducting the $5? What about taxes? Consequently, the step-by-step process can be far more detailed (and tedious). Luckily, many programming languages allow for a degree of data abstraction.

Modularity and Abstraction

Programming in the oldest procedural languages had two major disadvantages:

- The process involved so much detail that the programmer (and any person reading the program) lost sight of the big picture.
- Similar statements required in various parts of the program had to be rewritten in more than one place.

A helpful step in program writing occurred with the development of methods that allowed programmers to group statements together into modules. Modules are known in various programming languages as functions, procedures, subroutines, or simply routines. For example, you can create a module named PrintCompanyData that contains the following statements:

```
Print CompanyName
Print CompanyAddress
Print CompanyCity, CompanyState, and CompanyZipCode
```

You can then change the billing program.

```
Read in CustomerOrder from disk
While there are records on the disk
   PrintCompanyData
   Print NameOfCustomer
   Print CustomerAddress
   Print CustomerCity, CustomerState, and CustomerZipCode
   Get PriceOfItemOrdered
   Multiply PriceOfItemOrdered by QuantityOrdered giving BalanceDue
   If QuantityOrdered > 12 subtract $5 from BalanceDue
   Print BalanceDue
   Read in another CustomerOrder from disk
```

The program including this module is slightly shorter than the original program because three separate statements are "summarized" by a single module name. The use of the module name in the program represents a **call** to the module.

Modular programs are easier to read because one descriptive name represents an entire series of detailed steps. If more modules are created, the main program changes as follows:

```
Read in CustomerOrder from disk
While there are records on the disk
    PrintCompanyData
    PrintCustomerData
    CalculateBalance
    Print BalanceDue
    Read in another CustomerOrder from disk
```

Programming computers in the oldest programming languages—machine language and assembly language—is called **low-level** because you must deal with the details of how the machine works physically. In contrast, languages such as COBOL and BASIC are called **high-level** because the programmer need not worry about hardware details. Although C++ is a high-level language, it is sometimes referred to as **mid-level** because it contains features that allow you to use it on either a high or low level.

The new program is more concise and more understandable; it is also more abstract. **Abstraction** is the process of paying attention to important properties, while ignoring details. Of course, you must attend to the details at some point; the individual modules must eventually be written in a step-by-step process. However, the main program can be written by using abstract concepts to represent sets of finer details.

When working with real-world objects, you take abstraction for granted. For example, you can talk on the telephone without considering how the signals are transmitted. If you had to worry about every low-level detail, from how the words are formed in your mouth to how the phone charges are billed to your account, you would never complete a call.

Programming in a high-level programming language allows you to take advantage of abstraction. When you write a command to send output to a printer, you don't instruct the printer about how to actually function—how to form feed the paper, dispense ink, and print each character. Instead, you simply write an instruction such as `Print BalanceDue` and the hardware operations are carried out automatically.

Besides the advantage of abstraction, modular programs can be written more quickly because different programmers may be assigned to write different modules. If the program contains four modules, four programmers can work simultaneously, with each handling one-fourth of the job.

Finally, a well-written module may be called from another place within the same program or from another program. Many applications can use the module that prints a company's name and address, for example. Whether you are preparing job estimates, year-end tax returns, or stockholder reports, you need to print the company name and address.

Information Hiding

Besides a copy of a value, you can pass a memory address to a function.

Another advance in programming occurred when programming languages became capable of passing values from one module to another. **Passing a value** means that a copy of the data in one module of a program can be sent to another module for its use.

As noted earlier, a module that prints a company's name and address is useful in many applications within that company. A module that prints *any* name and address that is passed to it, on the other hand, has value in many applications for companies all over the world.

Passing values to a module represents the first step toward information hiding. **Information hiding** means that a programmer can write a program or module and use procedures developed by others without knowing the details of those procedures. Just as you need know only the correct telephone number to dial to reach a specific party, using a procedure requires that you know only the information it requires. You need to recognize the **interface** to the procedure—that is, what type and how much data to send it. You don't need to understand how the procedure uses the input data as long as it gives the desired results.

For example, imagine that you can create a NameAddress procedure for the billing program:

```
Print Name
Print Address
Print City, State, and ZipCode
```

The billing program uses this module twice:

```
Read in CustomerOrder from disk
While there are records on the disk
   NameAddress  (pass Company data)
   NameAddress  (pass Customer data)
   CalculateBalance
   Print BalanceDue
   Read in another CustomerOrder from disk
```

Languages that use only global variables typically call their modules **subroutines**. Languages that allow local variables and the passing of values are more likely to call their modules **procedures** or **functions**.

Global and Local Variables

All programming languages allow **global** variables—that is, variables whose names are known to all modules in the program. To beginning programmers, global variables seem like a highly useful option. If a variable holds the customer's zip code, why not call it CustomerZipCode and let every module in the program access the data stored there?

A large program with many routines, however, is unlikely to be written by a single programmer. If all variables are global, then each programmer working on a module must know the name of the CustomerZipCode variable for two reasons: to use it in that module and to avoid using that name for some other purpose.

You may want to use a useful and well-written module that includes CustomerZipCode in other programs in the company, for years to come. If it is a global variable, however, then all programmers working on subsequent programs must recognize the name and purpose of the CustomerZipCode variable.

What if the routine proves so useful that you want to sell it to other companies? Every programmer in the world would then need to know about the global CustomerZipCode variable name, and none could use it for any other purpose in a program.

Multiply those limitations by all variable names used in all possible programs, and you can see that using global variable names correctly would soon become impossible.

When you write the NameAddress procedure, you choose variable names that are **local**—that is, only known to, and available in, that procedure. When another module calls the NameAddress routine, ZipCode may receive a company zip code, customer zip code, supplier zip code, or employee zip code. To the NameAddress routine, each item is simply ZipCode; with each separate call to the NameAddress procedure, ZipCode holds a different value. A module that calls NameAddress could even include its own variable called ZipCode. Because NameAddress receives a copy of whatever data is passed to it, a ZipCode variable in the calling program would not conflict with the local ZipCode variable in the NameAddress routine.

Encapsulation

When procedures use local variables, the procedures become relatively autonomous "mini-programs." Routines that contain their own sets of instructions and their own variables remain independent of the program that calls them. The details within a routine are hidden and contained—that is, **encapsulated**—which helps to make the routine reusable.

Many real-world examples of encapsulation exist. When you build a house, you don't invent plumbing and heating systems. Rather, you reuse previously designed and tested systems. You don't need to know the fine details of how the systems work; they are self-contained units you incorporate in your house. This type of encapsulation certainly reduces the time and effort necessary to build a house. Assuming the plumbing and electrical systems you choose are already in use in other houses, using existing systems also improves your house's **reliability**. Besides not needing to know how your furnace works, if you replace one model with another, you don't care if its internal operations differ. The result—a warm house—is what's important.

Similarly, reusable software saves time and money and enhances reliability. If the NameAddress routine has been tested before, you can be confident that it will produce correctly spaced and aligned output. If another programmer creates a new and improved NameAddress routine, you don't care how it works as long as it prints the data correctly.

The concept of passing variables to procedures allows programmers to create variable names locally in a procedure without changing the value of similarly named variables found in other procedures. Procedural programming with procedures has limitations, however. You must know the names of the procedures, and you can't reuse those names within the same program. You also must know the type of data to pass to a procedure. If you need a similar procedure that works on a different type of data, you must create a new procedure with a different name. These limitations are eliminated in object-oriented programs.

Object-Oriented Programming

Object-oriented programming adds several new concepts to programming and requires a different way of thinking:

- You analyze the objects with which you are working and the tasks that need to be performed with and on those objects.
- You pass messages to objects, requesting the objects to take action.
- The same message works differently (and appropriately) when applied to the various objects.
- A procedure can work appropriately with different types of data it receives, without the need for separate procedures.
- Objects can share or **inherit** traits of previously created objects, thereby reducing the time it takes to create new objects.
- Information hiding is more complete than in procedural programs.

Object-Oriented Thinking

To see object-oriented thinking in action, consider your everyday life. The "real world" is full of objects. A door, for example, needs to be opened and closed. You pass messages by turning its knob. The same message (turning a knob) has a different result when applied to your radio. The "open" event works differently on a door than on a desk drawer, a bank account, or a computer file, but you can call all of these operations "open." A new door with a stained glass window inherits most of its traits from a standard door. When you use a door, you usually do not care about the latch or hinge construction features, and you don't have access to the interior workings of the knob or what may be written on the inside of the door panel.

Consider a typical object-oriented program, such as a Windows word-processing program, spreadsheet, or game. In each case, a window is an object that can be opened, closed, maximized, minimized, and dragged. A user may initiate several events (pass messages to a window) with a mouse or keyboard. The "click" event works differently when it occurs with a minimize button than when it relates to an item within the window. The effect of a particular keystroke combination differs according to the other keystrokes or mouse clicks that have come before it. When a programmer writes a new Windows program, the Windows features are not created from scratch; they are inherited. When you use a Windows application, you are relatively unconcerned with how minimization works; likewise, you usually can't change the size of the font used in the menu or eliminate the control box.

For another example of object-oriented thinking, consider our customer billing program. It might contain an object called PreferredCustomerBill. To think about a PreferredCustomerBill as an object, you must determine the tasks that it must perform. Perhaps you must add new transactions to, apply payments to, apply a discount to, and print the PreferredCustomerBill. A program may pass a message to the PreferredCustomerBill to instruct it to perform any of those tasks. Applying a payment works differently when the bill is overdue (interest is charged) or when the customer uses a credit card. When you create the PreferredCustomerBill, it may inherit the traits of the RegularCustomerBill. In turn, a new object called PreferredCustomerYearEndSummary may inherit the traits of the PreferredCustomerBill. Some applications that use the PreferredCustomerBill should not be allowed to alter a customer's balance or date due; these data items should remain hidden and inaccessible.

What You Should Know About Object-Oriented Programming

The basic principles behind using object-oriented programming techniques involve:

- objects
- classes
- inheritance
- polymorphism

If you have programmed in any object-oriented language, you should be familiar with each of these concepts. By working through the lessons and exercises in this text, you will gain mastery of these concepts as they apply to C++. For now, we will provide a brief overview of each.

Objects and Classes

It is hard to discuss objects without mentioning classes; it is equally difficult to discuss classes without bringing up objects. An **object** is any *thing*. A **class** consists of a category of things. An object is a specific item that belongs to a class; it is called an **instance** of a class. A class defines the characteristics of its objects and the methods that can be applied to its objects.

For example, Dish is a class. You know that you can hold a Dish object in your hand, and that you can eat from it. MyDilbertMugWithTheChip is an object and a member of—or an instance of—the Dish class. This situation is considered an **is-a** relationship because you can say, "My coffee mug is a dish." Each button on the tool bar of a word-processing program is an instance of a Button class. In a program used to manage a hotel, Penthouse and BridalSuite are instances of HotelRoom.

Inheritance

The concept of class is useful because of its reusability; you can create new classes that are descendants of existing classes. The descendent classes can **inherit** all of the attributes of the original (or **parent**) class or they can override inappropriate attributes. In geometry, a Cube is a descendent of a Square. A Cube has all Square attributes, plus one additional characteristic: depth. A Cube, however, has a different method of calculating TotalArea (or Volume) than a Square has. In business, an EmployeeWorkRecord class, created to hold and manipulate an employee's job history with the company, may be descended from the EmployeeInitialApplication class. EmployeeWorkRecord inherits methods for using Name and HireDate, but adds Promotion and SalaryHistory data.

Polymorphism

Functions may occasionally need to operate differently depending on the context. Object-oriented programs use the feature **polymorphism** to carry out the same operation in a manner customized to the object. Such differentiation is never allowed in languages that aren't object-oriented.

Without polymorphism you would have to use a separate name to multiply two integers or two floating-point numbers. A third function is needed also to multiply three numbers. Just as your blender can produce juice regardless of whether two fruits or three vegetables are inserted, the object-oriented multiplication function will give a product whether it receives two integers or three floating-point numbers. Similarly, the operation of a ComputePay function may vary according to whether the employee is salaried rather than paid hourly; likewise, a ComputeGradePointAverage uses different methods when a course is Pass-Fail rather than graded, and a word-processing program produces different results when you press Delete when one word in a document is highlighted than when a filename is highlighted.

What You Should Know About C++

This book expands your knowledge of object-oriented programming by guiding you through the design and testing of several related programs in C++, reviewing basic principles and introducing more advanced principles along the way. Just as you can use the piano as a basis for studying music theory and subsequently apply what you have learned to guitar, saxophone, or voice, you can apply the principles described here to other programming languages such as Java, SmallTalk, or Object Pascal.

Using C++ to write programs involves innumerable details. This book is directed to individuals who have used C++ or C to write programs in the past. For the finer details of the language, you should consult an introductory C++ text, although the major ideas and commands are summarized here.

The C++ Programming Environment

Depending on your C++ installation, the compiler may be accessed by clicking an icon, making a selection from a menu, or typing a command line from your operating system.

The main work area in any C++ programming environment is the editor. An **editor** is a simplified version of a word processor in which you can type your program statements, or **source code**. C++ source code files are typically saved with a .CPP extension.

In some programming environments, the file extensions may vary or not exist at all.

After you enter the code for a program, it must be compiled. **Compiling** is the process by which the code you have written becomes transformed into machine language—the language that the computer can understand. The output from the compilation is **object code**. When a C++ program is compiled, a file is created that has the same filename as the source code, but an .OBJ extension.

A runnable, or **executable**, program needs the object code as well as code from any outside sources (other files) to which it makes reference. The process of integrating these outside references is called **linking**. An executable file contains the same filename as the source code and the object code, but carries the extension .EXE to distinguish it as a program.

When you compile a C++ program, **error messages** and/or **warnings** may appear. A C++ program with errors will not execute; all such error messages must be eliminated before it will run. Although a warning will not prevent a program from executing, it should be examined closely, as it probably indicates a problem. For example, if you try to display a variable that does not exist, C++ will issue an error message, such as "Undefined symbol." If you attempt to display a variable that exists but has not been assigned a valid value, C++ will not issue an error message, but will issue a warning, such as "Possible use of variable before definition."

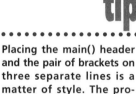

The main() Function

C++ programs consist of routines called modules or functions. Every function includes a function header and a function body. The initial line of code in a C++ function makes up the **function header**, which always has three parts:

- the type of variable that the function will return to the function that calls it
- the name of the function
- in parentheses, the types and names of any variables that the function receives

If you envision a butterfly's metamorphosis to a caterpillar as being a function, then the function header for metamorphosis would be `butterfly metamorphosis(caterpillar)`. In this case, butterfly is returned from the function, metamorphosis is the name of the function, and caterpillar is the input into the function.

Every C++ program contains at least one function called **main**. If the main function does not pass values to other programs or receive values from outside the program, then main() receives and returns a void type. (**Void** simply means "nothing.") Many C++ programs begin with the header `void main(void)` or, for simplicity, `void main()`.

The body of every function in a C++ program is contained in curly brackets. Therefore, the simplest program you can write has the following form:

```
void main()
    {
    }
```

C++ statements are placed between the opening and closing brackets. Every complete C++ statement ends with a semicolon. Often, several statements must be grouped together—for example, when several statements must occur in a loop. In such a case, the statements will have their own set of opening and closing brackets within the main brackets, forming a **block**. One universal C++ truth: Every C++ program must contain exactly the same number of opening brackets as closing brackets.

Working with Variables

In C++, variables (sometimes called **identifiers**) must be named and given a type before they can be used.

Names of C++ variables can include letters, numbers, and underscores, but must begin with a letter or underscore. No spaces or other special characters are allowed within a C++ variable name. Age, LastName, tax_1999, ready2go, salary, Salary, and SALARY are all valid variable names. Note that salary, Salary, and SALARY could all be used within the same C++ function without conflict because C++ is case-sensitive. C++ programmers typically use all lowercase letters for variable names or else capitalize only the first letter of each new word (after the first word) in a variable name (for example, lastYearGross).

A C++ keyword cannot be used as a variable name. Common C++ keywords are listed in Table O-1. Although keywords vary for each C++ compiler, it is better not to use any of these terms as variables. That way, your code will be portable to other compilers.

and	double	not_eq	this
and_eq	dynamiccast	operator	throw
asm	else	or	true
auto	enum	or_eq	try
bitand	explicit	overload	typedef
bitor	extern	private	typeid
bool	false	protected	typename
break	float	public	uchar_t
case	for	register	union
catch	friend	reinterpret_cast	unsigned
char	goto	return	using
class	if	short	virtual
compl	inline	signed	void
const	int	sizeof	volatile
constcast	long	state_cast	wchar_t
continue	mutable	static	while
default	namespace	struct	xor
delete	new	switch	xor_eq
do	not	template	

Table O-1: C++ Keywords

On some computer systems, only the first 31 characters of a variable name are actually used. Thus, variable names should be limited to 31 characters, or at least be unique within the first 31 characters.

Each named variable must have a type. C++ supports three simple types: integer, floating point, and character.

An **integer** is a whole number, either positive or negative. Examples are 4, 15, +5000, and -10. Integers do not include decimal points, and they may not be written with commas, dollar signs, or any symbols other than a leading + or -. (Of course, if a + symbol is not used, the integer is assumed to be positive.)

tip
• • • • • • • • • • • • • •
▶ **You can determine the size of variables in your system with the sizeof() operator. For example, to find how much memory an integer uses, you can place this statement in a program:**
```
cout<<"Integer size"
<<sizeof(int)
<<"on computer";
```
Output might then be: Integer size 2 on computer.

tip

When an integer is stored in two bytes, the 16 bits used can form only 65,536 combinations; thus, only 65,536 different integer values can be stored. One bit indicates whether the value is positive or negative; the other 15 bits can represent values from -32,768 through +32,767. Problems arise when a programmer forgets those limits. If you store a value of 60000 in an integer named salary and then print it out, C++ will not produce any error message, but will display –5536 rather than 60,000. Because 60,000 is larger than 32,767, C++ misinterprets salary as a negative number.

tip

A single character, such as 'D', is contained in single quotes. A string value such as "Donna" (see "Working with Strings" later in this overview) uses double quotes.

tip

Unlike most other programming languages, C++ allows you to assign values to several variables in one statement. For example, tot = sum = amount = 0; assigns a value of 0 to all three variables listed in the statement.

An integer value may be stored in an **integer variable** declared with the keyword **int**. Three other options exist for declaring an integer variable: **short int, long int,** and **unsigned int**. The amount of memory each requires depends upon the computer system, but a short int may take less memory than an int, and a long int may take more than an int. (But maybe not! The amount of memory used depends upon your system.) An unsigned int may be declared if the value in a variable will always be positive—for example, in the case of an annual salary.

Real or **floating-point numbers** are numbers that include decimal positions, such as 98.6, 1000.0002, and -3.85. They may be stored in variables with types **float, double,** and **long double**. The amount of storage required for each of these types varies from computer to computer. Usually, a double occupies more memory space than a float (allowing a double to provide greater precision), but not necessarily. A long double typically provides more memory space than a double. A double will always take no less storage space than a float, and a long double will invariably require no less space than a double.

Characters may be stored in variables declared with the keyword **char**. (Some people pronounce this keyword as "care" because it comes from "character"; others pronounce it "char" because of the way it is spelled.) A **character** may hold any single symbol in the ASCII character set. Often, it contains a letter of the alphabet, but it could include a space, digit, punctuation mark, arithmetic symbol, or other special symbol. In C++, a character value is always expressed in single quotes, such as 'A' or '&'.

To declare a variable, list its type and its name. A variable declaration is a C++ statement, so it must end with a semicolon. For example, int score; is a complete C++ statement that declares an integer variable named score.

Variables may be declared anywhere in a C++ program, but are often declared just after the opening curly brackets in a function. This traditional format makes the variables easier to locate when reading the function later.

Explicitly stating the value of a variable is called **assignment**. It is achieved with the assignment operator =. You may assign a value to a variable in the same statement that declares the variable, or you may wait until later. For instance, both

```
int testScore;
testScore = 98;
```

and

```
int testScore=98;
```

reserve a memory location for an integer named testScore and assign the value 98 there.

tip

• • • • • • • • • • • • • • • •

▶ Assignment always takes place from right to left; that is, a value on the right side of the assignment operator is stored in the memory location (variable) to the left of the assignment operator. Although `testScore = 98` **and** `98 = testScore` **are equivalent statements in algebra, the second statement is not allowed in C++.** `testScore` **cannot be stored in the memory location 98 because that location does not exist. C++ refers to locations in which values may be stored as Lvalues because these values may appear on the left side of assignment statements.**

tip

• • • • • • • • • • • • • • • •

▶ If you are using an older version of C++, the string type may not be defined. In such a case, add the following at the top of your program before declaring a string:

`#include<string.h>`
`typedef char string [40];`

The #include statement includes the header file that contains definitions of the functions used with strings. The typedef statement defines a new type, named string, consisting of 40 characters. You may change this number as needed.

If a C++ program includes more than one variable of the same type, the variables may be declared in the same statement or in separate statements. A declaration statement may include only one type, however. Some, none, or all of the variables may be given initial values. You must declare variables of different types in separate statements.

Once C++ programmers get used to placing a semicolon at the end of each statement, they may become carried away and put a semicolon at the end of every line. Sometimes a statement may extend across several lines; use a semicolon only when the entire statement is complete.

The const Qualifier

A variable that will not change in a program should not be declared as a variable. (After all, it is not going to vary.) Instead, it should be a constant. The statement `const double minimumWage = 4.75;` declares a constant named minimumWage that may be used like a variable, but may not be changed during a program. The keyword const is called a qualifier because it qualifies, or restricts, the ordinary capabilities of the named type (such as double).

Working with Strings

A string is actually an array of characters. An array is a series of contiguous memory locations, all holding data of the same type, and all of which can be referenced as a group via a single name.

Integers, floats, doubles, and strings are **scalar variables,** or variables that cannot be divided further into any legitimate type. A **string** is a nonscalar type that can be segmented into characters. A variable of type char can hold only one character. To store a name, address, product code, or description, you must use more than one adjacently stored character, or a string. To use all the operations and functions associated with strings, include the statement `#include<string>` or `#include<string.h>` at the top of your program. You can then declare a string such as `string firstName;`.

Creating Comments

Comments are statements that do not affect the compiling or running of a program. That is, they do not show up when the program runs. Comments are simply explanatory remarks that the programmer includes in a program to clarify what is taking place. These statements are useful to later users of a program because they may help explain the intent of a particular statement or the purpose of the entire program. In addition, comments may indicate who wrote the program and when. They may even help the programmer remember why she did something a certain way when she wrote the program weeks or months earlier.

tip

When using block comments, don't start a comment that never ends. Using a /* without a corresponding */ makes everything from that point on in the program a nonexecuting comment.

C++ supports both line comments and block comments. A **line comment** begins with two slashes (//) and continues to the end of the line on which it is placed. It may take up an entire line, or it may begin after some executable C++ code and take up the rest of the line. A **block comment** begins with a slash and an asterisk (/*) and ends with an asterisk and a slash (*/); it may be contained on a single line or continued across many lines. Like a line comment, a block comment may take up an entire line, or it may occur on a line along with executable code, either before or after the code. In the following example, the only executable code is the output of "Hello!".

```
// this is a comment on one line
/* this comment is on a different line */
/* this is in front */ cout<<"Hello!"; //this is in back
/* this comment runs across
    3 lines of code just to show
    that it can be done !      */
```

tip

Throughout this text, comments are used to point out features in code examples. Sometimes a comment will even indicate that a statement is invalid. This type of comment is for instruction; obviously, you wouldn't use such comments in professional programs.

Using Libraries and Preprocessor Directives

C++ programs will often refer to variables and code that lie outside the source code the programmer actually writes. C++ is powerful in part because many of its functions have already been written for you. For example, taking the square root of a number is a fairly complicated mathematical task, but the creators of C++ have written a function that calculates the square root of a number. You can include this function, sqrt(), in your own C++ programs—but only if the programs can find it when you link to outside files to create executable files.

Header files are files that contain predefined values and routines, such as sqrt(). Their file names usually end in .H. In order for your C++ program to use these predefined routines, you must include a **preprocessor directive**, a statement that tells the compiler to do something before compiling the program. In C++, all preprocessor directives begin with a pound sign (#), which is also called an **octothorp**.

The **#include** preprocessor directive tells the compiler to include a file as part of the finished product. In any program, you might include a special-purpose file you wrote, or you might include a file that is packaged with your C++ compiler. For example, to use the sqrt() function, you need to use #include<math.h>. You will need another include directive to use C++ input and output statements.

tip

The angle brackets in `#include<math.h>` indicate that the math.h file is found in the standard directory that holds "include" files.

C++ Output and Input

C++ provides several objects for producing output. The simplest is an object called **cout**, pronounced "see out." Its name comes from Console OUTput, and cout displays whatever is passed to it. When contained in a complete C++ program, the statement `cout<<"Hi there";` displays the phrase "Hi there" on the monitor. The insertion symbol (<<) says "insert whatever is to my right into the object cout."

The object cout is contained in the header file iostream.h. The term iostream is short for Input Output STREAM. The preprocessor directive `#include<iostream.h>` must appear at the top of any program that uses cout. Therefore, the complete program

```
#include<iostream.h>
void main()
  {
    cout<<"Hi there";
  }
```

will compile, execute, run, and produce output on the monitor.

You could replace the cout statement above with two cout statements:

```
cout<<"Hi";
cout<<"there";
```

Even though this version of the program uses two cout statements, nothing indicates that any output should be placed on a new line. To indicate a **newline** character, you can use the **escape sequence \n**. The backslash removes the usual meaning of the letter *n*, (which is simply to produce the letter *n*, as in the statement `cout<<'n';`) and causes the display to move to a new line. The statement `cout<<"Hi\nthere";` displays "Hi" and "there" on two separate lines.

Alternatively, you can use the end line manipulator **endl**. Inserting endl into the output stream causes \n plus all waiting output to display, a process called **flushing the buffer**. The following code produces "Hi" and "there" on two separate lines:

```
cout<<"Hi";
cout<<endl;
cout<<"there";
```

A single cout object may display more than one item, as long as each item is preceded by its own insertion symbol. For example, `cout<<"Hi there"<<endl;` displays "Hi there" and flushes the buffer.

A program in which the programmer predetermines all variable values is not very useful, however. Many programs rely on input from a user. The **cin** (pronounced "see in") object fetches values from the keyboard. It is used with the **extraction operator** >>. Like cout, cin is contained in the iostream.h header file.

Prior to a cin statement, it is almost always necessary to provide the user with a **prompt**, or a short explanation of what is expected. You may confirm that the data were actually entered and stored by echoing them, or displaying them in an unaltered form, soon after input.

```
cout<<"Enter score ";
cin>>score;
```

In the program segment above, a prompt displays and the program pauses until a user types in a score and presses Enter. As with cout, one cin object may be used to enter more than one value.

```
cout<<"Please enter three scores ";
cin>>score1>>score2>>score3;
```

At the prompt "Please enter three scores," the user may enter three integers with any white space between them. **White space** consists of spaces, tabs, and enters.

Arithmetic Operators

Often, after data values are input, you perform calculations with them or make decisions based on them.

C++ provides five simple arithmetic operators for creating arithmetic expressions: addition (+), subtraction (-), multiplication (*), division (/), and modulus (%). Each of these arithmetic operators is a **binary operator**. That is, each takes two operands, one on each side of the operator, as in 12 + 9.

The results of an arithmetic operation may or may not be stored in memory. For example,

```
cout<<12+9;
```

and

```
sum=12+9;
cout<<sum;
```

both result in 21 displaying on the monitor. In the second code fragment, however, sum contains the result of the addition and can be accessed again.

Addition, subtraction, multiplication, or division of any two integers results in an integer. For example, the expression 7+3 results in 10, and the expression 7/3 results in 2. When two integers are divided, any fractional part of the result is lost.

If either or both of the operands in addition, subtraction, multiplication, or division is a floating-point number, then the result is also a floating-point number.

The modulus operator (%), which gives the remainder of integer division, may be used only with integers. The expression 7%3 results in 1, because 3 goes into 7 two times with one remaining.

When more than one arithmetic operator is included in an expression, then multiplication, division, and modulus operations always occur before addition or subtraction. Multiplication, division, and modulus are said to have **higher precedence**. When two operations with the same precedence appear in an expression, then the operations are carried out from left to right. For example, the expression 2 + 3 * 4 results in 14 (not 20) because the multiplication of 3 and 4 takes place before 2 is added. All precedence rules can be overridden with parentheses. Thus, the expression (2 + 3) * 4 results in 20 (not 14) because the expression within the parentheses is evaluated first.

In addition to the standard binary arithmetic operators for addition, subtraction, multiplication, division, and modulus, C++ employs several shortcut operators.

A common programming procedure is to produce a total by adding a variable's value to a running total. In C++, you can add a variable named Num to a variable named Total with the statement

```
Total = Total + Num
```

or

```
Total += Num
```

Each expression means "Take the value in Num, add it to Total, and store the result in Total," or "Replace the value of Total with the new value you get when you add Num to Total."

Similarly, C++ provides the -= operator for subtracting a value from another and the *= operator for multiplying one value by another.

Another common programming task is to add 1 to a variable—for example, when keeping count of how many times an event has occurred. C++ provides four ways to add 1 to a variable:

```
count = count + 1;
count += 1;
++count;  // This ++ is called a prefix operator
count++;  // This ++ is called a postfix operator
```

Each of these options means "Replace the current value of count with the value that is 1 more than count," or simply "Increment count." As you might expect, you can use two minus signs (− −) before or after a variable to decrement it.

Evaluating Other Expressions

Determining the value of an arithmetic expression like 2 + 3 * 4 is straightforward. In addition, however, C++ evaluates many other expressions that have nothing to do with arithmetic.

C++ employs six relational binary operators, which are listed in Table O-2.

==	equivalent to
>	greater than
>=	greater than or equal to
<	less than
<=	less than or equal to
!=	not equal to

Table O-2: Relational operators

All false relational expressions are evaluated as 0. Thus, an expression such as 2 > 9 has the value 0. You can prove that 2 > 9 is evaluated as 0 by entering the statement cout<<(2>9); into a C++ program. A 0 will display on output.

All true relational expressions are evaluated as 1. Thus, the expression 9 > 2 has the value 1. You can prove this point by entering the statement cout<<(9>2); into a C++ program. A 1 will display on output.

The unary operator ! means **not**. It essentially reverses the true-false value of an expression. For example, cout<<(9>2); displays a 1 because "9 is greater than 2" is true. In contrast, cout<<!(9>2); displays a 0 because "not 9 greater than 2," although grammatically awkward, is a false statement.

The operator == deserves special attention. Suppose two variables, q and r, have been declared, and q = 7 and r = 8. The statement cout<<(q==r); produces 0 (false) because the value of q is not equivalent to the value of r. The statement cout<<(q=r);, however, produces 8. The single equal sign does not compare two variables; instead, it assigns the value of the rightmost variable to the variable on the left. As r is 8, q becomes 8, and the value of the entire expression is 8. A common C++ programming error is to use the assignment operator (=) when you actually intend to use the comparison operator (==).

Selection and Looping

Computer programs seem smart because of their ability to use selections. They gain power because of their ability to loop. C++ supports a variety of ways to perform selection and looping.

The if Statement

The primary C++ selection statement is an if statement. The **single-alternative** if takes the form

if (*expression*)

   statement;

where *expression* is any C++ expression that can be evaluated, and *statement* is any C++ statement or block of statements.

For example,

```
if(driverAge<26)
    premiumDue+=100;
```

If the expression in the parentheses is true, then the statement following the if will execute; if the driverAge is less than 26, then 100 will be added to the premiumDue. The parentheses surrounding the evaluated expression are essential.

If the execution of more than one statement depends upon the selection, then the statements may be blocked with curly brackets.

```
if(driverAge<26)
  {
    premiumDue+=100;
    cout<<"Driver is under 26";
  }
```

The **dual-alternative if** uses an **else** to determine the action to take when an if expression is evaluated as false. For example,

```
if(genderCode=='F')
  cout<<"Female";
else
  cout<<"Male";
```

Note the semicolon following the first statement and before the else; it is required.

An else must always be associated with an if. Of course, several statements may also be blocked in the else portion of the selection.

Any C++ expression may be evaluated as part of an if statement. If the expression is evaluated as 0, it is considered false, and the statement or statements following the if will not be executed. If the expression is evaluated as 0 and an else exists, then the statements in the else block will be executed. If the expression in an if statement is evaluated as *anything* other than 0, it is considered to be true. In that case, any statement associated with the if will execute.

Any C++ statements may appear in the block associated with an if, and any C++ statements may appear in the block associated with an else, including other ifs and elses.

The switch Statement

When different outcomes are desired for different specific values of an integer variable, a series of ifs may be used.

```
if(dept==1)
   cout<<"Human Resources";
else
  if(dept==2)
     cout<<"Sales";
   else
     if(dept==3)
       cout<<"Information Systems";
     else
        cout<<"No such department";
```

tip

The switch can contain any number of cases in any order. The values in the case statements do not have to occur in descending order as they do in this example, nor do they have to be consecutive.

As an alternative, you can use the **switch statement**. For example,

```
switch(dept)
       {
       case 1:
         cout<<"Human Resources ";
         break;
       case 2:
         cout<<"Sales";
         break;
       case 3:
         cout<<"Information Systems";
         break;
       default:
         cout<<"No such department";
       }
```

The keyword **switch** identifies the beginning of the statement. The variable in parentheses is then evaluated. Each case following the opening curly brackets is compared with dept. As soon as a case equaling the value of dept is found, all statements from that point on execute until either a break statement or the final curly bracket in the switch is encountered. If we remove the break statements from this code, all four cout statements will execute when dept is 1. The default option is executed when no cases are equivalent to the value of dept.

The if Operator

Another alternative to the if statement involves the **if operator** (also called the **conditional operator**), which is represented by a question mark (?). The if operator provides a way to express two alternatives in a concise manner. Consider the statements `cout<<((driverAge<26) ? "Driver is under 26" : "Driver is at least 26");`. If the driverAge is less than 26, the first message will display; if the driverAge is not less than 26, the second message will display. The question mark is necessary after the evaluated expression, and a colon must be included between the two alternatives.

Logical And and Logical Or

In some programming situations, two (or more) conditions must be true to initiate an action. For example, let's say you wish to display the message "Discount should apply" if a customer visits your store more than five times a year and spends at least $1000 during the year. Assuming the variables are declared and have been assigned reasonable values, the following code works correctly using a nested if—that is, one if statement within another if statement.

```
if(numVisits>5)
        if (annualSpent>=1000)
                cout<<"Discount should apply";
```

tip

You may not enter a space between the ampersands (&&) in a logical and; likewise, a space cannot separate the pipes (||) in a logical or.

If numVisits is not greater than 5, the statement is finished—the second comparison will not even take place. Alternatively, a **logical and (&&)** can be used:

```
if(numVisits>5 && annualSpent>=1000)
    cout<<"Discount should apply";
```

You read the above code as "If numVisits is greater than 5 *and* annualSpent is greater than or equal to 1000, display "Discount should apply"." As with the nested ifs, if the first expression (numVisits > 5) is not evaluated as true, then the second expression (annualSpent >= 1000) will not be evaluated.

In certain programming situations, only one of two alternatives must be true for some action to take place. Perhaps the store will deliver merchandise if a sale amounts to at least $300 or if the customer lives within the local area code, no matter what the sale total. Two if statements could be used to display a "Delivery available" message:

```
if (saleAmt >= 300)
    cout<<"Delivery available";
else
    if(areaCode==localCode)
      cout<<"Delivery available";
```

If the saleAmt is at least $300, the conditions for delivery are established, and the areaCode will not be evaluated. A **logical or** (||) could be used as well:

```
if(saleAmt >=300 || areaCode==localCode)
  cout<<"Delivery available";
```

Read this statement as "If the saleAmt is greater than or equal to 300 or the areaCode is equivalent to the localCode, then display 'Delivery available'." As with the code using the two ifs, if the first condition in the or expression is evaluated as true, then the second expression will not be evaluated.

The while Loop

Loops provide a mechanism with which to perform statements repeatedly and, just as importantly, to stop when warranted.

In C++, the **while** statement may be used to loop. For example,

```
count = 1;
while(count<5)
    {
     cout<<count;
    ++count;
    }
```

If you create an infinite loop, either on purpose or by accident, you can stop it by holding down the Ctrl key and pressing the Pause/Break key.

C++ also provides a do statement. It takes the form

do
  statement;
while (expression);

The do statement may be used when the statements in the body of the loop must execute at least once. In a do loop, the expression is not evaluated until the "bottom" of the loop.

Any C++ expression may be placed inside the required parentheses, and, just as with the if statement, the statements inside the while block will be executed if the expression is evaluated as true (nonzero). With a while statement, however, when the expression is evaluated as true, the statements that follow will execute repeatedly as long as the expression remains true.

When creating loops in a computer program, you always run the risk of creating an **infinite loop**, or a never-ending loop. For example,

```
e = 1;
while (e < 2)
 cout<<"Help! I can't stop! ";
```

Because e is initially evaluated as less than 2, and the statement in the body of the loop does nothing to change its value, the expression e < 2 will continue to be evaluated as true forever. As a result, "Help! I can't stop!" will display again and again.

The for Statement

The **for statement** represents an alternative to the while statement. It is most often used in a **definite loop**, or a loop that must execute a definite number of times. It takes the form

```
for(intialize;evaluate;alter)
        statement;
```

Inside the parentheses, semicolons separate the three items—initialize, evaluate, and alter.

Initialize represents any steps you want to take at the beginning of the statement. Most often, this step involves initializing a loop control variable, but it can consist of any C++ statement or even several C++ statements separated with commas.

Evaluate represents any C++ expression. Most often it compares the loop control variable with a limit, but it may include any C++ expression. If the evaluation is true (not 0), any statements in the for loop are executed. If the expression is evaluated as false (0), the for statement is completed, and program execution continues with the next statement, bypassing the body of the for statement.

If the evaluation of the expression between the semicolons is true and the statements in the body of the loop are executed, then the final portion of the for loop, represented by *alter*, takes place after the statements are complete. Most often, this step changes the value of the loop control variable in some way, but you can use any C++ statements.

For example, the while loop that produces the output **1 2 3**

```
j=1;
while(j < 4)
  {
    cout<<" "<<j;
    ++j;
  }
```

can be rewritten as a for loop:

```
for(j=1; j<4; ++j)
    cout<<" "<<j;
```

Although the code used in the for loop is more concise than that in the while loop, the execution is the same. With the for statement, you are less likely to make common looping mistakes, such as not initializing the variable that controls the loop or not changing the value of the loop control variable during loop execution. Those mistakes remain possibilities, however, because C++ allows you to leave empty any of the three items inside the for loop parentheses (the two semicolons are still required).

SUMMARY

- Computer equipment is considered hardware. The instructions written in a computer programming language that tell the computer what to do are called software or programs.
- Compilers or interpreters are translators that check a program for syntax errors. Logical errors can be found by running and testing a program.
- All programming languages provide methods for producing output, accepting input, and declaring variables. In declaring variables, you give them a name, a type, and, optionally, a value.
- Procedural programs consist of a series of steps or procedures that take place one after the other. They contain steps in sequence, loops, and selections.
- Reasonable programming units that perform smaller tasks are known as modules, functions, procedures, subroutines, or routines.
- The use of routines allows abstraction, the process of paying attention to important properties, while ignoring nonessential details.

- Functions or modules may use local variables (known only to the routine) rather than global variables (known to the entire program).

- The use of abstraction and local variables, combined with the capabilities of encapsulation or information hiding, makes code reliable and easy to reuse.

- Computer programs that focus on objects and events are called object-oriented programs. These programs focus on objects, the necessary tasks to be performed on the objects, and the messages sent to objects.

- The major principles involved in object-oriented programming are objects, classes, inheritance, and polymorphism.

- An object is an instance of a class, which defines the characteristics of the object.

- Classes can inherit attributes from parent classes.

- Polymorphism is the feature that enables the same operation to be carried out differently depending on the object involved.

- An editor is a simplified version of a word processor in which you can write your program statements (source code).

- The C++ compiler may issue error messages or warnings.

- C++ programs are made up entirely of functions, each of which includes a header and a body.

- C++ function headers have three parts: the type of variable that the function will return to the function that calls it, the name of the function, and the types of any variables that will be passed to the function (enclosed in parentheses).

- The body of every function in a C++ program is surrounded by curly brackets.

- Each C++ program must include a main() function. Most programs begin with `void main()`.

- Every complete C++ statement ends with a semicolon. When several statements need to be grouped together, the block of statements will have its own set of opening and closing brackets within the main opening and closing brackets.

- C++ variables can be named with letters, numbers, and underscores, but must begin with a letter or underscore. Although variables may be declared anywhere in a C++ program, they are commonly placed just after the opening curly brackets in a function.

- C++ supports three simple variable types: integer, floating point, and character.

- You assign a value to a variable with the assignment operator (=). Assignment always takes place from right to left.

- Strings require special include statements to enable the use of appropriate C++ operators and functions.

- Comments are program statements that provide explanatory remarks. A line comment begins with two slashes (//) and continues to the end of the line on which it is placed. A block comment begins with a slash and an asterisk (/*) and ends with an asterisk and a slash (*/); it may be contained on one line or continued across many lines.

- Header files contain predefined values and routines. Use of a header file requires the use of the preprocessor directive #include.

- The cout function displays whatever is passed to it and uses the insertion operator <<.

- \n indicates new line. The manipulator endl can be used to insert a '\n' and flush the buffer.

- The cin function fetches values from the keyboard, using the extraction operator >>. A prompt—that is, a short explanation of what is expected from the user—often precedes a cin statement.

- C++ provides five binary operators for creating arithmetic expressions: addition (+), subtraction (-), multiplication (*), division (/), and modulus (%).

- Shortcut operations include +=, -=, and *=. You may also use ++ or -- before or after a variable to increase or decrease its value by 1.

- C++ employs six conditional binary operators: ==, >, <, >=, <=, and !=.
- All true expressions are evaluated as 1. All false expressions are evaluated as 0.
- You use an if statement, a switch statement, or the ? operator to make a selection.
- Two or more conditions may be tested using the and (&&) or the or (||) operators.
- You can use a while or a for statement to loop.
- The const qualifier can be used with values that should not change.

QUESTIONS

1. Writing instructions that enable a computer to carry out a task or group of tasks is known as _____.
   a. processing
   b. programming
   c. editing
   d. compiling

2. The physical components of a computer system are called _____.
   a. hardware
   b. software
   c. firmware
   d. programs

3. Another term for programs is _____.
   a. input
   b. floppy disks
   c. hardware
   d. software

4. C++, BASIC, Pascal, COBOL, and RPG are all _____.
   a. operating systems
   b. codes
   c. programming languages
   d. hardware

5. The rules to any programming language are its _____.
   a. syntax
   b. interpretation
   c. logic
   d. customs

6. A translator that notes whether you have used a language correctly may be called a _____.
   a. thesaurus
   b. compiler
   c. coder
   d. decoder

7. Using a statement at the wrong time or with an inappropriate object creates a _____.
   a. logical error
   b. syntax error
   c. compiler error
   d. language error

8. A program that predicts the exact sequence in which events will take place is said to be _____.
   a. compiled
   b. interpreted
   c. procedural
   d. object-oriented

9. Which type of statement does not occur in computer programs?
   a. sequence
   b. loop
   c. denial
   d. selection

10. Paying attention to the important properties while ignoring inessential details is known as _____.
    a. selectiveness
    b. polymorphism
    c. abstraction
    d. summarizing

11. Sending a copy of data to a program module is called _____.
    a. passing a value
    b. making a reference
    c. recursion
    d. setting a condition

12. When you understand the type of data to send to a procedure, you understand the procedure's _____.
    a. limits
    b. hidden information
    c. interface
    d. protocol

13. Variable names known only to the procedure in which they are declared are _____.
    a. local
    b. global
    c. recent
    d. internal

14. Object-oriented programmers primarily focus on _____.
    a. procedures to be performed
    b. the step-by-step statements needed to solve a problem
    c. objects and the tasks that must be performed with those objects
    d. the physical orientation of objects within a program

15. A major advantage of inheritance is _____.
    a. reducing the time it takes to create new objects
    b. not having to think about how objects will be used
    c. reducing the amount of memory required to execute a program
    d. enabling people who have not studied programming to create useful applications

16. An object is _____.
    a. a category of classes
    b. a name given to a class
    c. an instance of a class
    d. the same as a class

17. Object is to class as _____.
   a. library is to book
   b. mother is to daughter
   c. Plato is to philosopher
   d. president is to Lincoln

18. Inheritance occurs when a class adopts all the traits of _____.
   a. an object
   b. a parent class
   c. a variable
   d. a function

19. The feature that allows the same operations to be carried out differently depending on the object is _____
   a. polymorphism
   b. polygamy
   c. inheritance
   d. multitasking

20. Which English language example best represents polymorphism?
   a. taking a nap as opposed to taking a bribe
   b. killing time as opposed to killing a bug
   c. ordering a pizza as opposed to ordering a soldier
   d. all of the above

E X E R C I S E S

1. List the steps or procedures for each of the following. Include at least one example of a loop and one example of a selection in this process.
   a. shopping for new shoes
   b. filling a customer's catalog order
   c. computing the amount of federal income tax you owe

2. Many systems are modular. Name some modules within each of the following systems:
   a. a stereo
   b. a college
   c. a payroll system

3. Name a class that contains each of these objects:
   a. William Shakespeare
   b. a customer letter indicating that an item has been backordered
   c. a refund check to a customer who has overpaid

4. Name three objects in each of these classes:
   a. vehicle
   b. business license
   c. year-end reports for a company

5. To review your C++ skills, write short procedural programs for the following:
   a. Write a program that lets the user input two integers. The output is the larger of the integers.
   b. Write a program that lets the user input two integers. The output is one of three messages:
   First integer is larger.
   Second integer is larger.
   Integers are the same.
   c. Write a program that displays "Go Team!" seven times.
   d. Write a program that asks the user for an integer and then displays "Go Team!" that many times.

debugging ▶ 6. Each of the following files in the OVERVIEW folder contains syntax and/or logical errors. Determine the problem in each case, and fix the program.
   a. DEBUGO-1
   b. DEBUGO-2
   c. DEBUGO-3

C++ Functions

case ▶ Teacher's Pet is a software firm that specializes in children's educational programs. You've just landed your first job there as a C++ programmer. The opportunity is perfect for you: the company needs someone who knows C++ syntax, but they are willing to teach you object-oriented concepts.

Your supervisor at Teacher's Pet is Audrey Burns. "Your first assignment is to create a simple program that displays a sum when a child enters two numbers," Audrey tells you. "This project won't be truly object-oriented, but object-oriented programming requires that you be very comfortable with C++ functions. You can begin by creating a program that uses functions extensively."

"Okay," you say. "Let me get to work."

Previewing the TWONUMS Program

The TWONUMS program gives directions, and then allows the user to input numbers. Next, the user guesses the sum of the two numbers. If he or she enters an incorrect sum, the correct answer is displayed. After the completion of five problems, session statistics are shown.

1   Start your C++ compiler and load the **TWONUMS.CPP** program.

2   Run the program and follow the on-screen directions to play. The program will ask for two numbers, and then wait for you to enter their sum. If you answer incorrectly, the correct answer will be displayed. (Make sure you compute some problems incorrectly so that you can see this feature work.)

3   After the fifth pair of numbers, a summary of your activity displays. Press any key when you have finished viewing the summary.

4   Examine the code to get a feel for the structure of the program. You will be creating this program in Tutorial 1.

LESSON A

objectives

In this lesson you will learn:

- What a function is
- What benefits are offered by procedural abstraction
- How to create global and local variables
- How to create a function prototype
- How to return values from functions
- How to pass values to functions

Functions

What Is a Function?

With any computer programming language, large programs are usually broken down into modules. This strategy allows you to think of the programming task more abstractly—that is, to establish an overview of the major procedures before determining the detailed steps within those procedures. Creating modules makes it easier to work with programs, allows several programmers to write or modify modules in the same program, and enables you to create reusable pieces. In C++, these modules are known as functions.

Functions are miniprograms that perform some task or group of tasks. Each function may include its own variables and its own statements. Any statement that is allowed in the main() function of a C++ program can be used in any other function. When you write a main() function, you may include other functions that are part of the same file; alternatively your functions may be stored in their own files and then included in other C++ programs with an #include statement.

Although the following program is very simple, it demonstrates how a function is used within a program that displays a company logo on the monitor. Imagine that a co-worker creates a function called displayLogo() and stores it in a file called logo.h. This function displays your company logo on the screen. To construct a program that uses the logo function, you would write:

```
#include<logo.h>
void main()
  {
    displayLogo();
  }
```

tip

One line is a very short function; 100 lines is a very long one. See Tutorial 4 for a discussion of function length.

That's it. You don't need to know how the function works; it may contain one line of code, or 100 lines. You need to know only the function's name and the name of the file in which it is stored.

The statement **displayLogo();** is known as the **call** to the function. When the call is made, the control of the program is transferred to displayLogo() and statements written in displayLogo() execute. When displayLogo() is complete, the control of the program returns to main(), which proceeds to the next instruction. When you write the main() function, you need not worry about whether displayLogo() will be a function you will write as part of the new program file or whether it will be stored in a separate file, requiring the #include statement.

When writing C++ programs that employ the input and output objects, cin and cout, you must use include files because cout and cin cannot be used without iostream.h. In addition, you may create your own include files. These files may contain functions or predefined constants. For example, if several of the new programs will use your company's minimum wage and minimum retirement age, you may create a file called myheader.h with the following contents:

```
const double minimumWage = 4.75;
const int minRetireAge = 60;
```

The following program would run correctly:

```
#include<iostream.h>
#include"myheader.h" // note the quotes
void main()
  {
    cout<<"Minimum wage is "<<minimumWage<<endl;
    // notice minimumWage is not defined in this program
    cout<<"Minimum retirement age is "<<minRetireAge
      <<endl;
    // notice minRetireAge is not defined in this program
  }
```

The program produces the following output:

```
Minimum wage is 4.75
Minimum retirement age is 60
```

You can override the constants declared in the header file by giving variables or constants in your program the same name. This method allows you to use header files for constants already defined there, but prevents you from having to recognize every other variable or constant name that might potentially be defined within the file.

The following program

```
#include<iostream.h>
#include"myheader.h"
void main()
{
   double minimumWage = 99.99;
      // overrides constant in myheader.h
   cout<<"Minimum wage is "<<minimumWage<<endl;
   cout<<"Minimum retirement age is "<<minRetireAge
      <<endl;
   // minRetireAge has not been overridden
}
```

produces the following output:

```
Minimum wage is 99.99
Minimum retirement age is 60
```

Library header files usually do not contain complete functions. Instead they provide function prototypes for functions stored in other files and already compiled. Their use speeds up the process of linking together all the files necessary to run a program.

Technically, an include file does not require the .h extension. Nevertheless, using this extension is a convention and helps other people recognize the file type.

The current directory is the one to which your programs automatically compile and save. Most compilers have a menu option called Options/Directories, through which you can specify the current directory.

When you include a header file that contains functions, you cannot use the same names for the functions in your main program. If you do, the compiler will issue an error message saying that you have two different bodies for the same function.

When using the standard files that come with the C++ compiler, angle brackets should surround the header filename. This format tells the compiler to search for the file in the standard directory that holds include files. When working with your own header files, use quotation marks instead. The compiler will then search in the current directory first. You can also give a full path name: #include "c:\headers\johnson\myheader.h".

Quotes are allowed surrounding the standard include filenames. Use of this format will cause the compiler to look for the file in the current directory first, however, and it will take a little longer to locate the appropriate file. As a result, programmers generally use angle brackets for standard files and quotes for their own files.

When you write the displayLogo() function itself, you create two parts:

■ a header
■ a body

The header of a function consists of three parts:

■ the type of variable that the function will return to the function that calls it
■ the name of the function
■ in parentheses, the types and names of any variables that will be passed to the function

For example, the displayLogo() function has the header

```
void displayLogo(void)
```

because it neither returns any values to the program that calls it nor takes any values from that program.

The **body** of a function consists of any C++ statement between a pair of curly brackets. These statements may include variable or constant declarations, input or output statements, arithmetic statements, and even calls to other functions. For an *extremely* simple company logo, the body of the displayLogo() function might consist of the following code:

```
{

  cout<<"ABC COMPANY"<<endl;
  //not much of a logo — but it's simple

}
```

The entire displayLogo() function follows:

```
void displayLogo(void)  // note no semicolon

  {

    cout<<"ABC COMPANY"<<endl;

  }
```

Just as with the main() function, no semicolon ever follows a function header.

Procedural Abstraction

Abstraction is the process of extracting the relevant attributes of an object. It simplifies your concept of the object, allowing you to ignore inessential details. To some extent, real life would be impossible without abstraction. You use all sorts of objects—pencils, keys, forks, and so on—every day, without worrying about their molecular structure. You use your telephone without understanding the transmission of voice signals. As a programmer, you have already used objects like cin without worrying about how each bit of the entered data is stored.

Using functions is one way (but certainly not the only way) to employ procedural abstraction in C++. When you construct a to-do list, you write down the main tasks to be accomplished.

Write letter to Better Business Bureau

Annual review with Harrison

Gift for Mom

Lunch with Ralph

You write down the main tasks to be accomplished. You don't decide until later whether you'll print the letter on office letterhead or plain paper, or whether you'll meet with Harrison in your office or in a conference room. You don't even think about what you'll order for lunch or where you will eat. If you got bogged down in such details, it would take too long to create the list.

When writing a main() function, you can use the names of other functions that perform a wide variety of tasks. You don't need to worry about their details. This tactic makes the main program easier to write and helps others to understand your program. Anyone reading a payroll program that uses the following functions can see the "big picture" of the program's purpose:

```
computeGross();

deductFederalTaxes();

deductLocalTaxes();

deductInsurance();

printPaycheck();
```

tip

By planning your programs with code reusability in mind, you train yourself to think in an object-oriented fashion. In the real world, reusing software components greatly facilitates maintenance programming—a hallmark of object-oriented programming.

Whenever possible, you should strive to use functions that have already been written. If a colleague has written, tested, and used the displayLogo() function, it would be a waste of time for you to reinvent it. If a programmer at another company has written a good deductFederalTaxes() module, it is probably less expensive to purchase it than to endure all the headaches associated with developing your own function. Similarly, when you design your own functions, keep the notion of reusability in mind. Future projects will go more smoothly if the functions you write and test now can be reused later.

You'll now begin to write your version of the TWONUMS program, which you will name MYNUMS.CPP. This program will allow users to enter numbers and guess their sum. In the final program, users will get three attempts at each of five problems. For now, however, users will have only one attempt at one problem.

1 Start your C++ compiler. Open a new file, and then on the editor screen, type a list of tasks that this program will perform. You will turn the list into program comments so that you can compile incomplete versions of this program as you work. At this stage, you don't worry about correct C++ syntax; you are simply employing procedural abstraction. These major tasks in the program will eventually become your function names.

tip
• • • • • • • • • • • • • • • • •

Instead of two functions, getFirstNum() and getSecondNum(), that fetch the user's two numbers, an equally acceptable solution would be to create a single function called getNum() and call it twice.

```
// displayDirections();
// getFirstNum();
// getSecondNum();
// displayNums();
// sumNums();
// getGuess();
// displayResults();
// finalStat();
```

2 Above this list of functions, add comments, such as your own name and the date:

```
// Program MYNUMS
// Written by:
// Date written:
```

3 Below the comments, add the #include statement needed for cin and cout, the main() function header, and the opening curly bracket:

```
#include<iostream.h>
void main()
    {
```

4 Immediately above the list of your future function names, add the comment

```
// declarations
```

5 At the end of the list of functions, add another comment, followed by a closing curly bracket:

```
// executable portion of program begins here
}
```

6 Save the program as **MYNUMS.CPP**. Resave it after every few steps as you work through this tutorial.

7 Compile the program to check for and correct any syntax errors.

Global Versus Local Variables

Some named objects in your life are **global**. At the office, if the conversation turns to "Roseanne," "Madonna," or "Cher," you probably assume that your co-workers are talking about the same people that workers in other offices mean when they use those names. The names are global in the sense that they are known to workers in every office and always refer to the same individuals. Similarly, global variables are those that are known to all functions in a program.

Some named objects in your life are **local**. When a co-worker speaks of "Jim in Accounting" or "The Task Master," you and other members of your office understand the reference. People in the company across the street do not recognize them, however. Those references are local, just as some variables are local to a function.

You may have a local co-worker who **overrides** a global one. If the sales manager in your company is named Roseanne, then co-workers are referring to her when they use the name, not the more famous actress Roseanne. Variables work the same way, too. A variable with a given name inside a function overrides any global variable with the same name, unless you take special action to specify use of the global variable.

Variables that are declared in a block (that is, between curly brackets) are local to that block. They have the following characteristics:

- Local variables are created when they are declared within a block.
- Local variables are known only to that block.
- Local variables cease to exist when that block ends.

Pairs of curly brackets may be placed anywhere in a C++ program and are always placed at the beginning and end of every function, including main(). Therefore, variables declared within a function remain local to that function. In contrast, variables declared within curly brackets within any function are local to that block.

In the following program, note that the variable b comes into existence when it is declared, but ceases to exist when the program ends. The variable c has a much shorter life; it is only "alive" between the interior, nested brackets. In other words, it is **in scope** between the brackets.

```
#include<iostream.h>
void main()
  {
    int b = 2;  // b comes into existence
    cout<<b;
      {
        int c = 3; // c comes into existence cout<<c;
      } // c dies
  } // b dies
```

No variable can be accessed outside of its scope. You wouldn't try to use a variable before it is declared; similarly, you can't use it after it goes out of scope.

```
#include<iostream.h>
void main()
  {
    int b = 2;
    cout<<b;
    cout<<c;
      // this won't work -- c hasn't been declared yet
      {
        int c = 3;
        cout<<c;   // this statement is fine
        cout<<b;
          // this is fine, too -- still inside b's set
          // of brackets
      }
    cout<<b; // this statement is still fine
    cout<<c;
      //this won't work; c is out of scope
  }
cout<<b;
  // won't work -- program is over; b is out of scope
```

tip

• • • • • • • • • • • • • • • •

The occasion on which C++ programmers commonly don't declare a variable at the beginning of a function is when they use a loop control variable in a for statement. For example,

```
for(int x=0;x<10;++x)
```

This program illustrates that variables can be declared anywhere within a C++ program, but it is not necessarily a good idea to do so. The variable c isn't declared until well into the program for illustrative purposes, allowing you to observe its local scope, but many programmers prefer to declare virtually all variables at the beginning of each function. If the variables are declared in the same place, it is easier to find them and to change them later if necessary. In addition, you can more easily see whether you are inadvertently giving two variables the same name.

All variables declared within any function are also in a block because a function body is a block; therefore these variables are local to the function. Consider this program with a sayHello() function:

```
#include<iostream.h>
void sayHello (void)
  {
    int x = 12;
      // x comes into existence within sayHello()
    cout<<"Hello";
    cout<<x; // 12 will display
  }  // sayHello()'s x dies
```

Now consider a main() function that calls sayHello():

```
void main()    // this declaration is not complete --
               // sayHello() should be prototyped

  {
    int y = 13;
    sayHello();
    cout<<y;  // statement OK -- y is local to main()
    cout<<x;  // this is not OK; x doesn't exist here
  }
```

Even though the main program calls the sayHello() function, and the sayHello() function declares x, the variable x cannot be used in main(). Instead, it is local to sayHello().

In the following program, x can be used in main(), but it is the x that is local to main(). The x in sayHello() has no effect on main()'s x, because the two are completely different variables.

```
#include<iostream.h>
void sayHello (void)
  {
    int x = 12;  // sayHello()'s x comes into existence
    cout<<"Hello";
    cout<<x; //  12 will display --
             // this variable is unrelated to the 77 in main
  }  // sayHello()'s x dies
void main()  // this function is not complete --
             // sayHello() should be prototyped
  {
    int y = 13;
    int x = 77; // main's x comes into existence
    cout<<x; // 77 will display
    sayHello();
    cout<<y; // 13 will display
    cout<<x;  // 77 will display -- main's x still exists
  } // main's x and y both die
```

If the sayHello() and main() functions are written by different programmers, no conflict will arise. Each programmer can use x as a variable name without destroying any values in the other's function. A major advantage of using local variables is that many programmers can work on a large program, each writing separate functions, and they can use any variable names inside their own functions. These variables will not affect data stored in variables with the same names in other functions.

Variables declared outside a block are **global**. Global variables are known to all functions in the file in which they are declared.

C++ provides even more complete encapsulation when using classes, which are discussed in Tutorial 3.

```
#include<iostream.h>
int WorldlyOne = 44;
void main()
  {
    cout<<WorldlyOne;
    WorldlyOne = 1732;
  }
```

A much better style is to use local variables than global ones. This strategy represents a preliminary example of a type of **encapsulation**. Local variables may be envisioned as "in a capsule," separated from the main () program, which cannot harm them. Beginning programmers often think it is easier to use global variables rather than local ones, because global variables are known to all functions. Using global variables, rather than creating local variables in functions, is actually disadvantageous for these reasons:

- If variables are global in a program and you reuse any functions in a new program, the variables must be redeclared in the latter program. They no longer "come along with" the function.
- Global variables can be affected by any function, leading to errors. In a program with many functions, finding the function that caused an error can prove difficult.

You may use a global variable even when a local variable with the same name exists, by using the **scope resolution** operator. This operator (the symbol **::**) is placed directly before the variable name. It causes the program to access global variable, rather than the local variable.

```
#include<iostream.h>
int someNum = 44; // someNum is a global variable
void main(void)
  {
    int someNum = 23; // someNum is a local variable
    cout<<someNum;  // output is 23
    cout<<::someNum; // output is 44;
  }
```

You can now add the variables that will be local to the main() MYNUMS program. In addition, you will add one global constant.

1 The main()'s function variables immediately follow the comment // declarations. You will need two integers for the two numbers the user will enter: int firstNum, secondNum;.

2 You will need a variable to hold the correct sum and the user's guess: int correctSum, guess;.

3 One constant that will eventually be used throughout this program is the number of summing problems. It represents a good candidate for a global variable because many functions may need to know the number of problems. If we ever modify the program to use more or fewer problems in the future, the change can be made in one place with a global variable. Above void main() place the constant const int problems = 5;.

4 Compile the program and correct any syntax errors.

tip

When you create a variable, you will get a warning until you create a program that uses the variable. You can safely ignore the warning.

Prototyping

Before a function can be used in a program, it must be prototyped. In **prototyping**, you create a sample function outline or a description of how the actual function will look. When you declare a variable, you give it a type and a name. When you prototype a function, you declare it, so you give it a type and a name as well. A prototype actually indicates three features about a function:

- the type of variable that the function will return to the function that calls it (also known as the function's type)
- the name of the function
- in parentheses, the types of any variables that will be passed to the function

This prototype resembles the list of items found in a function header. In fact, with minor differences, a function prototype must match very closely the function header to which it refers. For example, the function that displays a company logo named displayLogo() is written so that it neither needs information from the function that calls it nor sends any information back to this function. The displayLogo() function's header is void displayLogo(void) and its prototype is void displayLogo(void);. The function header does not end in a semicolon; the prototype does.

The complete main program that uses displayLogo() follows:

```
#include<iostream.h>
#include"logo.h"
void main()
  {
    void displayLogo(void);  // prototype of function
    displayLogo();  // call to function
  }
```

The statement `void displayLogo(void);` notifies the main program that the called function will need nothing and will return nothing. The statement `displayLogo();` actually calls the function.

Create the prototype, function call, and function for the displayDirections() function, which neither receives nor returns data.

1 In main(), in the section where the other variables are declared, create a prototype for a function to display the directions for the MYNUMS program to the user. Replace the comment `// displayDirections()` in your abstract list of procedures with the complete prototype. Because the function neither sends nor receives information, its prototype is `void displayDirections(void);`.

2 As the first instruction in the executable portion of main(), after the comment `// executable portion of program begins here`, call the displayDirections() function: `displayDirections();`.

3 Create the displayDirections() function. This function will display the game directions on the screen. After the closing bracket of main(), enter the following function:

```
void displayDirections(void)
  {
    cout<<"This program will ask you for two numbers"
      <<endl;
    cout<<"Try to guess their sum"<<endl;
  }
```

4 Compile the program and correct any syntax errors. Save the program.

5 Run the program. The directions will display on the screen.

Returning Values from Functions

The type of value that a function returns is also known as the function's type (or the function's return type). The functions we have used so far have been type void. That is, the displayLogo() function does not return anything to the program that calls it, nor does the main() function. Sometimes, however, a function should send a value back to the calling program.

```
double figureTaxes();
char askUserForInitial();
```

These are prototypes of functions that return a double value and a character value, respectively, to any program that uses them. Programmers would say that figureTaxes() is a function of type double and askUserForInitial() is a function of type char.

Functions used for data entry almost always return the entered data to a main() program or other calling function. For example, the purpose of the function askUserForInitial() is to prompt a user for a character entry. The following complete program, which uses the askUserForInitial() function, is followed by the complete function.

```cpp
#include<iostream.h>
void main()
   {
      char usersInitial;
      char askUserForInitial(void);
      usersInitial = askUserForInitial();
      cout<<"Your initial is "<<usersInitial<<endl;
   }
char askUserForInitial(void)
   {
      char letter;
      cout<<"Please type your initial and press enter"
         <<endl;
      cin>>letter;
      return(letter);
   }
```

The main program declares a character variable, usersInitial, and a character function, askUserForInitial(). Next, askUserForInitial() is called, and its return value is assigned to usersInitial. This variable then displays on the screen.

The function askUserForInitial() declares a local variable named letter. At the prompt, the user types in a character, which is stored in letter. The variable letter is local to the function. It goes out of existence when the function ends. Before the function ends, however, a copy of the contents of letter is returned to the main() program, where it is assigned to another variable, usersInitial.

The programmer who writes this function does not need to know the variable names used by the programmer who writes main(). If main() and askUserForInitial() have the same variable names, then we have:

```
#include<iostream.h>
void main()
  {
    char initial;
    char askUserForInitial(void);
    initial = askUserForInitial();
    cout<<"Your initial is "<<initial<<endl;
  }
char askUserForInitial(void)
  {
    char initial;
    cout<<"Please type your initial and press enter"
      <<endl;
    cin>>initial;
    return(initial);
  }
```

The variable initial in the main() function differs from the initial in askUserForInitial(). The two variables may or may not share the same name. Sue Johnson on Oak Street and Sue Johnson on Elm Avenue, for example, have the same name, yet have different addresses. Similarly, two variables with the same name in different functions have different memory addresses; they are different variables.

Add a function to the MYNUMS program to fetch the player's first number.

1 In the **MYNUMS** program, create a prototype for a getFirstNum() function. The function does not need any data from the main program, but it must return the integer entered by the player. Modify the getFirstNum() comment line in your abstraction list to become a complete prototype: `int getFirstNum(void);`

2 In the executable section of main(), call the function getFirstNum() and assign its return value to the variable firstNum: `firstNum = getFirstNum();`

3 Below the end of the displayDirections() function, add a new function to obtain the first number. This function will have its own local variable, num, in which to store the integer before it is returned to the main program.

```
int getFirstNum(void)
  {
    int num;
    cout<<"Enter the first number "<<endl;
    cin>>num;
    return(num);
  }
```

4 Compile the program and correct any syntax errors. Because you have not yet written the functions that require firstNum, you may receive a warning that firstNum is assigned a value that is never used. This warning may safely be ignored.

5 Run the program. Directions will display and you will be prompted to enter a number.

6 Create your own prototype, call, and function for a function getSecondNum(), which should prompt for, get, and return the second player number.

7 Compile the program and correct any syntax errors. Run the program.

A severe limitation of functions is that each function may have only one type; as a consequence, it may return only one value. Instead of two separate functions for getFirstNum() and getSecondNum(), you may prefer to write a single function that gets both of the values. You will be able to use this option in Lesson B, later in this tutorial.

Passing Values to Functions

Some functions need information from the main() program. For example, consider a program that should compute your paycheck. After entering your hours worked and hourly rate, you can create a function called netPay() to compute the product, deduct your withholding, and display the results.

```
#include<iostream.h>
void main(void)
  {
    int hours;
    double hourlyRate;
    // the prototype for the function will go here
    cout<<"Enter hours worked "<<endl;
    cin>>hours;
    cout<<"Enter rate per hour "<<endl;
    cin>>hourlyRate;
    // you want the function to compute and print the
    // net pay here
  }
```

The netPay() function is type void, as it does not return anything to the main() program. It does, however, need to obtain the hours and the pay rate from the main() program. The prototype for this function can be written as follows:

```
void netPay(int, double);
// you list only the types of the variables passed to
// the function
```

or it can be written

```
void NetPay(int hours, double hourlyRate);
// you list types and variable names used in the program
```

or it can be written

```
void(int hoursWorked, double rateOfPay);
// you list types and other descriptive names, which
// are not necessarily the same as the variables
```

The parentheses of the prototype enclose a list of the variable types that will be passed to the netPay() function. This list simply notes the types that will be passed, separated by a comma. A type must be listed for each variable that will be passed, even if two or more variables have the same type. For example, a function that computes the sum of four integers may have the prototype: void funcToAddFourIntegers(int a, int b, int c, int d);

tip

The variable names used in the prototype are immaterial, because a function should be reusable. That is, a function that adds two integers should work for any two integers. Thus, sumFunction (int a, int b) can be used with the variables a and b or with the variables c and d.

Each type may also be associated with a name for the variable that will be passed. These names may be identical to the names of the variables that will be actually used when the function call occurs. For example,

```
void netPay(int Hours, double HourlyRate);
```

The names may also be simply descriptive, albeit different from the variables that will actually be used:

```
void netPay(int hoursWorkedThisWeek, double rateOfPay);
```

You can omit variable names in the prototype if desired. (The names will be necessary when we call the function, however.) Nevertheless, the names give someone looking at the prototype an idea of the kind of data expected by the function. In the prototype, the variable names actually play the same role as comments.

A function call is placed in a program at the point where function processing should occur. For example, the netPay() function appears after hours and hourly rate have been entered because the net pay calculations take place there. The parentheses in the call to netPay() surround the variables netPay() will need. This list of variables is sometimes called the **parameter list**.

Both hours and hourlyRate are passed to the function by placing their names between the parentheses. These variables are called **actual parameters** because they hold the values that will actually be used by the function netPay(). The order in which the two actual parameters are listed within the parentheses is very important. The function prototype for netPay() states that the function will receive an integer and a double, *in that order*. Thus, the function netPay() will expect to receive the data *in that order*. If variables are not sent to a function in the correct order, data may be lost, incorrect results may be produced, or the program may refuse to run.

```
#include<iostream.h>
void main()
  {
    int hours;
    double hourlyRate;
    void netPay (int hours, int rate);    // prototype
    cout<<"Enter hours worked "<<endl;
    cin>>hours;
    cout<<"Enter rate per hour "<<endl;
    cin>>hourlyRate;
    netPay(hours, hourlyRate); // call to function --
    // passing it an integer and a double
    // hours and hourlyRate are the actual parameters

  }
```

When you call the netPay() function, you need not indicate the types for hours and hourlyRate. The function prototype indicates the types expected, and the function header specifies which types will be accepted; only the variables that actually hold data to be sent to the function are needed in the function call.

The header of netPay() indicates that it will return nothing to the program that calls it, but that it will accept an integer and a double, in that order. The integer and the double that are accepted from main() are new variables that have been declared locally within this netPay() function. Consequently, these variables can have either different or the same names as the variables in the calling program. The local variables receive a copy of the data stored in the variables in the actual parameters when this function was called. The list of variable types and names in the function header is known as the **formal parameters**. These parameters serve as local variables for the function. They will cease to exist when the function ends; for now, however, they hold copies of the values from the actual parameters in the main program.

In the body of netPay(), a local variable is declared, some arithmetic is performed, and an output statement is issued.

```
void netPay(int time, double money)
  {
    const double withholdingPct = 0.15;
      // withholding is 15%
    double withholdingAmount, netAmount;
    netAmount = time * money; // compute gross
    withholdingAmount = netAmount * withholdingPct;
      // withholding is a percentage of the gross
    netAmount -= withholdingAmount;
      // subtract withholding from the net amount
    cout<<"Net pay is "<<netAmount<<endl;
  }
```

In the following steps, you will add the displayNumbers() function to the MYNUMS program. This function will pass the firstNum and SecondNum values entered by a player to a function that echoes the numbers.

1   Add the prototype for a displayNumbers() function, replacing the displayNumbers() comment in your list of abstractions. Because this function returns nothing, it is type void. The function accepts two integer numbers that have been entered by the player.

```
void displayNumbers(int firstNum, int secondNum);
```

2 In the main() function, add a function call to displayNumbers() just after the two numbers have been entered.

```
displayNumbers(firstNum,SecondNum);
```

3 At the end of the file, after the getSecondNum() function, add the displayNumbers() function. This function contains two formal parameters to hold the two passed values.. The parameters may have the same names as the variables in main(), or they may have different names.

```
void displayNumbers(int numOne, int numTwo)
  {
    cout<<"Now guess the sum of "<<numOne;
    cout<<" and "<<numTwo<<"."<<endl;
  }
```

4 Compile and test the program. Don't forget to save the program periodically.

Of course, any combination of actions in a function is possible. Some functions return and receive nothing. Others return values, receive values, or both. Functions may receive any number of variables, but may return, at most, only one variable of one type.

In the next steps, you will develop the functions to sum the numbers, get the player's guess, and display the results.

1 Add the prototype for the sumNums() function. It will receive two integers and return their sum.

```
int sumNums(int firstNum, int secondNum);
```

2 Add the call to sumNums().

```
correctSum = sumNums(firstNum, secondNum);
```

3 Add the function sumNums(). It will have a local variable, named total, that holds the sum of the two integers until a copy of its value is returned to main().

```
int sumNums(int a, int b)
  {
    int total;
    total = a + b;
    return(total);
  }
```

4 Compile and test the program.

5 Add the prototype for getGuess():

```
int getGuess(void);
```

6 Add the call for getGuess():

```
guess = getGuess();
```

7 Add the function for getGuess():

```
int getGuess(void)
  {
    int guess;
    cout<<"What is your guess?"<<endl;
    cin>>guess;
    return(guess);
  }
```

8 Compile and test the program.

9 Add the prototype, call, and function for displayResults(). They are

```
void displayResults(int correctSum, int guess);
```

```
displayResults(correctSum, guess);
```

```
void displayResults(int sum, int guess)
  {
    (guess == sum) ? cout<<"Correct!"<<endl :
      cout <<"Wrong!"<<endl;
  }
```

10 Compile and test the program. Run it several times, giving both correct and incorrect answers.

11 Save the program.

S U M M A R Y

- In C++, a function is a module or miniprogram that performs some task or group of tasks.
- When you call a function, program control is transferred to the function.
- When you write a program that uses a function, you need not worry about whether the function will be written as part of the new program file or stored in a separate file. You care only that the function accomplishes the desired task.
- Besides functions, you may want to include constants in separate header files.
- A function has two parts: a header and a body.
- The header of a function includes three parts: the type of variable that the function returns to the function that calls it, the name of the function, and, in parentheses, the types and names of any variables passed to the function. The function header is not followed by a semicolon.
- The body of a function consists of any C++ statements placed between a pair of curly brackets.
- The last statement in a function is often a return statement.
- Abstraction is the process of extracting the relevant attributes of an object, thereby simplifying the view of the object.
- Local variables are created when variables declared in a block remain known only to that block. They cease to exist when that block ends.
- Traditionally, all variables are declared together, at the beginning of a block.
- Variables declared outside a block are global; that is, they are known to all functions in the file in which they are declared.
- Prototyping means creating a sample function outline or description for the actual function. Functions must be prototyped before you can use them.
- A prototype indicates the type of variable that the function will return to the function that calls it, the name of the function, and, in parentheses, the types of any variables that will be passed to the function.
- The type of value that a function returns to the calling program is referred to as the function's type. A function may return only one value.
- The prototype of a function that receives values contains, in parentheses, a list of the variable types that will be passed to it, separated by commas. A type must be provided for each variable to be passed, even if multiple variables have the same type.
- A function call is placed in a program at the spot where the function processing should occur.

■ The variables passed to a function are actual parameters, and the order in which they are listed is crucial.

■ The variables listed in a function header that receive copies of data from the calling program are the formal parameters. These variables can have either different or the same names as the variables in the calling program.

QUESTIONS

1. Modules in C++ programs are _____.
   a. functions
   b. procedures
   c. subroutines
   d. miniprograms

2. Any #include files may contain _____.
   a. constants
   b. variables
   c. functions
   d. all of the above

3. Library header files usually contain _____.
   a. complete functions
   b. parts of functions
   c. function prototypes for functions stored in other files
   d. function bodies, but not function headers

4. When using the standard files that come with the C++ compiler, you should surround the header file name with _____.
   a. square brackets
   b. angle brackets
   c. parentheses
   d. quotes

5. The two parts of a function are the _____.
   a. header and footer
   b. declarations and statements
   c. legs and feet
   d. header and body

6. The body of a C++ function is surrounded by _____.
   a. parentheses
   b. angle brackets
   c. curly brackets
   d. square brackets

7. The last statement in a function is often a(n) _____.
   a. return
   b. goodbye
   c. finish
   d. endfunction

8. Which of the following is NOT included in the header of a function?
   a. the type of variable returned by the function to the function that calls it
   b. the name of the program or function that calls the function
   c. the name of the function
   d. the types and names of any variables that will be passed to the function

9. A function that returns no values to the program that calls it is _____.
   a. not allowed in C++
   b. type void
   c. type empty
   d. type barren

10. The process of extracting the relevant attributes of an object is known as _____.
    a. polymorphism
    b. inheritance
    c. abstraction
    d. data hiding

11. Software that can be used in applications other than the one for which it was originally written is called _____.
    a. recyclable
    b. inherited
    c. reusable
    d. cheating

12. Variables that are declared in a block are known as _____ variables to that block.
    a. confined
    b. local
    c. global
    d. immediate

13. Local variables _____.
    a. are created outside a block
    b. are known only to that block
    c. continue to exist when their block ends
    d. are illegal in C++

14. When a variable exists or is accessible, it is said to be _____.
    a. immediate
    b. in the path
    c. available
    d. in scope

15. Programmers prefer to declare almost all variables _____.
    a. at the beginning of each function
    b. globally
    c. on one line
    d. with cryptic names

16. An advantage of using local variables is that _____.
    a. they are known to all functions in the file
    b. names used in one function do not affect data stored in variables with the same names in other functions
    c. values given to local variables are retained when those parameters go out of scope
    d. the program does not become "crowded" with too many variable names

17. Variables declared outside a block are called _____.
    a. global
    b. universal
    c. stellar
    d. external

18. Separating parts of a program into units that remain unaffected by other parts of a program is the concept known as _____.
    a. intrusion
    b. volatility
    c. encapsulation
    d. protection

19. The outline or the definition of a function is called its _____.
    a. beta test
    b. forerunner
    c. outline
    d. prototype

20. The type of value that a function sends back to the function that calls it is known as its _____.
    a. type
    b. return value
    c. reference data
    d. sentinel

E X E R C I S E S

1. Write a program in which the main() function calls a MarysLamb() function. Write the MarysLamb() function, which should display the words to the song "Mary Had a Little Lamb."

2. Write a program that asks the user to input an integer, and then calls a function that should multiply the integer by the numbers 2 through 10 and then display the results.

3. Write a program that asks the user for the most expensive and least expensive restaurant bills he or she anticipates. A function tipTable() should calculate and display 15% of each whole-dollar amount between the two entered limits.

4. Write a program that asks the user for two integers and a character, 'A', 'S', or 'M'. Call one of three functions that adds, subtracts, or multiplies the user's integers based on the character input.

5. Write a program including two functions. The first function should ask a salesperson for the dollar value of daily sales and return this figure to the main program. The second function should calculate the salesperson's commission based on the following rates:

Sales	Commission
0 – 999	3%
1000 – 2999	3.5%
3000 – up	4.5%

The dollar value of the calculated commission should be returned to the main program, which then displays it.

LESSON B
objectives

In this lesson you will learn how to:

- Work with pointers
- Pass addresses to functions
- Use reference variables with functions
- Pass arrays to functions
- Create inline functions
- Use default arguments with functions
- Overload functions

Working with Functions

Passing Addresses to Functions

Just as variable values may be passed to and returned from functions, so may variable addresses. Passing an address to a function allows you to avoid having the function copy the passed object, a process that takes time and memory. You might also pass addresses to a function if you wanted a function to change multiple values. Recall that a function may return only one value (and that value must be the function's type). If you pass addresses to a function, however, it can change the contents at those actual memory addresses, eliminating the need to return any values at all.

You can view the memory address of any variable by using the **address operator**, &.

tip

A printed address may appear meaningless because it is expressed as a base 16 (hexadecimal) number rather than as a more familiar base 10 number. Don't worry about the base 10 value; just be aware that you are viewing a memory address.

```cpp
#include<iostream.h>
void main()
  {
    int myValue = 16;
    cout<<"myValue is "<<myValue<<endl;
    cout<<"It is stored at address "<<&myValue<<endl;
  }
```

The output of this program depends on your computer, but it might take the following form:

```
myValue is 16
It is stored at address 0x8ea0fff4
```

You can access the value of any variable by using the variable's name. In contrast, inserting an ampersand in front of its name allows you to access its address.

You may also declare variables that can hold memory addresses. These variables are called pointer variables, or simply **pointers**. You declare a pointer with a type, just like other variables. The type indicates the type of variable whose address will be held by the pointer. To indicate that a variable is a pointer, begin the variable's name with an asterisk. For example, `int *aPointer;` declares an integer pointer variable named aPointer. The aPointer variable may hold the address of any integer, as in aPointer = &myValue;. You can then output the contents of myValue in one of two ways:

```
cout<<myValue;
```

or

```
cout<<*aPointer;
```

The asterisk used in the last cout statement is called the **indirection operator**. It is read as "the contents stored at aPointer" or "the contents pointed to by aPointer."

Consider, for example, a function that determines the result of an integer division as well as its remainder. You could write two functions to perform the two tasks, making two separate function calls:

```
#include<iostream.h>
void main()
  {
    int a = 19, b = 7, dividend, modulus;
    int resultDiv(int a, int b); // prototype of the
    // function that divides a and b
    int remainder(int a, int b); // prototype of the
    // function that determines the remainder
    dividend = resultDiv(a,b); // call resultDiv function
    modulus = remainder(a,b); // call remainder function
    cout<<"dividend is "<<dividend<<" and modulus is "
      <<modulus;
  }
int resultDiv(int oneNumber, int anotherNumber)
  {
    int result;
    result = oneNumber / anotherNumber;
    return(result); // function returns one thing --
    // the result of division
  }
int remainder(int oneNumber, int anotherNumber)
  {
    int result;
    result = oneNumber % anotherNumber;
    return(result); // function returns one thing --
    // the result of modulus
  }
```

Alternatively, you could pass two addresses to one function, making a single function call:

```cpp
#include<iostream.h>
void main()
  {
    int a = 19, b = 7, dividend, modulus;
    void results(int a, int b, int * d, int *m);
    // prototype of the function that divides and determines the remainder
    results(a, b, &dividend, &modulus);
    cout<<"Dividend is "<<dividend<<" and modulus is "<<modulus;
  }
void results(int oneNumber, int anotherNumber, int *oneAddress, int *anotherAddress)
  {
    *oneAddress = oneNumber / anotherNumber;
      // change the contents at oneAddress
    *anotherAddress = oneNumber % anotherNumber;
      // change the contents at anotherAddress
  }
```

In this program, four items are passed to the results() function: the value of a, the value of b, the address of dividend, and the address of modulus. In turn, the results() function receives four items:

- oneNumber, which holds the value of a
- anotherNumber, which holds the value of b
- oneAddress, a pointer that holds the address of dividend
- anotherAddress, a pointer that holds the address of modulus

When values are stored in oneAddress and anotherAddress, the values of dividend and modulus are also changed because they have the same address.

In the following steps, you will change the getFirstNum() function in the MYNUMS program to accept the address of firstNum.

1 Change the prototype of getFirstNum() to indicate that a pointer will be passed to the function and nothing will be returned:

```cpp
void getFirstNum(int *firstNum);
```

2 Change the function call to pass the address of firstNum to the getFirstNum() function:

```
getFirstNum(&firstNum);
```

Because getFirstNum() is now a void function, it returns nothing, and you cannot assign its value to any variable.

3 Change the function header of getFirstNum() to agree with the prototype:

```
void getFirstNum(int *num)
```

4 In this version of getFirstNum(), num is a pointer that is passed to the function. Therefore, you should remove the line that declares num as a local integer variable in the function.

5 In the getFirstNum() function, change the input statement so that it accepts data into the address held in the num pointer:

```
cin>>*num;
```

6 The function is now a void function and returns nothing. Remove the return statement in the function.

7 Compile and test the program. It should run just as it did in the previous version.

8 When a function receives addresses as parameters, the values at all addresses may change. Instead of two separate functions, getFirstNum() and getSecNum(), you could create one function, getNums(), that receives both input values. Remove both the getFirstNum() and the getSecNum() functions from your program by removing (or commenting out) the following items:

   ■ the function prototypes
   ■ the function calls
   ■ the functions

9 Create a new prototype for getNums() that receives two parameters: the addresses of both firstNum and secondNum.

```
void getNums(int *firstNum, int *secondNum);
```

10 Place a call to getNums() in the location once occupied by the two removed calls, just before the call to displayNums():

```
getNums(&firstNum, &secondNum);
```

11 Write the getNums() function that uses pointers for the data entry:

```
void getNums(int *num1, int *num2)
  {
    cout<<"Enter the first number "<<endl;
    cin>>*num1;
    cout<<"Enter the second number "<<endl;
    cin>>*num2;
  }
```

12 Compile, test, and save the program.

Using Reference Variables with Functions

A criminal who uses two names is said to have an **alias**. To create a second name for a variable in a program, you can generate an alias. A **reference variable** is a variable that acts as an alias for a second variable.

A reference variable is declared with a type and an ampersand in front of its name:

```
double someMoney = 34.78;
double &cash = someMoney; // cash is a reference variable
```

The variables someMoney and cash now both refer to the same variable. Any change to cash will modify someMoney, and any change to someMoney will alter cash.

```
cash = 6.58;
cout<<someMoney; // output is 6.58
someMoney = 1.25;
cout<<cash; // output is 1.25
```

As a reference variable refers to the same memory address as a variable, and a pointer holds the memory address of a variable, what's the difference between the two?

- Pointers are more flexible.
- Reference variables are easier to use.

Pointers are more flexible because they can store the address of any variable of the correct type. You declare a pointer to a variable by placing an asterisk in front of the pointer's name. You assign a value to a pointer by inserting an ampersand in front of the name of the variable whose address you want to store in the pointer.

```
int var = 20;

int anotherVar = 45;

int *pointVar;

pointVar = & var;  // pointVar is a pointer; store the
   // address of var there

cout<<*pointVar<<endl; // output is 20

pointVar = &anotherVar; // store the address of anotherVar there

cout<<*pointVar;/ // output is 45
```

tip

You must assign a value to a reference variable when you declare it.

```
int &badReference;
//no assignment --
//illegal
```

Reference variables are easier to use because you don't need any extra punctuation to output their values. You declare a reference variable by placing an ampersand in front of its name. You assign a value to a reference variable by using another variable's name. The value in the reference is then output by using its name.

```
int var = 20;

int anotherVar = 45;

int &refVar = var;  // refVar is a reference; it holds
   // the same memory address as var

cout<<refVar;  // output is 20, the value of var

&refVar = anotherVar; // illegal -- refVar is a
   // reference for var only
```

When you want to pass the address of a variable to a function, allowing the function to alter the variable's memory location or to save the overhead incurred in making a copy, it can prove easier to use a reference variable than a pointer. To work with the stored value, you don't need the asterisk. If you require another name for a variable, a reference is preferable. If you must hold the addresses of several different memory locations, then a pointer is required.

The following function uses two pointers to change the contents of two variables:

```
void results(int oneNumber, int anotherNumber, int *oneAddress, int *anotherAddress)
  {
    *oneAddress = oneNumber / anotherNumber;
      // change the contents at oneAddress

    *anotherAddress = oneNumber % anotherNumber;
      // change the contents at anotherAddress

  }
```

The same function can use two reference variables, thereby avoiding the use of the dereferencing asterisks for oneAddress and anotherAddress.

```
void Results(int oneNumber, int anotherNumber, int &oneAddress, int &anotherAddress)

  {

oneAddress = oneNumber / anotherNumber;
  // change the contents at oneAddress

anotherAddress = oneNumber % anotherNumber;
  // change the contents at anotherAddress

  }
```

When you pass a variable's address to a function, whether with a pointer or a reference, any changes to the variable made by the function alter the actual variable as well. In addition, the function no longer needs to make a copy of the variable. Passing an address is a double-edged sword, however. A function that receives an address may change the variable—but sometimes you may not want the variable changed.

To pass an address (thus eliminating the copy of a variable) while still protecting the variable from change, you may pass a reference as a constant.

tip

••••••••••••••••••

▶ If a function receives a variable as a constant, but then passes it to another function that does not receive the variable as a constant, most compilers will not issue an error message. You may inadvertently change a variable that should remain constant.

```
#include<iostream.h>

void main()

  {

    int x = 8;

    void someFunction(const int &refx);
      // function prototype

    someFunction(x); // call to function cout<<x;

  }

void someFunction(const int &refx)
// function receives an alias reference

  {

    refx = 99;
      // illegal -- refx cannot be changed because it
      // is a constant

    cout<<refx;
      // legal -- refx can be used even though it can't
      // be changed; — output is 8

  }
```

Use the const modifier for all variables passed to functions that should not change within the function. This practice provides safety, in that the compiler will check to ensure that the variable is not changed inadvertently. In addition, this tactic makes your intentions clear to anyone reading your program.

In the following steps, you will change the getNums() function in the MYNUMS program to accept reference variables, rather than pointers, as parameters.

1 Change the prototype of getNums() to indicate that reference variables will be passed:

```
void getNums(int &firstNum, int &secondNum);
```

2 Remove the ampersands from the call to getNums():

```
getNums(firstNum, secondNum);
```

3 Change the function header of getNums() to agree with the prototype. The function will now receive references to the two integers.

```
void getNums(int &num1, int &num2)
```

4 Remove the indirection operators from the cin statements inside the getNums() function:

```
cin>>num1;
cin>>num2;
```

5 Compile, test, and save the program.

Working with Arrays

Although the scalar data types—int, char, double, and float—suffice to describe the data used in many programs, it is sometimes convenient to create groups of variables that you can manipulate as a unit. A list of individual scalar items that all have the same type is called an **array**. An array holds two or more variables with the same name and type in adjacent memory positions. The variables with the same name are distinguished from one another by their **subscripts**; the subscript is a number that indicates the position of the particular variables being used.

In C++, you declare an array by using the form

```
type arrayName[size];
```

where type is any simple type, arrayName is any legal identifier, and size (in the square brackets) represents the number of **elements** the array contains. For example,

```
double moneyCollected[15];
```

declares an array of 15 variables, each of which is type double. The first variable in the array (or element of the array) is moneyCollected[0]. The last element is

tip

C++ may not issue warnings or errors if a subscript exceeds the size of the array. Instead, it will simply access memory outside the array, with unpredictable results. The programmer is responsible for ensuring that the subscript remains within the intended range.

moneyCollected[14]. The number in square brackets, the subscript, should be either a whole number or a variable of type integer.

An array name actually represents a memory address. Thus, an array name is a pointer. The subscript used to access an element of an array indicates how much to add to the starting address to locate a value.

The array declaration int nums[5]; declares an array that holds five integers. You can view the address of the array with the statement

```
cout<<nums;
```

The statement

```
cout<<&nums[0];
```

produces identical output. In the first statement, the name of the array represents the beginning address of the array. In the second statement, the address of nums[0] is the beginning address of the array as well.

Similarly,

```
cout<<(nums + 1); // address of nums plus one more integer
```

produces output identical to that of

```
cout<<&nums[1]; // address of second element of nums array
```

These two examples produce the same output because nums is the beginning address of the array. As nums is an array of type integer, nums + 1 is one integer away from the beginning address of the array. That is, the address one integer away from the beginning address of the array is the address of nums[1].

	nums[0]	nums[1]	nums[2]	nums[3]	nums[4]
	33	45	67	78	99
Address	nums or nums + 0	nums + 1	nums + 2	nums + 3	nums + 4

Figure 1-1: How nums[5]={33,45,67,78,99}; appears in memory

Because an array name is a memory address, when you pass an array name to a function, you are actually passing an address. Therefore, any changes made to the array within the function will also affect the original array.

```cpp
#include<iostream.h>
void main()
  {
    int someNumbers[4] = {2,5,8,24};
      // initialize an array with four values
    void addOneToEach(int someNumbers[]);
      // prototype -- note the empty brackets
    addOneToEach(someNumbers);
      // function call -- note that the beginning
      // address of array is passed
    for(int a = 1; a< 4; ++a)
      cout<<" "<<someNumbers[a];  // output is 3 6 9 25
  }
// function to add 1 to each element of the array
void addOneToEach(int funcArray[])
// function header -- note the empty brackets
  {
    for(int b =0; b<4; ++b)
      ++funcArray[b];
  }
```

When an array name is passed to a function, the function "knows" the starting address of the array. Therefore, you don't need to indicate a size for the array in the function header. It doesn't matter whether funcArray consists of four elements or 400; the starting address is the same in either case. When you modify funcArray within the function, you are actually changing someNumbers in the main program—funcArray is an alias for someNumbers.

In the following steps, you will change the MYNUMS program so that it can maintain statistics for five summing problems and then display them at the end of the game.

1 In main(), add a declaration for an array that will hold an integer for each summing problem. We will use 1 if a guess is correct and 0 if a guess is incorrect.

```cpp
int guessWasCorrect[problems];
```

2 Change the main() program so that the user can attempt five problems rather than just one. After `displayDirections();`, add the beginning of a for statement:

```
for(int tries =0; tries<problems; ++tries)

  {
```

3   Place the final curly bracket of the for loop after the call to displayResults();

4   Modify the displayResults() function so that it returns an integer indicating whether the user's sum is correct or incorrect. Change the prototype for displayResults() as follows:

```
int displayResults(int correctSum, int guess);
```

5   Change the call to displayResults() so that an integer is returned to the guessWasCorrect array:

```
guessWasCorrect[tries] =
  displayResults(correctSum, guess);
```

6   Modify the displayResults() function body so that a 0 or 1 is returned:

```
int displayResults(int sum, int guess)

  {
    int right;
    if(guess==sum)

      {
        cout<<"Correct!"<<endl;
        right =1;
      }
    else

      {
        cout<<"Wrong!"<<endl;
        right=0;
      }
    return(right);

  }
```

7   Create a function to display the statistics at the end of the game. The function needs to know the contents of the guessWasCorrect array, but should not alter the contents of the array.

Start by creating a prototype for the function that accepts the address of the array, but does not change its contents. Change the finalStats prototype comment as follows:

```
void finalStats(int guessWasCorrect[]);
```

8 Place the call to the finalStats() function after the end of the for loop, but before the closing curly bracket to main():

```
finalStats(guessWasCorrect);
```

9 Write the finalStats() function:

```
void finalStats(const int correct[])
  {
    cout<<"Final statistics"<<endl;
    for(int x =0; x< problems; ++x)
      {
        cout<<"Problem "<<x+1<<" was ";
        (correct[x]==0) ? cout<<"wrong."<<endl :
          cout<< "right."<<endl;
      }
  }
```

10 Compile, test, and save the program.

Inline Functions

Each time you call a function in a C++ program, the computer must do the following:

- Remember where to return when the function eventually ends.
- Provide memory for the function's variables.
- Provide memory for any value returned by the function.
- Pass control to the function.
- Pass control back to the calling program.

This extra activity constitutes the **overhead**, or cost of doing business, involved in calling a function. When a program calls a function many times, the overhead is relatively small because you no longer need to write the function's lines of code many times in different locations in the program. If a group of statements is very small or is not used very many times, however, placing the statement in a function may be convenient but not worth the overhead. An **inline** function is a small function with no overhead. Overhead is avoided because program control never transfers to the function. Rather, a copy of the function statements is placed directly into the compiled calling program.

tip

• • • • • • • • • • • • • • • • •

When you inline a function, you merely make a request to the compiler; the compiler does not have to honor this request, however. This limitation may pose a problem if the function is included in a header file accessed by two different source files. If the compiler generates a message saying that an inline function has duplicate definitions, put the function in its own source file and include it just once in the compilation.

```cpp
#include<iostream.h>
inline double computeGross(double hours, double rate)
  // note the keyword inline
  {
    return(hours * rate);
  }
void main()
  {
    double hrsWorked=37.5, rateOfPay=12.45, gross;
      // main's local variables
    gross = computeGross(hrsWorked, rateOfPay);
// call to the inline function --
// looks like a regular function call
    cout<<"\nGross pay is "<<gross;
  }
```

The inline function appears prior to main(), which calls it. Any inline function must precede any function that calls it, which eliminates the need for prototyping in the calling function. When you compile the program, the code for the inline function is placed directly in main(). When you run the main() program, it executes more rapidly than a version with a non-inline function because of the lack of overhead. The size of the main program, however, exceeds the size of a program with a non-inline function. If you use the inline function many times within the same program, the program could grow dramatically because the function statements are copied at the location of each call. Therefore, you should use an inline function in the following situations:

- when you want to group statements together so that you can use a function name
- when the number of statements is small (one or two lines in the body of the function)
- when the function is called on few occasions

In the following steps, you will add an inline function to the MYNUMS program that takes care of calculating the sum of two numbers.

1 In the **MYNUMS** program, above the void main() line, rewrite sumNums() as an inline function for summing the two integers:

```cpp
inline int sumNums(int j, int k)
  {
    return(j+k);
  }
```

2 Remove the prototype for sumNums() from the main() function (or comment it out).

3 Remove the non-inline function sumNums() from the file (or comment it out).

4 Compile, test, and save the program.

Using Default Arguments

When you don't provide enough arguments in a function call, you usually want the compiler to issue a warning message for this error. For example, the following code is lacking a character parameter:

```
#include<iostream.h>
void main(void)

  {
    int FunctionNeedsThree(int, double,char);
      // function prototype
    FunctionNeedsThree(12, 4.5);
      // Error -- character parameter is missing
  }
```

Sometimes, however, it is useful to create a function that supplies a **default value** for any missing parameters. For example, you might create a function to calculate either the volume of a cube or the area of a square. When you want a cube's area, you pass three parameters to the function: length, width, and height. When you want a square's area, you pass only two parameters, and a default value of 1.0 is used for the height. The height is a default parameter; the length and width are **mandatory parameters**.

```
#include<iostream.h>
void main()

  {
    double calculate(double l, double w, double h = 1.0);
    cout<<calculate(4.0, 4.0, 4.0); // this call to the
    // function uses three values -- result is 64
    cout<<calculate(4.0, 4.0);  // this call to the
    // function uses two values and 1.0 -- result is 16
  }
double calculate(double l, double w, double h)

  {
    return(l * w * h);
  }
```

Two rules apply to default parameters:

■ If you assign a default value to any variable in a function prototype's parameter list, then all parameters to the right of that variable must also have default values.

■ If you omit any argument when you call a function that has default parameters, then you must leave out all arguments to the right of that argument.

For example, examine the following program and notice how the default values are applied:

```cpp
#include<iostream.h>
void main()
  {
    void badFunc(int var1 = 1, int var2);
    // illegal -- if var1 has a default, then var2 must
    void functionWithDefaults(int var1,int var2=2,int var3=3);
      // legal
    functionWithDefaults();
      // illegal -- a value for var1 is mandatory
    functionWithDefaults(4); // output is 423
    functionWithDefaults(4, 5);  // output is 453
    functionWithDefaults(4, 5, 6); // output is 456
  }
int functionWithDefaults(int one, int two, int three)
  {
    cout<<one<<two<<three;
  }
```

The function called functionWithDefaults() has one mandatory parameter and two default parameters. Therefore, you must pass at least one—but no more than three—values to the function.

Overloading Functions

In most computer programming languages, each variable used in a function must have only one name. As you have already seen, C++ allows you to employ an alias. Similarly, in most computer programming languages, each function used in a program must have a unique name. For example, if you want a function to display a value's square, you could create a function that squares integers, a function that squares floats, and a function that squares doubles; each function receives a unique name:

tip
••••••••••••••••••
C++ can apply the same
name to different func-
tions because the compiler
generates a different name
for each function based on
the type of data being
passed. This feature is
called *name mangling*. As
a programmer, you don't
have to worry about how
it works.

```
void squareInteger(int x)

  {

    cout<<"In integer function "<<x*x<<endl;

  }

void squareFloat(float x)

  {

    cout<<"In float function "<<x*x<<endl;

  }

void squareDouble(double x)

  {

    cout<<"In double function "<<x*x<<endl;

  }
```

Instead of using three function names for functions that perform basically the same task, C++ allows you to reuse, or **overload**, function names. For example, each function that squares a value can bear the same name. C++ determines which function to call by reviewing the parameters submitted.

```
#include<iostream.h>
void squareValue(int x)

  {

    cout<<"In integer function "<<x*x<<endl;

  }

void squareValue(float x)

  {

    cout<<"In float function "<<x*x<<endl;

  }

void squareValue(double x)

  {

    cout<<"In double function "<<x*x<<endl;

  }

void main()

  {

    int i = 5;

    float f = 2.2;

    double d = 3.3;

    squareValue(i); // output is "In integer function 25"

    squareValue(f); // output is "In float function 4.84"

    squareValue(d); // output is "In double function 10.89"

  }
```

Overloading a function's name allows you to use it for more than one function. The benefit derives from your ability to use one easy-to-understand function name without regard to the data types involved. Of course, you still must write each function separately. While functions with the same name need not perform similar tasks, your programs will be clearer if overloaded functions perform essentially the same tasks.

In the following steps, you will create two functions that demonstrate default arguments and overloading. Each function will sum the values passed to it, and each receive one, two, or three arguments. One function adds integers; the other adds doubles.

1 Open a new C++ program file. Enter comments, such as your name and the date. Add the statement `#include<iostream.h>`.

2 Write a function named sum() that will accept one, two, or three integers and return their sum. The first integer is mandatory; the last two integers must have default values of 0.

```cpp
int sum(int a, int b =0, int c = 0)
  {
    return(a+b+c);
  }
```

3 Write another function named sum() that will sum one, two, or three doubles.

```cpp
double sum(double a, double b = 0.0, double c = 0.0)
  {
    return(a+b+c);
  }
```

4 Write a main() function to test the new functions.

```cpp
void main()
  {
    cout<<sum(1)<<endl;
    cout<<sum(2,3) <<endl;
    cout<<sum(4,5,6) <<endl;
    cout<<sum(7.8) <<endl;
    cout<<(12.2,34.0,6.0) <<endl;
  }
```

> **5** Compile and test the program, confirming that the functions work correctly in each instance.
>
> **6** Save the program as **OVERLOAD.CPP**.

S U M M A R Y

■ You can view the memory address of any variable by using the address operator, &.

■ You may declare pointer variables, also known as pointers, that can hold memory addresses.

■ A pointer is declared with a type that indicates the type of variable whose address it will hold. To indicate that a variable is a pointer variable, place an asterisk in front of the variable's name.

■ You may use the indirection operator, the asterisk, to access the contents stored in an address held by a pointer.

■ You cannot change the address of a declared variable, but you can alter the contents of a pointer variable.

■ You pass addresses to a function to avoid having the function copy the passed value, and to have the function change more than one value.

■ A reference variable is a variable that serves as an alias for another variable. It is declared with a type, by placing an ampersand in front of its name.

■ A reference variable is easier to use than a pointer; a pointer is more flexible than a reference variable.

■ To pass an address, thereby eliminating the copy of a variable but protecting the variable from change, you may pass a variable pointer as a constant.

■ An array name is a memory address. The subscript used to access an element of an array indicates distance from the beginning address.

■ The work involved in calling a function is known as overhead.

■ An inline function is a small function with no overhead. It places a copy of the function statements directly into the calling program when it is compiled.

■ Any inline function must precede any function that calls it; the calling function does not require a prototype.

■ Functions may include mandatory parameters and default parameters.

■ If you assign a default value to any variable in a function prototype's parameter list, then all parameters to the right of that variable must have default values as well.

■ If you omit any argument when you call a function that has default parameters, you must leave out all arguments to the right of that argument.

■ C++ allows you to overload function names, so that the same name can be applied to more than one function.

Q U E S T I O N S

1. In C++, the address operator is the following symbol _____.
   a. >>
   b. &
   c. *
   d. !

2. Variables that hold memory addresses are called _____.
   a. subscripts
   b. holders
   c. pointers
   d. indicators

3. When you declare a pointer, you must give it a _____.
   a. type
   b. type and name
   c. type, name, and value
   d. name and value

4. You indicate a variable is a pointer variable by placing a(n) _____ in front of the variable's name.
   a. asterisk
   b. ampersand
   c. dollar sign
   d. exclamation point

5. You have declared an integer pointer called point. You have also declared an integer called number. Which statement is the correct format?
   a. point = number;
   b. point = *number;
   c. point = &number;
   d. point = +number;

6. You have assigned the address of Value to the pointer P. Which statement will display the value stored in Value?
   a. cout<<P;
   b. cout<<*Value;
   c. cout<<&P;
   d. cout<<*P;

7. The indirection operator is the _____.
   a. asterisk
   b. ampersand
   c. dollar sign
   d. plus sign

8. Which is a good reason for passing a variable's address to a function?
   a. the function will have a copy of the variable
   b. the function cannot change the value of the variable in the calling function
   c. C++ requires that all variables used in a function be passed by address
   d. the function needs to change multiple variable values

9. A variable that is an alias for another variable is known as a(n) _____.
   a. reference variable
   b. actual parameter
   c. formal variable
   d. sneaky variable

10. A difference between reference variables and pointers is that _____.
    a. reference variables are easier to use
    b. pointers are easier to use
    c. reference variables are more flexible
    d. no difference exists between reference variables and pointers

11. Passing a variable pointer as a constant _____.
   a. protects the contents pointed to by the pointer from change
   b. eliminates the need to name the pointer in the function
   c. eliminates the need to give the pointer a type in the function
   d. causes a copy of the pointer to be produced in the function

12. An array name is a _____.
   a. subscript
   b. formal parameter
   c. memory address
   d. prototype

13. The time and memory involved in calling a function represent the function's _____.
   a. prototype
   b. overhead
   c. cost
   d. burden

14. When the compiler places a copy of a small function's statements directly into a program, the function is said to be _____.
   a. overloaded
   b. mangled
   c. inline
   d. redundant

15. When you omit parameters from a function call, values can be provided by _____.
   a. formal parameters
   b. reference parameters
   c. overloaded parameters
   d. default parameters

16. If you assign a default value to any variable in a function prototype's parameter list, then _____.
   a. all other parameters in the function prototype must have default values
   b. all parameters to the right of that variable must have default values
   c. all parameters to the left of that variable must have default values
   d. no other parameters in that prototype can have default values

17. When a program calls a function that has default parameters, if you omit an argument, you must _____.
   a. not omit any other arguments
   b. omit all arguments
   c. omit all arguments to the right of that argument
   d. omit all arguments to the left of that argument

18. Having more than one function with the same name is called _____.
   a. overloading
   b. defaulting
   c. casting
   d. referencing

19. A C++ program contains a function with the header `int function(double d, char c)`. Which of the following function headers could be used within the same program?

a. char function(double d, char c)

b. int function(int d, char c)

c. both (a) and (b) would be allowed

d. neither (a) nor (b) would be allowed

20. Overloaded functions are required to _____.

a. have the same return type

b. have the same number of parameters

c. perform the same basic functions

d. none of above

EXERCISES

1. Given the following declarations and statements:

```
int arrayOfInts[25] = {33,55,77};
int *pointer;
Pointer = &arrayOfInts[0];
```

and assuming that arrayOfInts is stored at memory address 4000, and that integers are two bytes, is each of the following legal or illegal? If legal, what is its value?

a. arrayOfInts[0]

b. arrayOfInts[1]

c. arrayOfInts[2]

d. arrayOfInts[3]

e. arrayOfInts[24]

f. arrayOfInts[25]

g. &arrayOfInts[0]

h. pointer

i. *pointer

j. *pointer + 1

k. *(pointer +1)

2. Write a program that calculates the cost of building a desk. The program consists of three functions:

■ a function to accept as input the type of wood desired and the number of drawers in the desk

■ A function to calculate the cost of the desk based on the following:
Pine desks are $100.
Oak desks are $140.
All other woods are $180.

In addition, a $30 surcharge is charged for each drawer.

■ A function to display the final price

Pass all variables by value.

3. Rewrite the desk program from problem 2, passing all variables as reference variables.

4. Rewrite the desk program from problem 2, changing the function that displays the final price to an inline function.

5. Write a program that accepts 10 values and stores them in an array. Pass the array to a function that determines the smallest and largest of the values.

6. Write a program that asks a student how many tests he or she has taken so far in a course. The program should accept any number from 1 to 5; the user can then enter the appropriate number of test scores. Write an overloaded function to average the student's test scores. The function should compute a correct average whether the student has taken one, two, three, four, or five tests.

debugging ▶ 7. Each of the following files in the TUT01 folder contains syntax and/or logical errors. Determine the problem in each case, and fix the program.
   a. DEBUG1-1.CPP
   b. DEBUG1-2.CPP
   c. DEBUG1-3.CPP
   d. DEBUG1-4.CPP
   e. DEBUG1-5.CPP

Structures and Classes

case Teacher's Pet is achieving huge success with sales of the TWONUMS program, and young children are clamoring for more. After surveying grade-school teachers, you discover that fractions are universally difficult for children. You plan to create a series of products that will help children discover the properties of fractions.

As you plan the program series, you realize two things:

1. A fraction has two data parts: a numerator and a denominator. It will be most convenient to deal with these two parts as a single entity.

2. Not only does a fraction have two data parts, but there is also a set of tasks that are performed on all fractions. In other words, a particular fraction is really an object that is a member of a class.

You can begin to use a fraction as a single unit by creating a structure. You can then graduate to making a fraction a true object by adding methods to use with it.

Previewing the FRACCLS Program

The FRACCLS program is not very interesting to run—all it does is display some fractions. Nevertheless, it is a first step toward object-oriented programming. Each fraction is an object with its own data and its own behaviors. It is also a member of a class.

1   Load the **FRACCLS.CPP** program and execute it.

2   Examine the code. You will be creating this code yourself in this tutorial.

LESSON A
objectives

In this lesson you will learn:

- What advantages structures offer
- How to define a structure type
- How to declare a structure
- How to pass structures to functions
- How to use your own #include files
- How to return structures from functions

Structures

Why Use Structures?

In a small program, you deal with a few integers, a few doubles, or a few characters at one time. When you write a function that receives two or three variables, it is a simple matter to list the variables in the prototype and function header. In many applications, however, dozens of variables go together logically, perhaps to form a **record**.

For example, an employee record typically consists of the following information:

- social security number
- last name
- first name
- middle initial
- street address
- city
- state
- zip code
- area code
- phone number
- date of hire
- rate of pay
- number of dependents

and so on, for perhaps 50 or 60 more items.

Imagine the call to a function that deals with an employee record:

```
dealWithEmployee(socSecNo, last, first, middle, street,etc.
```

The following statement is a much clearer function call:

```
dealWithEmployee(oneEmployeeRecord);
```

In this call, oneEmployeeRecord contains all the information pertaining to the employee, and you pass the entire record to the dealWithEmployee() function.

It is often more convenient to group large numbers of variables together, because they go together logically and are easier to handle as a single entity. A simple integer or character has a scalar type, also known as **fundamental type**. You can also create objects that have more complicated types known as **programmer-defined types**.

Determining the attributes of an object, and subsequently dealing with the object as a whole, are preliminary steps toward object-oriented programming. When you use a real-world object, like a radio, you don't think or care about how it works. Sometimes, however, you change some of the states of the attributes of the radio, such as volume level or frequency selection.

When you write a program and create a name for a group of associated variables, you hide, or encapsulate, the individual components. Sometimes you want to change the state of some of these components; often you want to think about the entity as a whole.

One C++ construct for grouping variables that enables you to deal with them as a unit is the structure, which groups variables that belong together logically. If all variables are of the same type, they can form an array. A structure, however, can consist of variables of different types, which are known as **members** of the structure.

A structure is not the only C++ construct for encapsulating data, or even the one most commonly used. A **class** can also be used to encapsulate data. Classes have advantages relative to structures in what they can contain and what they can do, and C++ programmers use classes far more frequently. Structures, however, are the predecessors of classes, and are slightly easier to manage. As the major concepts you learn about structures will also apply to classes, the former represent a good starting point.

Defining a Structure Type

Declaring a structure type requires you to use the keyword **struct**, followed by a name for the structure type, followed by (within curly brackets) a list of the data types and names of all elements of the structure. For example, the following is a very simple employee record structure type:

```
struct EmployeeRecord
  {
    int employeeNumber;
    string lastName;
    double rateOfPay;
}; // notice the semicolon at the end of the declaration
```

Using this knowledge, you can now begin to create a C++ program that uses a fraction. First, you will create a structure to hold a fraction.

1   Open a new source file.
2   The structure type is called Fraction, so name the structure type struct Fraction.
3   On a new line, type the opening curly bracket.

tip

· · · · · · · · · · · · · · · · ·

▶ Just as you can declare more than one variable of a fundamental type in the same statement,

```
double oneAmount,
  anotherAmount;
```

you can also declare multiple structures in the same statement:

```
struct EmployeeRecord
  onePerson,
  somebodyElse;
```

tip

· · · · · · · · · · · · · · · · ·

▶ C++ programmers would say that EmployeeRecord is an **abstract data type** (ADT). This term simply indicates that EmployeeRecord is a type you define, as opposed to types like char and int that are defined by C++.

4 On new lines, type two variable declarations:

```
int numerator;
int denominator;
```

5 Type the closing curly bracket, followed by a semicolon.
6 Compile the program segment, and correct any errors.
7 Save the file as **MYFRAC.CPP**.

The definition of the EmployeeRecord type shows that it consists of an integer, a string, and a double. Note that the definition of the EmployeeRecord type does not set aside any memory for storage, just as writing "int" or "double" does not set aside any memory for storage. Defining the EmployeeRecord type simply shows what attributes the new type will contain if and when any actual structures are declared. Just as no memory is reserved for an integer until you actually name an integer,

```
int oneInteger;  // now enough memory to hold one
  // integer (named oneInteger) is set aside
```

no memory is reserved for a structure until you actually assign a name to a structure,

```
EmployeeRecord theGuyInAccounting;
        // enough memory to hold one EmployeeRecord
        //(named theGuyInAccounting) is set aside
```

Add a declaration for one fraction to the MYFRAC program.

1 Because the program is now going to include an output statement, add an include statement at the top of the file:

```
#include<iostream.h>
```

2 Below the struct definition in the **MYFRAC** file, begin the program with the following format:

```
void main()
  {
```

3 Declare one fraction structure as

```
Fraction oneFraction;
```

4 Add the closing curly brackets and compile the program. Depending on your compiler, you may receive a warning that you have a local variable that is not referenced. The message appears because you have declared oneFraction, but have not done anything with it (referenced it) at this point. The warning can safely be ignored.

Once a structure is declared, you can refer to specific attributes of it by using the structure's name, a dot, and the attribute's name. For example, to display the last name of theGuyInAccounting, the correct statement is

```
cout<<theGuyInAccounting.lastName;
```

It is never correct to work with the attribute of a structure without indicating the structure to which it belongs.

Assignment to a structure can be made attribute by attribute:

```
EmployeeRecord mySecretary;
mySecretary.employeeNumber = 345;
strcpy(mySecretary.lastName,"Allen");
  // strcpy is a function used to copy one string to another
mySecretary.rateOfPay = 12.50;
```

The function strcpy takes two string arguments and copies the second to the first. It is prototyped in the file string.h.

Assignment can also be made at the time of declaration:

```
EmployeeRecord mySecretary = {345, "Allen", 12.50};
```

Give a value to the fraction you declared in MYFRAC.

1 After the declaration of oneFraction, enter the following assignment statements:

```
oneFraction.numerator = 2;
oneFraction.denominator = 3;
```

tip
················
▶ To use cout, don't forget that you need to insert `#include<iostream.h>` as the first line in the program.

2 To confirm that the assignments are correct, add statements to echo the values:

```
cout<<"Numerator is "<<oneFraction.numerator<<endl;
cout<<"Denominator is "<<oneFraction.denominator<<endl;
cout<<"Fraction is "<<oneFraction.numerator<<"/"
  <<oneFraction.denominator<<endl;
```

3 Compile and test the program. The output is as follows:

```
Numerator is 2
Denominator is 3
Fraction is 2/3
```

Obviously, it would not be very practical if every EmployeeRecord for a company needed its own name, such as theGuyInAccounting or mySecretary. Structures usually become useful when they are used in arrays.

When EmployeeRecord is declared as a structure, then

```
EmployeeRecord employee[200];
```

tip
················
▶ Do not make the mistake of trying to refer to the first employee's last name as `employee.lastName[0]`. It's `employee[0]` you want, not `lastName[0]`.

declares an array that has room to store data for 200 employees.

The first employee is employee[0] and the second employee is employee[1]. The surname of the first employee is employee[0].lastName and the employee number of the second employee is employee[1].employeeNumber. You can display all 200 employee numbers with the following instructions:

```
for(int x = 0; x < 200; ++x)
  cout<<employee[x].employeeNumber<<endl;
```

Add an array of fractions to the MYFRAC program. The array will hold nine values representing ¹⁄₁₀, ²⁄₁₀, ³⁄₁₀, and so on.

1 Add a declaration:

```
Fraction fracArray[9];
```

2 Add steps to fill the array of structures with values representing $\frac{1}{10}$, $\frac{2}{10}$, and so on:

```cpp
for(int x = 0; x <9; ++x)
  {
   fracArray[x].numerator = x+1; // element 0 has
    // numerator 1, element 1 has numerator 2, and so on
   fracArray[x].denominator = 10; // for this
    // example, the denominator is 10 for each fraction
  }
```

3 To confirm that the values are stored correctly, write a loop to echo the values:

```cpp
for(x=0; x<9;++x)
{
  cout<<fracArray[x].numerator<<"/";
  cout<<fracArray[x].denominator<<endl;
 }
```

4 Compile and test the program.

The members of any C++ structure can be any data type, including other structures. For example, most employee records contain more than just the last name of the employee. You may want to store a first name and a middle name or initial, too. You can create a structure just for names:

```cpp
struct Name
 {
  string last;
  string first;
  string middle;
 };
```

A structure definition for an employee record is then:

```
struct EmployeeRecord
  {
    int employeeNumber;
    Name employeeName;
    double rateOfPay;
  };
```

When you declare one employee as

```
EmployeeRecord employee;
```

you can refer to their middle initial as `employee.employeeName.middle`. Notice the two dots; they signal that `middle` is a member of the Name structure, and `employeeName` is a member of the EmployeeRecord structure. Defining Name as a separate structure type provides two advantages:

- You save time when declaring the EmployeeRecord structure because the individual parts of the name are declared as part of the Name structure.
- You can reuse the Name structure in other applications. Programs that work with customer orders, distributors, and advertising mailing lists, for example, might use the Name structure, and you will not have to redefine first, middle, and last in each application.

You have already learned that reusability is a major feature of thinking in an object-oriented manner. Developing this type of a structure is a good example of planning ahead for reuse.

In the following steps, you will create a structure for mixed numbers. A mixed number is one like 7⅛, which consists of a whole part and a fractional part.

1   Just after the complete `struct Fraction` definition in your program, create a structure definition for mixed numbers:

```
struct MixedNum
  {
    int wholeNum;
    // to hold whole number part of mixed number

    Fraction partNum;
    // to hold fractional part of mixed number

  };  // don't forget the semicolon
```

Each partNum is a structure with both a numerator and a denominator.

2 To your main() program, add a declaration for one mixed number:

```
MixedNum oneMix;
```

3 To give the mixed number a value representing 7⅛, add assignment statements at the end of the program:

```
oneMix.wholeNum = 7;
oneMix.partNum.numerator = 1; // notice the two dot operators
oneMix.partNum.denominator = 8;
```

4 Add a statement to display the number in mixed number format:

```
cout<<oneMix.wholeNum<<" "<< oneMix.partNum.numerator
  <<"/"<<oneMix.partNum.denominator<<endl;
```

5 Compile and test the program.

Passing Structures to Functions

You can pass copies of individual structure members to functions, or you can pass copies of entire structures to functions.

Passing an individual structure member to a function is no different than passing any other scalar variable. For example, you can define a structure to hold a student ID number and a grade-point average with the following statements:

```
struct StudentRec
  {
    int idNum;
    double gpa;
  };
```

You can declare one student's record as follows:

```
StudentRec oneStudent;
```

You can then pass the student's grade-point average to a function,

```
testProbation(oneStudent.gpa);
```

as long as the function is prepared to receive a double, such as

```
void testProbation(double avg)
 {
  if (avg<2.0)
     cout<<"On probation";
 }
```

Alternatively, you can pass a copy of an entire structure to a function, as long as the function is prepared to receive the same type of structure:

```
#include<iostream.h>
struct StudentRec  // this type is global
  {
    int idNum;
    double gpa;
  };
void main()
  {
    StudentRec oneStudent = {6143, 3.6};
    // declare one student
    void probationMessage(StudentRec scholar);
    // function prototype
    probationMessage(oneStudent); // call function
  }
void probationMessage(StudentRec scholar)
  // this is the function -- it receives a
  // StudentRec structure
  {
  if (scholar.gpa<2.0)
    cout<<"Student "<<scholar.idNum<<" is on probation";
  }
```

Both the main() function and the probationMessage() function use the global type StudentRec. The structures oneStudent and scholar are local to their respective functions. The scholar structure receives a copy of the data in the oneStudent structure and, in turn, can access idNum and gpa.

The StudentRec type in this example does not have to be global; you can define the StudentRec type in main() and again in probationMessage(). Nevertheless, it makes sense to define the structure type globally for two reasons:

■ You save many lines of code by not rewriting the identical structure definition in each function that uses it.

■ A change to the format of an organization's student record (or employee record, or inventory record)—for example, when a new field is added—is made only once.

The second point is very important. More than half of most programmers' time on the job (and almost all of new programmers' time on the job) is spent **maintaining**, or making changes to, existing programs. For example, an administrator may decide that a StudentRec should contain a new field to hold earned credit hours. If StudentRec is redefined in several functions, then this change must be made in each of those locations. The more places a change must be made, the more time it takes, the more likely that an error will occur when making a change, and the greater the chances that one of the necessary changes will be overlooked. By the same token, because you may use specific structure definitions, such as a student record, within many applications in an organization, it makes sense to store the structure definitions in a single, separate file that can be included with all appropriate programs.

Using Your Own #include Files

You have already used #include files—for example, cout and cin could not be used without iostream.h. You may also create and include your own header files. For example, if several of your programs require use of a student record, you may create a file called myheader.cpp with the following contents:

```
struct StudentRec
   {
      int idNum;
      double gpa;
   };
```

An #include file does not have to carry the .h extension, but this convention helps other people understand the type of file it is. Because some compiler problems may result when you compile your own header files using a .h extension, we will follow the convention of using a .cpp extension.

The following program runs correctly:

```
#include<iostream.h>
#include"myheader.cpp"  // note the quotes
void main()
   {
         StudentRec aSophomore = {3315, 2.7};
         cout<<"student "<<aSophomore.idNum;
         cout<<" has a gpa of "<<aSophomore.gpa<<endl;
   }
```

When using the standard files that come with the C++ compiler, the angle brackets are used surrounding the header filename. This format tells the compiler to search for the file in the standard directory that holds #include files. When using your own header files, use the quotation marks. The compiler will then search in the current directory first. You can also give a full path name:

```
#include "c:\hjohnson\headers\myheader.cpp"
```

tip

Quotes are allowed around the standard include filenames. This format will cause the compiler to look for the file in the current directory first, however, and it will take a little longer before the appropriate file is located.

In the following steps, you will create a header file for the fraction structure.

1 Cut (do not delete) the statements that define the Fraction and MixedNum structures from the **MYFRAC** program.

```
struct Fraction
  {
    int numerator;
    int denominator;
  };
struct MixedNum
  {
    int wholeNum;
    Fraction partNum;
  };
```

Paste them into a new file.

2 Compile the new file, correct any errors, and save the file as **FRAC.CPP**.

3 Add an #include statement at the top of the **MYFRAC** program to include the **FRAC.CPP** file:

```
#include"frac.cpp"
```

4 Compile and run the **MYFRAC** program. It should work the same way as before; the only difference is that the structure definitions of Fraction and MixedNum are now physically located in their own file.

Returning Structures from Functions

You can return changes to a structure made in a function in any of several ways: the function can return a copy of the structure, you can use a reference variable, or you can use a pointer.

Returning a Copy of a Structure

You can write a function that returns a structure using the same format as that employed for any function that returns a value. Rather than being a scalar type such as double or int, the function type is a structure type.

For example, you can create a structure to hold an inventory item and store it in a file named inven.cpp:

```
struct ItemSoldType
  {
    int stockNum;
    char nameOfItem[20];
    double price;
  };
```

In the following program, you use the function getData() to obtain values for the structure members and pass the values back to main(), where they are displayed.

```
#include"inven.cpp"
  // includes the definition of ItemSoldType
#include<iostream.h>
void main()
  {
   ItemSoldType oneItem;   // a structure to hold one item
   ItemSoldType getData(void);
   // a function prototype whose return type is ItemSoldType
   oneItem = getData();    // get the data and put it in oneItem
   cout<<"Stock num is "<<oneItem.stockNum;
   cout<<" Item is "<<oneItem.nameOfItem<<endl;
   cout<<"Price is "<<oneItem.price<<endl;
  }
ItemSoldType getData(void)  // the function begins here
  {
   ItemSoldType item;   // a local structure
   cout<<"Enter item number "<<endl;
   cin>>item.stockNum;
   cout<<"Enter name of item "<<endl;
   cin>>item.nameOfItem;
   cout<<"Enter price "<<endl;
   cin>>item.price;
   return(item);   // a copy of the structure returns
  }
```

Now you will add a function to MYFRAC that adds 1 to a mixed number.

1 Add a new structure declaration to your program. This structure will hold a mixed number that is 1 larger than the oneMix number.

```
MixedNum biggerMix;
```

2 Prototype a function that receives a MixedNum structure and returns a MixedNum structure.

```
MixedNum addOneToMix(MixedNum m);
```

3 As the last statement in your current **MYFRAC** program, call the addOneToMix() function to add 1 to the mixed number stored in oneMix, and store the result in biggerMix.

```
biggerMix = addOneToMix(oneMix);
```

4 Next, add a statement to display biggerMix:

```
cout<<biggerMix.wholeNum<<" "
  <<biggerMix.partNum.numerator
  <<"/"<<biggerMix.partNum.denominator<<endl;
```

5 At the end of your **MYFRAC** file, write the function itself.

```
MixedNum addOneToMix(MixedNum m)
 {
 m.wholeNum++;
 return(m);
 }
```

6 Compile and test the program. If your original oneMix is 7⅛, your new biggerMix should be 8⅛. The output is as follows:

```
Numerator is 2
Denominator is 3
The fraction is 2/3
1/10
2/10
3/10
4/10
5/10
6/10
7/10
8/10
9/10
7 1/8
8 1/8
_
```

Passing a Reference to a Structure

Instead of passing a structure back from a function, you can pass a reference to a structure. For example, in the inventory program, the prototype for getData() indicates the return type is ItemSoldType:

```
ItemSoldType getData(void);
```

The getData() function creates a temporary local structure, fills it with data, and passes a copy of the structure back to the main() program, where the copy is stored in oneItem:

```
oneItem = getData();    // get the data and put it in oneItem
```

An alternative is to pass the address of oneItem to the getData() function. If this function has access to the actual memory address of oneItem, values can be assigned to the actual memory locations of oneItem's data members. You need not make a temporary local structure within getData() or pass anything back to main().

Using this approach, you can change the inventory program as follows:

```
#include"inven.cpp"  // includes definition of ItemSoldType
#include<iostream.h>
void main()
  {
   ItemSoldType oneItem;  // a structure to hold one item
   void getData(ItemSoldType &oneItem);
    // prototype of a function whose return type is void
    // it receives a reference
   getData(oneItem);   // send a reference to oneItem
   cout<<"Stock num is "<<oneItem.stockNum;
   cout<<" Item is "<<oneItem.nameOfItem<<endl;
   cout<<"Price is "<<oneItem.price<<endl;
  }
void getData(ItemSoldType &item)  // function begins here
  {
  // no local structure necessary
   cout<<"Enter item number "<<endl;
   cin>>item.StockNum;
   cout<<"Enter name of item<<endl;
   cin>>item.nameOfItem;
   cout<<"Enter price "<<endl;
   cin>>item.price;
  // nothing to return; the function "knows" address of
    // oneItem
  }
```

In this program, the getData() function receives a reference to the oneItem structure in main(). Therefore, the function receives input to the actual structure—not a copy of it—and you don't have to pass anything back to main(). This strategy saves the overhead involved in making a duplicate local structure in getData(). Although ItemSoldType is a small structure without many data members, the savings of not creating local copies of a structure become even more significant with a large structure.

Using a Pointer to a Structure

When you want a function to have access to a structure's members, you can also use a pointer to the structure. Consider a function that increases the price of an item by 25 percent. The function prototype for a function that receives a pointer to an ItemSoldType structure is `void  increase(ItemSoldType *point);`.

This function, named increase, returns nothing. It receives a pointer (arbitrarily named point) that points to a structure whose type is ItemSoldType. The function call is `increase(&oneItem);`. You pass the address of the oneItem structure (whose type is ItemSoldType) to the increase function. The entire program is shown below:

```
#include"inven.cpp" // contains the definition of ItemSoldType
#include<iostream.h>
void main()
  {
   ItemSoldType oneItem = {6712, "Hammer", 10.00};
    // a structure initialized with some data
   void increase(ItemSoldType *point);
    // a function whose return type is void; it receives
    // a pointer
   increase(&oneItem);    // send the address of oneItem
   cout<<"Stock num is "<<oneItem.stockNum<<" Item is"
     <<oneItem.nameOfItem<<endl;
   cout<<"Price is "<<oneItem.price<<endl;
    // price is changed to 12.50
  }
void increase(ItemSoldType *itemPointer)
  // function receives a pointer
  {
    // no local structure necessary
    (*itemPointer).price=(*itemPointer).price * 1.25;
    // nothing to return; function "knows" address of oneItem
  }
```

The statement in the increase() function that deserves comment is

```
(*itemPointer).price=(*itemPointer).price*1.25;
```

You read this awkward statement as "Take the price member of the structure whose address is stored in itemPointer, or pointed to by itemPointer, and multiply it by 1.25." The parentheses in the code are necessary. Without them, the statement becomes

```
*itemPointer.price=*itemPointer.price * 1.25;
```

This statement would read as "Take the address that is stored in the pointer *itemPointer.price, and multiply it by 1.25." This operation is illegal because no address is stored in itemPointer.price (it's a double value, not an address).

Because this syntax for using pointers to structures is so awkward, another, simpler notation exists. The itemPrice member of the structure pointed to by the itemPointer can be increased with the statement

```
itemPointer->price = itemPointer->price * 1.25;
```

SUMMARY

- You can group variables together by creating a structure, which is a nonscalar, programmer-defined type.
- Creating a structure allows you to encapsulate data.
- The variables within a structure are members of that structure.
- When you declare a structure, you use the keyword struct, followed by a name for the structure type, followed by (within curly brackets) a list of the data types and names of all elements of the structure.
- No memory is reserved for a structure until you actually assign a name to it.
- You refer to a specific attribute of a structure by using the structure's name, a dot, and the attribute's name.
- Assignment to a structure can be made either at the time of declaration or later, in an attribute-by-attribute format.
- Structures are typically most useful when they are stored in arrays.
- The members of any C++ structure can be any data type, including other structures. Thus, you can reuse existing structure definitions.
- You can pass copies of individual structure members to functions, and you can pass copies of entire structures to functions.
- Often, you define structure types globally, allowing you to save many lines of code and make global record format changes in just one location.
- Structure definitions are often stored in a separate file that can be included with all appropriate programs.
- When using your own header files, use the quotation marks surrounding the filenames used in #include statements.
- You can receive changes to a structure made in a function in any of several ways: the function can return a copy of the structure, you can use a reference variable, or you can use a pointer.
- You can reference an item in a structure that is pointed to by pointer p as (*p).item or p->item.

QUESTIONS

1. When variables refer to attributes of an entity (such as name, address, and phone number of a person), those attributes form a _____.
   a. file
   b. record
   c. field
   d. program

2. A fundamental type such as int or double is a _____.
   a. programmer-defined type
   b. complex type
   c. nonscalar type
   d. scalar type

3. Hiding individual components of an entity is _____.
   a. polymorphism
   b. encapsulation
   c. scaling
   d. not recommended in C++

4. One way in which a structure differs from an array is that _____.
   a. a structure may have members of more than one type
   b. a structure must have members that are all the same type
   c. an array may have members of more than one type
   d. there is no difference between a structure and an array

5. The keyword used to define a structure is _____.
   a. stru
   b. stt
   c. struct
   d. structure

6. The number of structures than can be declared in a single statement is _____.
   a. one
   b. two
   c. three
   d. unlimited

7. Consider this structure definition:

```
struct Wardrobe
  {
   double collarSize;
   int waistSize;
   int inseamSize;
  };
```

If doubles are four bytes and integers are two bytes, the amount of memory set aside by this definition is _____.
   a. zero bytes
   b. four bytes
   c. eight bytes
   d. unknown

8. Consider this structure declaration:

```
struct Wardrobe
  {
     double collarSize;
     int waistSize;
     int inseamSize;
  };
Wardrobe DadsClothing;
```

If doubles are four bytes and integers are two bytes, the amount of memory set aside by this declaration is _____.
a. zero bytes
b. four bytes
c. eight bytes
d. unknown

9. Consider this structure declaration:

```
struct Wardrobe
  {
   double collarSize;
   int waistSize;
   int inseamSize;
  };
Wardrobe DadsClothing;
```

You refer to DadsClothing's waistSize as _____.
a. DadsClothing(waistSize)
b. DadsClothing->waistSize
c. DadsClothing.waistSize
d. DadsClothing&&waistSize

10. Consider this structure declaration:

```
struct Wardrobe
  {
   double collarSize;
   int waistSize;
   int inseamSize;
  };
Wardrobe family[8];
```

You refer to the first family member's collarSize as _____.

a. family[0].collarSize

b. family.collarsize[0]

c. family[0].collarSize[0]

d. family.collarSize

11. Consider this structure declaration:

```
struct Wardrobe
  {
    double collarSize;
    int waistSize;
    int inseamSize;
  };
struct ShopList
  {
    int spendLimit;
    string favoriteStore;
    Wardrobe sizes;
  };
ShopList Jerry;
```

You refer to Jerry's collarSize as _____.

a. Jerry.collarSize

b. Jerry.ShopList.collarSize

c. Jerry.Wardrobe.collarSize

d. Jerry.sizes.collarSize

12. Using the wardrobe structure within the ShopList structure is an example of a good programming principle, known as _____.

a. reusability

b. polymorphism

c. redundancy

d. recursion

13. You can pass _____ to functions.

a. copies of individual structure members

b. copies of entire structures

c. pointers to structures

d. all of the above

14. You define a structure type globally because _____.

a. you save many lines of code by not rewriting an identical structure definition in each function that uses it

b. you will never change its definition

c. it is required in C++

d. all of the above

15. Consider this structure declaration:

```
struct Item
  {
     int invenNum;
     double cost;
     int quantity;
  };
Item tool;
```

Which function prototype can be used for a function that displays tool's cost?
a. void display(Item tool);
b. void display(double tool.cost);
c. either (a) or (b)
d. neither (a) nor (b)

16. The function whose prototype is Item getData(void); returns _____.
a. the address of a structure
b. a copy of a structure
c. a pointer to a structure
d. nothing

17. The function whose prototype is void getData(Item &thing); receives _____.
a. a pointer to a structure
b. a reference to a structure
c. a copy of a structure
d. nothing

18. The function whose prototype is void getData(Item *thing); receives _____.
a. a pointer to a structure
b. a reference to a structure
c. a copy of a structure
d. nothing

19. The C++ expression p->val means the same thing as _____.
a. *p.val
b. *(p.val)
c. (*p).val
d. p.val

20. In the expression p->val, p is a(n) _____.
a. address
b. pointer
c. structure
d. header

EXERCISES

1. Define a structure type that can hold a student's ID number, last name, first name, and credit hours completed. Write a program that declares a structure variable of that type, accepts appropriate data, and echoes the input.

2. Declare an array of structures to hold data for five students. Write a program that accepts data for five students and then echoes the input.

3. Write a function that adds 15 credit hours to each of the five student records from exercise 2.

4. Define a structure type that holds years, months, and days on the job. Write a program that declares one such structure, and allows you to enter and echo data.

5. Define a structure that holds an employee number, last name, and time on the job (using the structure from exercise 4). Write a program that accepts and echoes data from a declared structure.

6. Write a function that adds one month on the job to an employee's record. If an employee has 12 months of experience, this time should be converted to an additional year. Add this function to the program file from exercise 5, and test it.

In this lesson you will learn:

- How to define a class
- More about data hiding and encapsulation
- How public and private members differ
- What types of scope considerations apply
- How to create member functions

Technically, structures may contain methods as well. Because structures do not have many of the other capabilities of classes, however, C++ programmers rarely use structures for their objects.

Class names may be any legal C++ identifier. As with structure names, however, many programmers begin class names with a capital letter.

Classes and Members

Defining a Class

A **class**, like a structure or an array, is a programmer-defined data type. It is superior to a structure or an array because in addition to holding data members (or structures), it may also contain methods (or functions). When you begin to use classes, you truly begin to think in an object-oriented manner.

Recall two of the major aspects of object-oriented programming:

- You analyze the objects with which you are working and the tasks that need to be performed with and on those objects.
- You pass messages to objects, requesting that the objects take action.

Class creation requires object-oriented thinking. When you create a class, you consider all of its attributes, the tasks you will need to do with the class, and the communication that will initiate those tasks.

You can think of the built-in scalar types of C++ as classes. You do not have to define those classes; the creators of C++ have already done so. When, for example, the int type was first created, the programmers who designed it had to think of the following:

Q: What shall we call it?
A: int.
Q: What are its attributes?
A: An int is stored in two bytes; it holds whole-number values.
Q: What methods are allowed?
A: A method to assign a value to a variable (for example, num = 32;).
Q: Any other methods?
A: A method to perform arithmetic with variables (for example, num + 6;).
Q: Any other methods?
A: Of course, there are even more attributes and methods of an int, but these are a good start.

Your job in constructing a new class is similar. If you need a class for employee data, you should ask:
Q: What shall we call it?
A: Employee.
Q: What are its attributes?
A: It has an integer employee number and a double salary.

Q: What methods are allowed?

A: A method to assign values to a member of this class (for example, one employee's number is 3232 and her salary is 13.45).

Q: Any other methods?

A: A method to display data in a member of this class (for example, display one employee's employee number and salary).

Q: Any other methods?

A: Probably, but this is enough to get started.

You construct a class in two parts: a **declaration section**, which contains the class name as well as variables (attributes) and function prototypes, and an **implementation section**, which contains the functions themselves (tasks). The class definition shell for Employee follows:

```
// declaration section -- attributes and function
  // (task) prototypes
class Employee
  {
  int idNumber;
  double salary;
  void assignValues(int id, double sal);
    // prototype for assigning values
  void displayValues(void);
    // prototype for displaying values
  };
// implementation section -- functions will go here
```

In the following steps, you will create a class definition for fractions. The class definition will have the same attributes as the structure created in Lesson A, but it will also contain methods, or functions.

1 Open a new file for the class definition. You will initially create a class that can hold integer values for the numerator and denominator for a fraction. The class has functions that can receive values for the numerator and denominator and then display them. Type the following:

```
// declaration section
class Fraction
  {
    int numerator;
    int denominator;
    void getData(int n, int d);
    void showData(void);
  };
// implementation section -- the functions will go here
```

2 Compile the program, fix any errors or warnings, and save the file as **MYCLASS.CPP**.

Just as with a structure definition, this class definition (when it is complete) does not refer to any objects. You must create an instance or an object of the class. The statement

```
Employee MySecretary;
```

is an **instantiation** of the class Employee. An object, MySecretary now exists.

You can now create an instantiation of the Fraction class.

1 Below the class definition, begin a program and create one fraction:

```
void main()
  {
    Fraction oneFraction;
  }
```

2 Compile and save the program.

tip
• • • • • • • • • • • • • • •

▶ Depending on your compiler, you may get a warning that one variable is unreferenced. You may safely ignore it because it will be referenced later in the program.

Data Hiding and Encapsulation

One of the major assets of object-oriented programming is that information hiding is more complete than with the procedures used in procedural programs. You employ a primitive form of information hiding when you write a program using functions to which you know only the interface, rather than the details of how the function works. C++ classes allow you to take data hiding a step further.

In terms of C++ classes, data hiding means that you can make data members of a class inaccessible to functions that are not part of the class; that is, you can make them **private**. In the Employee class, for example, you can prevent idNumber and salary from being displayed by any function except displayValues(). You can make it illegal in any main() function, or any other function in which mySecretary is instantiated, to write the statement

```
cout<<mySecretary.salary;
```

Instead, you make the statement

```
mySecretary.displayValues();
```

which calls the displayValues() function that is a function of ("belongs to") mySecretary.

Once you create a class, including writing and debugging all of its member functions, no outside function over which you have no control can ever modify or use the private member data of any object in the class in an erroneous manner—a major benefit. When you create and test a class, and store its definition in a file, programs that use that definition can be prevented from using member data incorrectly. If a private member of your Employee class must have a four-digit employee number, or if you require that the employee number always be displayed preceded by a pound sign, no function that is not a member of your class can ever change that designation (either intentionally or by accident).

You don't actually need to tell the compiler which data members are private because private is the default **access specifier.** That is, if you do nothing, all data and functions in a class will be private, or inaccessible.

Of course, if you cannot access any data or functions in a class, the class isn't much use. Usually, you want at least some functions to be **public**—that is, accessible by both member and nonmember functions. If the offices at your firm are all private and you cannot communicate with the executives in them, the company won't function for long. Usually, at least a receptionist is public, and you can communicate with the private executives through him or her. You communicate with the private members of a class by sending messages to the public member functions.

To do so, you write the access specifier public or private, followed by a colon, followed by the class members to which the specifier applies:

```
// declaration section
class Employee
  {
   private:
      int idNumber;
      double salary;
  public:
      void assignValues(int id, double sal);
        // prototype for assigning values
      void displayValues(void);
        // prototype for displaying values
  };
// implementation section -- the functions will go here
```

You can now add the private and public sections to the MYCLASS function class.

1   Add the keyword `private:` just prior to the integer numerator and denominator declarations.
2   Add the keyword `public:` after the integer declarations and just prior to the function declarations.
3   Compile the program and save it.

tip

Besides private and public, class members can be protected. The specifier protected is most often used when member functions of new classes are inherited from existing classes. (See Tutorial 7.)

tip

You can use public and private specifiers in structures, too. Unlike a class, the default in a structure is public.

tip

If private members are declared first, the keyword private is optional, because the members will be private by default. The specifier public, however, is required when you begin your list of public members.

tip

You can use the access specifiers public and private as many times as you wish in a class definition—for example, two private members, followed by one public member, followed by two more private members. It's better style, however, to group the private and public members together.

Scope Considerations in Defining Member Functions

You already know about scope; a local variable is "in scope" only within the function in which it is declared. The **scope resolution operator** is a C++ operator that identifies a member function as being "in scope" within a class. It consists of two colons (::). In the Employee class, one public member function is assignValues(). The header for the function signals that assignValues() is a member of Employee:

```
void Employee::assignValues(int id, double sal)
```

The header for the function indicates that nothing will be returned, Employee is the class, assignValues() is the name of the function, and an integer and a double will be passed to the function.

The complete assignValues() function is

```
void Employee::assignValues(int id, double sal)
  {
    Employee::idNumber = id;
    Employee::salary=sal;
  }
```

The assignValues() function is a member function of the Employee class, so it can assign values to idNumber and salary, even though both are private to the Employee class. The scope resolution operators in

```
Employee::idNumber = id;
Employee::salary=sal;
```

show that idNumber and salary are members of the Employee class. They are not necessary in this example, so you can replace the two statements with

```
idNumber = id;
salary=sal;
```

Using the scope resolution operator leaves no doubt as to what is happening, however, and it is required if the local variables you use for passing data to the function have the same names.

```
void Employee::assignValues(int idNumber, double sal)
  {
    Employee::idNumber = idNumber;
    // the scope resolution is required on idNumber
    salary=sal; // scope resolution not required on salary
  }
```

In the following steps, you will add the functions getData() and showData() that are part of the Fraction class.

1 At the end of the **MYCLASS** file, write the function getData().

```
void Fraction::getData(int n, int d)
  {
    Fraction::numerator = n;
    Fraction::denominator = d;
  }
```

2 Create the showData() function:

```
void Fraction::showData(void)
  {
    cout<<"Fraction is "<<Fraction::numerator;
    cout<<"/"<<Fraction::denominator<<endl;
  }
```

3 Add two statements to the main() function to assign values to oneFraction and to display them. Don't forget you need #include<iostream.h> at the top of the file, because this program now uses cout.

```
oneFraction.getData(3,4);
oneFraction.showData();
```

4 Compile, test, and save the program. The output is as follows:

```
Fraction is 3/4
```

Just like structures, objects that are members of classes may be stored in arrays. Once you create the Employee class, you may declare an array of Employee objects in which to store data about 100 workers:

```
Employee worker[100];
```

You can then fill the array with data. For example, to set each employee number to a consecutive number, and to set each salary to 6.00, use the following code:

```
for(int x = 0; x<100; ++x)
  {
   worker[x].assignValues(x,6.00);
  }
```

As with the array of structures, the object is subscripted.
Add an array of Fraction objects to the MYCLASS program.

1 At the top of the main() function, declare an array to hold nine Fraction objects:

```
Fraction nineFrac[9];
```

2 Add code to set each of the nine fractions to $\frac{1}{10}$, $\frac{2}{10}$, $\frac{3}{10}$, and so on. You accomplish this goal by calling getData() nine times.

```
for(int x =0; x<9; ++x)
  nineFrac[x].getData(x+1,10);
```

3 Next, display each of the values by calling showData() nine times.

```
for(x=0; x< 9; ++x)
  nineFrac[x].showData();
```

4 Compile, run, and save the program. The output is as follows:

```
Fraction is 3/4

Fraction is 1/10

Fraction is 2/10

Fraction is 3/10

Fraction is 4/10

Fraction is 5/10

Fraction is 6/10

Fraction is 7/10

Fraction is 8/10

Fraction is 9/10
```

SUMMARY

- A class is a programmer-defined data type that contains data members (states) and functions (methods).
- When you create a class, you consider all attributes of the class, all tasks you will need to perform with the class, and all communication that will initiate those tasks.
- You construct a class in two parts: a declaration section, which contains the class name as well as variables (attributes) and function prototypes, and an implementation section, which contains the functions themselves (tasks).
- When you create an object, you are creating an instantiation of a class.
- You can make members of a class private by using the private access specifier. The data then remain hidden, or are accessible only to member functions. This technique eliminates incorrect use of members in the future.
- You can make members of a class public by using the public access specifier. Public members are accessible by both member and nonmember functions.
- The scope resolution operator (::) identifies a member function as belonging to a class.
- Like other data types, objects can be placed in an array.

QUESTIONS

1. Which (if any) of the following is NOT a programmer-defined type?
   a. an array
   b. a structure
   c. a class
   d. all of the above are programmer-defined types

2. Classes hold _____.
   a. data
   b. methods
   c. both data and methods
   d. neither data nor methods

3. When you create a class, you must create _____.
   a. a name for the class
   b. all programs that will use the class
   c. both (a) and (b)
   d. neither (a) nor (b)

4. You construct a class in two sections, known as the _____.
   a. header and body
   b. type and parameters
   c. declaration and implementation
   d. pointer and variable

5. The declaration section holds _____.
   a. data members
   b. data members and function prototypes
   c. data members, function prototypes, and the functions themselves
   d. none of the above

6. The functions go in the _____ section of a class definition.
   a. declaration
   b. implementation
   c. prototype
   d. functioning

7. An object is a(n) _____ of a class.
   a. owner
   b. function
   c. definition
   d. instance

8. Making class members inaccessible to nonmember functions is an example of _____.
   a. polymorphism
   b. data hiding
   c. redundancy
   d. recursion

9. Two access specifiers in C++ are _____.
   a. public and private
   b. int and double
   c. formal and informal
   d. void and free

10. The major advantage of data hiding is that _____.
   a. your programs can include more data
   b. you no longer need functions
   c. no one can ever use your data
   d. your data will be used correctly

11. Which of the following is an access specifier?
   a. particular
   b. shielded
   c. protected
   d. safe

12. The default access specifier is _____.
   a. shielded
   b. private
   c. protected
   d. public

13. The best-written classes have _____.
   a. all functions private
   b. all data public
   c. no functions
   d. none of the above

14. Access specifiers are followed by _____.
   a. a comma
   b. a semicolon
   c. a colon
   d. two colons

15. The scope resolution operator is _____.
   a. a comma
   b. a semicolon
   c. a colon
   d. two colons

16. Consider this function prototype:

```
void Data::listValues(void);
```

Which is true?
a. Data is a member of listValues
b. listValues is a member of Data
c. Data is a function
d. listValues is a class

17. Consider this function prototype:

```
void Data::listValues(void);
```

Which is true?
a. Data is a variable
b. listValues is a variable
c. Data is a class
d. void is a member of listValues

E X E R C I S E S

1. Define a class that represents a student. Its data include a student's ID number, last name, first name, and credit hours completed. Its member functions include one that assigns values to a student object and one that displays the values in a student object.

2. Write a program that assigns values to oneStudent, an object of the student class. Display the values.

3. Declare an array of objects to hold data for five students. Fill the objects with data, giving students consecutive idNumbers. Give all students the name Michael Davis and 30 credit hours.

4. Modify the program in exercise 3 so that you can enter student idNumbers, names, and hours from the keyboard. Display the data in the five objects.

5. Define a class that holds years, months, and days on the job. Its functions assign values to years, months, and days, and then display the values. Write a program to test the class.

6. Add a member function to the class defined in exercise 5. Add a function to add 1 month to an object. Once months exceeds 12, years should be increased. Write a program that tests the function.

debugging ▶ **7.** Each of the following files in the TUT02 folder has syntax and/or logical errors. Determine the problem in each case, and fix the program.
a. DEBUG2-1.CPP
b. DEBUG2-2.CPP
c. DEBUG2-3.CPP
d. DEBUG2-4.CPP
e. DEBUG2-5.CPP

Class Features

case ▶ As part of your effort to eventually write a program that will handle fractions, you have created a class that represents a fraction. Your class includes two data members and two member functions. To create a more professional class, you will add a static data member and additional member functions, including constructors and a destructor.

Previewing the New FRACTION Program

The FRACNEW program displays 14 fractions, along with their decimal equivalents. The purpose of this tutorial is to teach you several useful class features; the sole purpose of the FRACNEW program is to demonstrate these features so that you can incorporate them into future programs.

1   Load the **FRACNEW.CPP** program and execute it.

2   Examine the code. You will be creating this code yourself in this tutorial.

LESSON A
objectives

In this lesson you will learn

- Why and how to declare static class members
- How to use the *this* pointer
- How to apply polymorphism in new ways
- What roles are played by member functions

Introduction to Class Features

tip

Static variables are sometimes called class variables because they don't belong to a specific object; they belong to the class.

Static Class Members

A C++ object is an instantiation of a class that can contain both data members and methods. When you create an object, a block of memory is set aside for the data members. Just as `int x;` reserves enough space to hold an integer in your system, `Employee oneWorker;` reserves enough storage to hold an Employee in your system (assuming Employee has been defined as a class). Each class object gets its own block of memory for its data members when it is created. When you create an array of 100 objects, for example, 100 such blocks of memory are set aside.

Sometimes every instantiation of a class may require the same value. For example, an employee record might have a data member that holds a company ID number that is the same for all employees, or an invoice record might contain a local sales tax that is the same for every member of the invoice class. If you declare 100 employees or 100 invoices, you will repeat the same information 100 times, wasting memory. Another option is to make the company ID and sales tax global variables, but then they could be changed anywhere in the program. This approach would violate the principle of data hiding—one of the major points of object-oriented programming is to protect data members from accidental or intentional change by functions that are not members of the class.

A better solution is to declare a class variable to be **static**, meaning that it will remain unchanged. A class variable that you declare to be static is the same (doesn't change) for all objects that are instantiations of the class. All members of the class share one storage location for a static data member of the same class. Although all members of the class appear to be storing a copy of the same value, they actually just have access to the same memory location.

For example, assume a four-digit company identification number is an attribute of every employee in your organization. You can define Employee as

```
// declaration section
class Employee
  {
   private:
     static int companyID;
     int idNumber;
     double salary;
   public:
     void assignValues(const int id, const double sal);
     // prototype for assigning values
     void displayValues(); //prototype for displaying values
  };
// implementation section -- functions will go here
```

You may then declare 100 employees:

```
Employee emps[100];
```

Memory is reserved for 100 integer idNumbers and 100 double salaries, but only one companyID.

Because a static data member uses only one memory location, it is defined (given a value) in a single statement outside the class definition. Most often this statement appears just before the class implementation section. Consider this complete program:

```cpp
#include<iostream.h>
// declaration section
class Employee
 {
  private:
    static int companyID;
    int idNumber;
    double salary;
  public:
    void assignValues(const int id, const double sal);
    // prototype for assigning values
    void displayValues(); //prototype for displaying values
 };
// definition of the static class member
int Employee::companyID = 1234;
// implementation section
void Employee::assignValues(const int id, const double sal)
 {
  Employee::idNumber=id;
  Employee::salary=sal;
 }
void Employee::displayValues()
 {
  cout<<"Employee ID "<<Employee::idNumber;
  cout<<" Salary "<<Employee::salary;
  cout<<" Company ID "<<Employee::companyID<<endl;
 }
// the program that uses the class
void main()
  {
    Employee people[4];   // declare 4 people
    double money = 5.25;
    for(int x = 0; x<4; ++x)   // give each person an ID 1001
    // through 1004, and a salary 6.25 through 9.25
      people[x].assignValues(x+1001, money +=1.00);
    for(x=0;x<4;++x)
      people[x].displayValues();

  }
```

The output is as follows:

```
Employee ID Salary 6.25 1001 Company ID 1234
Employee ID Salary 7.25 1002 Company ID 1234
Employee ID Salary 8.25 1003 Company ID 1234
Employee ID Salary 9.25 1004 Company ID 1234
```

Figure 3-1: Output Using static Company ID

Even though each employee has a unique employee ID and a unique salary, all employees share the same company ID, which was assigned a value just once. Notice that the keyword static is used when the symbol is declared, but not in the assignment statement in which it is assigned a value.

In the following steps, you will add a static class member to the fraction class created in Tutorial 2. Because every fraction uses the slash symbol (/) between the numerator and denominator, it makes sense to store a slash only once in memory, and use it to display every fraction.

1   Open the **MYCLASS** program from Tutorial 2 or key in the following program, which defines a fraction class, declares a single object and an array of objects that are members of the class, assigns values to them, and displays them:

```
#include<iostream.h>
// declaration section
class Fraction
  {
    private:
      int numerator;
      int denominator;
    public:
      void getData(const int n, const int d);
      void showData(void);
  };
// implementation section
void Fraction::getData(const int n, const int d)
  {
    Fraction::numerator = n;
    Fraction::denominator = d;
  }
void Fraction::showData(void)
  {
    cout<<"Fraction is "<<Fraction::numerator;
      <<"/"Fraction::denominator<<endl;
  }
void main()
  {
    Fraction oneFraction;
    Fraction nineFrac[9];
    oneFraction.getData(3,4);
    oneFraction.showData();
    for(int x =0; x<9; ++x)
      nineFrac[x].getData(x+1,10);
    for(x=0; x< 9; ++x)
      nineFrac[x].showData();
  }
```

2 In the private section of the Fraction class definition, add a static character
variable that will hold the slash:

```
static char symbol;
```

This statement declares a character named symbol. Only one symbol will exist,
no matter how many fraction objects are subsequently defined.

3   Just before the class implementation section, add the statement that assigns the correct value to the slash symbol:

```
char Fraction::symbol = '/';
```

Notice that you do not use the keyword static in this definition.

4   Change the output statement in the showData() function to

```
cout<<"Fraction is "<<Fraction::numerator
  <<Fraction::symbol<<Fraction::denominator<<endl;
```

This statement is no shorter than the previous version—in fact, it's actually a little longer. The cout statement is more readable now; it says "Output the fraction's numerator, the fraction's symbol, and the fraction's denominator." In addition, no matter how many fractions you eventually define, you will store the symbol in memory only once.

5   Compile and test the program. The appearance of your screen should resemble Figure 3-2.

```
Fraction is 3/4
Fraction is 1/10
Fraction is 2/10
Fraction is 3/10
Fraction is 4/10
Fraction is 5/10
Fraction is 6/10
Fraction is 7/10
Fraction is 8/10
Fraction is 9/10
```

Figure 3-2: Output of Fractions

6   Save the program as **MYCLASS2.CPP**.

The this Pointer

Static data variables are stored only once, regardless of how many instances of a class you declare. The other member variables that belong to a class are stored in a separate data structure for each instance of a class defined. If you create a class that includes one integer data member and then create 100 instances of that class, you will need storage for 100 separate integers. This technique allows each instance of the class to have its own state or value.

Consider a simple employee class:

```
// declaration section
class Employee
   {
      private:
        int idNumber;
        double salary;
      public:
        void assignValues(const int id, const double sal);
        // prototype for assigning values
        void displayValues(); //prototype for displaying values
   };
```

When you create two instances of the class,

```
Employee Clerk, Driver;
```

separate structures in memory are set aside for Clerk and Driver. Each has its own unique starting memory address. Space is allocated for an idNumber and salary for the Clerk as well as for the Driver. Just as it would be wasteful to store a shared company ID number separately for these two employees however, it would also waste space if you stored the code for the member functions assignValues() and displayValues() separately for each employee. Imagine a program that stores data for 100 employees, or imagine an employee class with 20 member functions. If the same function code were stored repeatedly for every instance of a class, the storage requirements would be enormous.

Luckily, C++ does not store member functions separately for each instance of a class. Instead, one copy of each member function is stored, and each instance of a class uses the same function. Whether you make the statement

```
Clerk.displayValues();
```

or

```
Driver.displayValues();
```

you will call the same copy of the function displayValues().

Because only one copy of each function exists, when you call a function it needs to know which object it should use. To ensure that the function uses the correct object, you use the name of the object:

```
Clerk.displayValues();
```

The address of the object Clerk is then automatically passed to the displayValues() function. Within the function, the address of the Clerk object is stored in a special pointer called the **this** pointer. The this pointer is automatically supplied for you every time you call a member function. For example, when you make the function call

```
Clerk.displayValues();
```

the actual argument list used by the compiler for displayValues() is

```
displayValues(Employee *this)
```

The actual function call used by the compiler is

```
displayValues(&Clerk);
```

When you make the function call

```
Driver.displayValues();
```

the actual function call is

```
displayValues(&Driver);
```

The assignValues() function receives an integer and a double. In addition, it receives a pointer to the object it will manipulate. When you make the statement

```
Clerk.assignValues(3445,8.75);
```

the actual argument list used by the compiler for assignValues() is

```
assignValues(Employee *this, const int id, const double sal);
```

The actual function call used by the compiler is

```
assignValues(&Clerk, 3445,8.75);
```

tip

••••••••••••••••••

▶ The this pointer is a constant. You cannot modify it as in

```
this = &someOtherObject;
// illegal!
```

tip

••••••••••••••••••

▶ One type of member function does not have a this pointer: the static member function. You make a class member function static when you want to call it from outside the source file in which it is defined, or when you want to call it even if no instances of a class exist. For example, if you wanted to display the symbol used in the Fraction class, even though you hadn't instantiated any Fraction objects, you could use a static function.

In each case, the first argument passed to the function (and sometimes the only argument) is a pointer that holds the address of the object to which you are referring.

Most often, you do not have to be concerned with the this pointer. Although it's nice to understand how the function knows which object to use, the reference is made automatically, and you don't have to dwell on it. At other times, you may want to use the this pointer explicitly within member functions. For example, to demonstrate that the this pointer exists, you could rewrite the displayValues() function as

```
void Employee::displayValues()
 {
 cout<<"Employee ID "<<this->idNumber;
 cout<<" Salary "<<this->salary<<endl;
}
```

This function works in exactly the same way as a function that does not use the this pointer. Because the function doesn't require the this pointer, you don't need to use it in this case, and the code given above is not recommended. About the only time you ever need to use the this pointer is when, within a function, you want to return the pointer that was sent to the function. For example,

```
return(*this);
```

To demonstrate that the this pointer exists, you can modify the showData() member function of your Fraction class.

1 Change the showData() function to

```
void Fraction::showData(void)
  {
    cout<<"Fraction is "<<this->numerator
      <<this->symbol<<this->denominator<<endl;
  }
```

2 Compile and test the program. Its performance should remain the same.

3   Change the cout statement back to

```
cout<<"Fraction is "<<Fraction::numerator
  <<Fraction::symbol<<Fraction::denominator<<endl;
```

4   Compile and test the program again. Although the functionality is the same, this syntax is preferred. Save the program.

Polymorphism

You first encountered polymorphism in the Overview to this book. Polymorphism is the feature in object-oriented programs that allows the same operation to be carried out differently depending on the object. When you speak English, you use the same instructions with different objects all the time. For example, you interpret a verb differently depending on the object to which it is applied. You catch a ball, but you also catch a cold. You run a computer, a business, a race, or a stocking. The meanings of "catch" and "run" are different in each case, but you can perform each operation correctly because the combination of the verb and the object makes the command complete.

When you write C++ (and other object-oriented) programs, you can send the same message to different objects and different types of objects. Suppose you have two members of the employee class, Clerk and Driver. You can display the data members of each with the following statements:

```
Clerk.displayValues();
Driver.displayValues();
```

No confusion arises as to which member's values should be displayed because the correct pointer is passed as a this pointer each time you call the displayValues() function.

Similarly, suppose you have three different objects that are members of different classes: a Clerk who is a member of the Employee class, a Shirt that is a member of the Inventory class, and XYZCompany, a member of the Supplier class. Each object can certainly have different numbers and types of data members: the Clerk has an employee idNumber and a salary; the Shirt has a sleeveLength, neckSize, and price; and the XYZCompany has a president, phoneNumber, dateOfLastOrder, and annualSalesFigure. Even though these objects are very different, occasionally you may need to display each of their data members. In such a case, it seems appropriate to call each function displayValues().

C++ allows you to create three very different member functions, one for each of the classes in question. For example, you might use the following functions:

```cpp
void Employee::displayValues(void)
  {
    cout<<"Employee ID is "<<Employee::idNumber
      <<".Salary is $"<<Employee::salary<<endl;
  }
void Inventory::displayValues(void)
  {
    cout<<"This shirt has a sleeve of "
      <<Inventory::sleeveLength;
    cout<<" and a neck size "<<Inventory::neckSize<<endl;
    cout<<"It sells for $"<<Inventory::price<<endl;
  }
void Supplier::displayValues(void)
  {
   cout<<"President: "<<Supplier::president
      <<" at phone"<<Supplier::phoneNumber<<endl;
   cout<<"Last order "<<Supplier::dateOfLastOrder;
   cout<<"  Annual sales "<<Supplier::annualSalesFigure
      <<endl;
  }
```

These three functions contain statements with different content, but they all have the name, displayValues(). You can write three function calls as follows:

```cpp
Clerk.displayValues();
Shirt.displayValues();
XYZCompany.displayValues();
```

tip

The concept of polymorphism includes far more than using the same function name for different function bodies. In Tutorial 7, you will learn about the role polymorphism plays in inheritance.

Each of these functions displays the intended object in a unique, appropriate format. The this pointer sends the appropriate address so the function uses the correct object. Because of the object's type (Employee, Inventory, or Supplier), you call the displayValues() function that is a member of the appropriate class.

When you can apply the same function name to different objects, your programs become easier to read and "make more sense." It takes less time to develop a project; you can also make later changes more rapidly. C++ programmers often can write programs faster than programmers who use non–object-oriented programming languages, and polymorphism is one of the reasons why.

Some Roles of Member Functions

Obviously, you can create an infinite number of classes and write an infinite number of functions. You use the data members of a class to describe the state of an object, and you use the member functions to work with those members. So far, we have dealt with functions that assign values to data and then display those values. Eventually, you will want to add many other specialized functions to your classes. You can classify the roles of member functions into four basic groups:

- **Inspector functions**, also called access functions. These functions return information about an object's state; they display some or all of an object's attributes. An inspector function typically has a name like displayValues().
- **Mutator functions**, also known as implementors. These functions change an object's state or attributes. A mutator function typically has a name like getData(), which obtains values for an object's data members from an input device, or computeGross(), which calculates a data member based on values in other data members.
- **Auxiliary functions**, also known as facilitators. These functions perform some action or service, such as sorting data or searching for data. A typical name for an auxiliary function is sortAscending() or findStudentsLowestScore().
- **Manager functions**. These functions create and destroy objects for you. They perform initialization and cleanup. Called constructors and destructors, they are the topic of Lesson B.

Your Fraction class already contains an inspector function, showData(), and a mutator function, getData(). In the following steps, you will add another mutator function, named convert(), that will compute the floating-point, or decimal, value of a fraction. You will call the convert() function from getData() as soon as the numerator and denominator values have been assigned.

1   To the private section of the Fraction class, add a new data member:

```
double floatingPoint;
```

2   To the private section of the Fraction class, add a new function prototype. The function, which is named convert(), will return a double value that is the floating-point equivalent of the fraction. The function belongs in the private section (although it would work just as well if placed in the public section) because it is accessed from within another member function, getData(). You will not call convert() from the main() program; rather, you will call getData() from the main() program and getData() will, in turn, call convert().

```
double convert(void);
```

3   To the implementation section of the Fraction class, add the function:

```
double Fraction::convert(void)
{
  double floatingPoint; // to hold floating-point value
  floatingPoint = double(Fraction::numerator);
  //this is a cast
    // numerator becomes a floating-point value
    //so division works; integer division loses
    //fractional part
  floatingPoint = floatingPoint/Fraction::denominator;
  return(floatingPoint);
}
```

4   To the getData() function, add a statement that.calculates the floatingPoint value for each fraction. After the values have been assigned for numerator and denominator, add the statement

```
Fraction::floatingPoint = convert();
```

5   To confirm that the correct conversions have taken place, add an output statement to the showData() function. Place this statement before the one that displays the fraction, so that output for each fraction will appear on a single line:

```
cout<<"Decimal is "<<Fraction::floatingPoint<<"   ";
// spaces at end for readability
```

6   Compile, test, and save the program. Compare your screen's appearance to Figure 3-3.

```
Decimal is 0.75 Fraction is 3/4
Decimal is 0.1 Fraction is 1/10
Decimal is 0.2 Fraction is 2/10
Decimal is 0.3 Fraction is 3/10
Decimal is 0.4 Fraction is 4/10
Decimal is 0.5 Fraction is 5/10
Decimal is 0.6 Fraction is 6/10
Decimal is 0.7 Fraction is 7/10
Decimal is 0.8 Fraction is 8/10
Decimal is 0.9 Fraction is 9/10
```

Figure 3-3: Fractions with decimal conversions

> Step 3 involves a cast. A statement such as `floatingNum = double(integerX);` ensures that integerX will be converted to a double before the assignment to floatingNum is made. In reality, C++ would make this particular conversion automatically, but your intentions are made clearer with the explicitly stated cast.

> The convert() function will not work correctly if you create a fraction that has 0 as its denominator, because division by 0 is always illegal. If you want to protect against this possibility, compare the Fraction::denominator to 0 before performing convert(). If the denominator is 0, assign 0 to floatingPoint.

SUMMARY

- You use a static variable, sometimes called a class variable, when you want all members of a class to share one storage location for a data member; all instantiations of the class will then have the same value for that data member.
- You define, or give a value to, a static data member in a single statement outside the class definition, most often just before the class implementation section.
- You use the keyword static when you declare a static data variable, but not when you assign a value to it.
- Data members of classes are stored separately for each instantiation of a class, with each having a unique starting memory address. Functions that are members of classes are stored only once, no matter how many instantiations of the class you create.
- Because only one copy of each member function exists, when you call a function it needs to know which object it should use. The function selects the correct object because the first argument in the function becomes a special pointer called *this* when you use the name of the object.
- Polymorphism is the feature in object-oriented programming that allows the same operation to be carried out differently, depending on the object.
- Polymorphism makes your programs easier to read and shortens project development time.
- When you create different classes, member functions of the different classes can have the same name, and C++ will execute the appropriate function based on the class.
- You can classify member functions into four basic groups: inspector functions, mutator functions, auxiliary functions, and manager functions.
- Inspector functions, also called access functions, return information about an object's state.
- Mutator functions, also known as implementors, change an object's state.
- Auxiliary functions, also known as facilitators, perform some action or service.
- Manager functions, which include constructors and destructors, create and destroy objects for you.

QUESTIONS

1. When you define an object that is a member of a class, such as `Student Abby;` _____.
   a. a block of memory is set aside and all data members are assigned valid values
   b. a block of memory is set aside
   c. no memory is set aside until values are defined
   d. no memory is set aside, but valid values are assigned to data members

2. If you want only one memory location to be reserved for a class variable, no matter how many objects are instantiated, you should declare the variable as _____.
   a. dynamic
   b. unary
   c. static
   d. volatile

3. Static variables are sometimes called _____.
   a. class variables
   b. functional variables
   c. dynamic variables
   d. auto variables

4. A static data member is given a value _____.
    a. within the class definition
    b. outside the class definition
    c. when the program is executed
    d. never

5. If you declare two objects as `Customer firstCust, secondCust;` which of the following must be true?
    a. Each object will store a separate copy of any static member data.
    b. Each object will store a separate copy of any member functions.
    c. Each object will store a separate copy of any nonstatic data members.
    d. You cannot declare two objects of the same class.

6. If you declare two objects as `Customer firstCust, secondCust;` which of the following must be true?
    a. Each object's nonstatic data members will be stored in the same memory location.
    b. Each object will be stored in the same memory location.
    c. Each object will have a unique memory address.
    d. You cannot declare two objects of the same class.

7. A class `StockItems` has four data members and three function members. You define 50 objects as members of the class. Which is true?
    a. Only one copy of each of the three functions exists.
    b. Only one copy of each of the four data members exists.
    c. Both (a) and (b) are true.
    d. Neither (a) nor (b) is true.

8. A member function uses the correct object when you call it because _____.
    a. a copy of the object is passed to the function
    b. the address of the object is passed to the function
    c. the address of the function is passed to another function
    d. the address of the object is returned from the function

9. To use the this pointer with a member function, you _____.
    a. declare `this` as static
    b. declare `this` as global
    c. define `this` as equal to the address of the appropriate object
    d. do nothing; it is automatically supplied for you

10. A class `MyClients` contains a member function `void printClientInfo()`. You define an object `SunriseCorp`. When you make the function call `SunriseCorp.printClientInfo();`, the actual argument list for `printClientInfo` is _____.
    a. printClientInfo(MyClients *this)
    b. printClientInfo(SunriseCorp *this)
    c. printClientInfo(MyClients)
    d. printClientInfo(SunriseCorp)

11. A class `MyClients` contains a member function `void printClientInfo()`. You define an object `SunriseCorp`. When you make the function call `SunriseCorp.printClientInfo();`, the actual function call to `printClientInfo` is _____.
    a. printClientInfo(this);   c. printClientInfo(SunriseCorp);
    b. printClientInfo(&this);   d. printClientInfo(&SunriseCorp);

12. Which functions do not have a `this` pointer?
   a. access functions   c. member functions
   b. inspector functions   d. static functions

13. The feature in object-oriented programming that allows the same operation to be carried out differently, depending on the object, is _____.
   a. inheritance   c. overfunctioning
   b. polymorphism   d. overriding

14. Functions that return information about an object's state can be classified as _____.
   a. inspector functions   c. auxiliary functions
   b. mutator functions   d. manager functions

15. The function printDataMembers() is most likely a(n) _____.
   a. inspector function   c. auxiliary function
   b. mutator function   d. manager function

16. A function that changes an object's state belongs to the category of _____.
   a. inspector functions   c. auxiliary functions
   b. mutator functions   d. manager functions

17. An auxiliary function _____.
   a. returns information about data members
   b. changes the state of data members
   c. performs an action or service
   d. creates and destroys objects

E X E R C I S E S

1. Write the class definition for dates that contain three integer data members: month, day, and year. Create a static member to hold a slash. Create two member functions, getDate() and showDate(). Write a main() program that instantiates an object of your class for 10/15/1999 and tests the functions.

2. Modify the program in exercise 1 to create an array of 20 dates. The first date is 10/15/1999. Each subsequent date should be one day later than the preceding date. Make sure the date following 10/31/1999 is 11/1/1999.

3. Modify the program in exercise 2 so the array contains 100 dates. Make sure the date following 12/31/1999 is 1/1/2000.

4. Write the class definition for vehicles owned by a car dealer. Data members are an ID number, a model year, and a price. Create two member functions, setData() and displayData(). Create a static data member to hold the dealer number. Write a main() program that instantiates at least three objects of type vehicle and tests the functions.

5. Modify the program in exercise 4 to explicitly use the this pointer in the functions.

6. Write the class definition for a pet. Data members are pet breed, age, and price. Create two member functions, setData() and displayData(). Write a main() program that also uses the vehicle definition from Exercise 4, and create one object for a vehicle you would like to own (use a descriptive object identifier such as red67Jaguar and one object for a pet you would like to own (use a descriptive object identifier such as greatDaneNamedSpike). Display the data for each object in your program.

LESSON B
o b j e c t i v e s

In this lesson you will learn

■ What a constructor is

■ How to make your own constructors

■ How to override the constructor's default arguments

■ How to overload constructors

■ How to use destructors

Constructors and Destructors

Constructors

A **constructor** is a function that is called automatically each time an object is created. You have been using constructors all along in your programs, even if you haven't realized it. When you declare a simple scalar variable, such as

```
int number;
```

C++ calls an internal constructor that reserves a memory location of the correct size for an integer and attaches the name "number" to that location. The value at the number location might be anything; C++ does not automatically initialize the variable. The definition

```
int number = 23;
```

calls a constructor that reserves memory, attaches a name, and assigns a value. It sends the constant 23 to the constructor function. Although this definition does not look like a function call, the following one does:

```
int number(23);
```

As a matter of fact, this definition does exactly the same things as the first one: it allocates memory, attaches a name, and assigns a value.

In the same way, if you have defined a class named Employee, then

```
Employee Clerk;
```

reserves memory and assigns a name, but does not initialize the values of any data members of Clerk. Similarly,

```
Employee Clerk(23);
```

reserves memory, attaches a name, and assigns a value to some data member of Employee. Because an integer is a scalar variable, only one memory location in the variable number can have a value. When you write

```
int number(23);
```

you know where the integer constructor is assigning the 23. In contrast, because Employee is a class, it may have many data members. When you write

```
Employee Clerk(23);
```

you don't know which data member will receive the 23 unless you can look at the code for the constructor.

Until now, we have let C++ provide its own constructor for our class objects, and we have subsequently used a mutator function such as getData() to assign values to data members. Sometimes, however, you may want to initialize an object's data members immediately upon creation or perform other tasks. In that case, you must write your own constructor.

Making Your Own Constructors

You want to write your own constructors so as to properly define or initialize all data members in an object. Constructor functions differ from other member functions in two ways:

- You must name a constructor function with the same name as the class for which it is a constructor.
- You cannot give a constructor function a return type (it's really not necessary because constructors always return an object of the class to which they belong).

Consider this class:

```
// declaration section
class Employee
  {
    private:
      int idNumber;
      double salary;
    public:
      void assignValues(const int id, const double sal);
      // prototype for assigning values
      void displayValues();
      // prototype for displaying values
  };
// implementation section -- the functions will go here
```

tip

Constructor functions are not coded with a return type. That format doesn't mean the return type is void; void is a type, so you should not use the term void when coding a constructor. Constructors always return one object of their class type.

Rather than define objects of class Employee to have meaningless values, or **garbage values**, until you call assignValues(), you might choose to assign a 0 to idNumber and 4.65 to salary as default values. You can accomplish this assignment by writing the following constructor prototype and placing it in the public section of the Employee class:

```
Employee(); // notice no return type
```

tip

You should almost always provide initial values for the data members in your objects. Even if you simply set all numeric attributes to zeros and all character attributes to spaces, the results will be better than the random, meaningless data that happen to be held in the memory locations where your objects are instantiated.

Next, you write the constructor function itself and place it with the other member functions:

```
Employee::Employee()
  {
    idNumber = 0;
    salary = 4.65;
  }
```

tip

idNumber=0;
can also be written
Employee::idNumber=0;
Similarly, you can use the class name with salary.

The constructor function Employee() is called a **default constructor** because it does not require any arguments. The data members in an employee object will be set by default. Any subsequent object instantiation such as

```
Employee Clerk;
```

results in an object with an idNumber of 0 and a salary of 4.65. Of course, these values can be changed later with the assignValues() function.

Most C++ programmers prefer this style of providing default values for the constructor. Your intentions are made clear in the prototype and, as you will learn in the next section, you can override these default values if necessary.

An alternative way of creating a default constructor is with the prototype

```
Employee(const int id=0, const double sal = 4.65);
```

The constructor function then is

```
Employee::Employee(const int id, const double sal)
 {
  Employee::idNumber =id;
  Employee::salary=sal;
 }
```

This format is also called a default constructor because all arguments have been given default values and any subsequent definition, such as

```
Employee Clerk;
```

also results in an object with an idNumber of 0 and a salary of 4.65.

In the following steps, you will create a constructor for the Fraction class. First, to show that the constructor function is called automatically, you will create a constructor that simply prints a message.

1 Open the **MYCLASS2** program, if it is not still open from Lesson A.
2 To the public section of the Fraction class, add the Fraction class constructor prototype for a constructor that takes no arguments:

```
Fraction();
```

3 In the implementation section, with the other member functions, add a constructor that displays a message:

```
Fraction::Fraction()
  {
    cout<<"Inside the constructor!"<<endl;
  }
```

4   To reduce the output of this demonstration program, comment out the three lines needed to call displayValues(). First, place // in front of

```
oneFraction.showData();
```

Next, place comment indicators in front of the two lines

```
for(x=0; x< 9; ++x)
    nineFrac[x].showData();
```

5   Compile and run the program. As the main() program defines a single fraction named oneFraction, and an array of nine fractions defined as nineFrac[9], the constructor is called 10 times. You should see 10 copies of "Inside the constructor!" on the screen, as shown in Figure 3-4.

```
Inside the Constructor!
Inside the Constructor!
Inside the Constructor!
Inside the Constructor!
Inside the Constructor!
Inside the Constructor!
Inside the Constructor!
Inside the Constructor!
Inside the Constructor!
Inside the Constructor!
```

Figure 3-4: Constructor Demonstration

6   Remove the cout statement from the constructor function, which you inserted only to prove that the constructor was called. Remove the comment indicators from the three lines to which you added them in step 4.

7   The default values assigned by your constructor can be anything you choose. For a fraction, it makes sense to create a default numerator of 0 and a default denominator of 1. The floatingPoint data member could be set to 0.0, though a better approach is to allow the convert() function to calculate the floatingPoint. Add the following statements to become the body of the constructor function:

```
Fraction::numerator = 0;

Fraction::denominator = 1;

Fraction::floatingPoint = convert();
```

8   Change the code in the main() program that calls getData(). Rather than setting all nine array fractions to 1/10, 2/10, 3/10, and so on, change the for statement to read

```
for(x=0;x<3;++x)
```

Run the program to confirm that it now sets only the first three elements of the array to 1/10, 2/10, and 3/10; the other six elements will be 0/1 because of the constructor.

9 Change the constructor prototype to the style in which it receives arguments:

```
Fraction(const int n = 0, const int d = 1);
```

10 Change the constructor function header to

```
Fraction::Fraction(const int n, const int d)
```

11 Change the constructor function body to

```
Fraction::numerator = n;
Fraction::denominator = d;
Fraction::floatingPoint = convert();
```

12 Test the program. The output should be the same as before. The program now passes two arguments to the constructor function, where they are assigned to the numerator and denominator.

13 Save the program.

tip

• • • • • • • • • • • • • • •

▶ **Do not make the mistake of defining an employee for whom you want to accept all of the default values as**

```
Employee Welder();
```

The C++ compiler will think you are prototyping a function named Welder() that takes no arguments and returns an Employee object. That's legal; you just would not end up with a defined object named Welder. The correct way to define an employee with all the default values is

```
Employee Welder;
// no parentheses above
```

Overriding the Constructor's Default Arguments

In Tutorial 1, you learned to create functions that have default values; these values are used if you fail to pass parameters to the function. Constructor functions are no different. They use their default values, unless you decide to override them.

Two rules apply to the use of default parameters with constructor functions:

- If you want to override constructor default values for an object you are instantiating, you must also override all parameters to the left of that value.
- If you omit any constructor argument when you instantiate an object, you must use default values for all parameters to the right of that argument.

For example, if the prototype for the constructor for an employee class is

```
Employee(const int id = 0, const double sal = 4.65);
```

then the following employees can all be defined:

```
Employee Clerk;  // both default values used
Employee Driver(111); // one default value used
Employee Secretary(222,8.95); // no default values used
```

The result of these three instantiations is as follows:

- A Clerk with the default idNumber of 0 and a salary of 4.65
- A Driver whose idNumber of 111 overrides the default idNumber, but whose salary is the default 4.65
- A Secretary whose idNumber of 222 and salary of 8.95 both override the default values in the constructor

In the following steps, you will add some objects to your fraction program that don't use the constructor default values. Currently, the constructor function prototype for Fraction is

```
Fraction(const int n = 0, const int d = 1);
```

The function itself is

```
Fraction::Fraction(const int n, const int d)
  {
    Fraction::numerator = n;
    Fraction::denominator = d;
    Fraction::floatingPoint = convert();
  }
```

tip

A minor problem with the Fraction class is that a fraction that receives a negative denominator will be displayed as 4/-5 or -4/-5. You may add code at the beginning of the constructor function to correct this error. For example,

```
if(d<0)  // if the
//denominator is negative
    {
        d = -d;
        //reverse the sign
        //on both the
        //denominator
        n = -n;
        // and the numerator
    }
```

Similar code can be added to the getData() function.

1 Add two new fraction definitions to the main() program by changing the statement that defines oneFraction to

```
Fraction oneFraction, secondFraction, thirdFraction(4),
    fourthFraction(4,7);
```

Upon construction, the objects oneFraction and secondFraction will assume the default values of 0 and 1 for the numerator and denominator, respectively. The object thirdFraction will have a numerator of 4 and a denominator of the default value, 1. The construction of the fourthFraction object will result in a numerator of 4 and a denominator of 7, overriding both constructor defaults.

2 At the end of main(), add the following display statements:

```
cout<<"secondFraction — 2 defaults ";
secondFraction.showData();
cout<<"thirdFraction — 1 default ";
thirdFraction.showData();
cout<<"Fourth fraction — no defaults ";
fourthFraction.showData();
```

3 Compile and test the program. The object oneFraction and the array nineFrac are displayed as before, but the output should now resemble that shown in Figure 3-5.

```
Decimal is 0.0 Fraction is 0/1
Decimal is 4 Fraction is 4/1
Decimal is 0.571429 Fraction is 4/7
```

Figure 3-5: Demonstration of Default Values

tip
....
You will learn about a special case of an overloaded constructor, the copy constructor, in Tutorial 6.

Overloading Constructors

Just like other C++ functions, constructors can be overloaded. Recall that overloading a function name allows you to use the same function name for separate functions that have different argument lists. Constructor functions for a given class must all have the same name; they must have the same name as their class. Therefore, if you provide two or more constructors for the same class, they are overloaded by definition. As with other overloaded functions, two constructor functions used in the same program must have different argument lists so the compiler can tell them apart.

For example, suppose you have two kinds of employees: regular hourly employees, who get an ID number and a salary, and contractual employees, who do not get an ID number or a salary. (In an expanded class definition, both kinds of employees would get attributes like name, address, and phone number.) The class definition for employee could contain two separate constructors: one for employees with ID numbers and one for employees without such numbers.

```
// declaration section
class Employee
  {
    private:
       int idNumber;
       double salary;
    public:
       Employee(); // one constructor for contract employees
       Employee(const int id);
       // another constructor for regular (with id) employees
       void assignValues(const int id, const double sal);
       // prototype for assigning values
       void displayValues(); // prototype for displaying values
  };
// implementation section goes here
```

The two constructor functions are

```
Employee::Employee() // constructor for contract employees
   {
   Employee::idNumber = 0;
   Employee::salary = 0.0;
   }
Employee::Employee(const int id) // constructor for
   //regular employees
   {
   Employee::idNumber = id;
   Employee::salary=4.65;
   }
```

When you make the following statements,

```
Employee Attorney;
Employee Clerk(762);
```

the instantiation of Attorney causes the constructor with no arguments to be called, and the Attorney object is assigned an idNumber of 0 and a salary of 0.0 (presumably to be changed later with another function). The instantiation of the Clerk object calls the constructor with one argument, resulting in an idNumber of 762 and a salary of 4.65.

You cannot define the constructor for the regular employees with a default value for the idNumber, such as

```
Employee(const int id = 999);
```

Both constructors would then become default constructors, because neither requires arguments. When you define

```
Employee Attorney;
```

the compiler does not know which constructor to call. When the compiler cannot differentiate between two overloaded constructors, they are considered to be **ambiguous**.

In the following steps, you will declare an overloaded constructor for the Fraction class. A mixed number is a number that has a whole-number part as well as a fractional part, such as 2 1/8. You will create the constructor for the Fraction class that will treat three integer arguments in the definition of a Fraction object as a whole-number part, a numerator, and a denominator. In other words,

```
Fraction fifthFraction(2,1,8);
```

is interpreted as 2 1/8.

1   In the public section of the Fraction class declaration section, add a prototype for the new Fraction constructor. This constructor will take three arguments: the whole-number part, a numerator, and a denominator. Because the first constructor you created in the last section of this lesson takes no more than two arguments, no ambiguity will exist.

```
Fraction(const int w, const int n, const int d);
```

Class Features   **tutorial 3**   **143**

2 In the implementation section, add the constructor function:

```
Fraction::Fraction(const int w, const int n, const int d)
  {
    Fraction::numerator = w * d + n;  // this is the only
    // hard part -- take the whole-number value
    // multiply by the denominator, and add the numerator
    Fraction::denominator = d;
    Fraction::floatingPoint = convert();
  }
```

3 Add a new object to the end of main(), a fraction equivalent to 2⅛:

```
Fraction fifthFraction(2, 1, 8);
```

4 Add statements to display the value:

```
cout<<"fifthFraction — 3 constructor arguments "<<endl;
  cout<<fifthFraction.showData();
```

5 Compile and test the program. It should produce the following output:

```
fifthFraction — 3 constructor arguments
Decimal is 2.125   Fraction is 17/8
```

Destructors

An object's destructor is also called when you use the C++ keyword delete to disallocate memory you obtained with the C++ keyword new. These topics will be discussed in Tutorial 10.

A **destructor** is a function that is called automatically each time an object is destroyed. An object is destroyed when it goes out of scope. For example, local variables are destroyed at the end of their function. Just as with constructors, you have been using destructors in your programs whether you realized it or not. When you declare a simple scalar variable, such as

```
int aNumber;
```

A destructor must have the same name as its class (plus the tilde) because it is called automatically when an object is destroyed. If you created your own name for a destructor, C++ would not know that it was the correct function to call.

Destructor functions have no return type. That doesn't mean the return type is void; void is a type.

Programmers usually do not need to perform as many tasks in destructor functions as they do in constructor functions. The most common case in which code is needed in a destructor arises when an object contains a pointer to a member.

aNumber goes out of scope at the end of the block in which you declare it, and a destructor is called automatically. Similarly, when you declare an object such as

```
Employee Clerk;
```

Clerk ceases to exist at the end of the block in which you declare it.

Just as with constructors, C++ provides a destructor if you don't declare one.

The rules for destructor function names are similar to the rules for constructor function names:

■ As with constructors, you must give a destructor function the same name as its class (and therefore the same name as any constructor for that class). Unlike with constructors, you must precede the destructor name with a **tilde** (~).

■ As with constructors, you cannot give a destructor function a return type (it's really not necessary because destructors never return anything).

■ Unlike with constructors, you cannot pass any values to a destructor.

Unlike with constructors, only one destructor can exist for each class. Because destructors can neither accept nor return values, C++ would have no way to distinguish between multiple destructors.

Consider this employee class with a destructor function declared:

```
// declaration section
  class Employee
    {
      private:
         int idNumber;
         double salary;
      public:
         Employee(const int id, const double sal);
         // prototype for constructor

         ~Employee(); // prototype for destructor

         void assignValues(const int id, const double sal);
         // prototype for assigning values

         void displayValues();
         // prototype for displaying values

    };
// implementation section -- the functions will go here
```

For purposes of illustration, you can write a destructor function whose only purpose is to let you know it is working:

```
Employee::~Employee()
  {
    cout<<"Employee just went out of existence!"<<endl;
  }
```

The following main() program defines an employee

```
void main()
  {
    Employee Clerk;(8134,7.95);
    Clerk.displayValues();
  } // scope of Clerk ends here
```

The Clerk is constructed, the values display, and, at the end of the program, the message "Employee just went out of existence!" displays, proving that the destructor function was called.

To illustrate that a destructor is called in your program, you will now add a destructor to the Fraction class.

1   In the public data section, add the destructor prototype

```
Fraction::~Fraction();
```

2   In the implementation section, write a destructor function that displays a statement when an object is destroyed:

```
Fraction::~Fraction()
  {
    cout<<"Object gone! ";
  }
```

3   Compile and test the program. Because the program currently constructs a total of 14 objects (5 individual objects and an array of 9 objects), when the program ends you see "Object gone!" 14 times.

4   Remove the cout statement from the destructor function, leaving behind just the shell. You now have a destructor that does nothing, but it remains in place in case you want to add more code later.

5 Compile and test the program again. The fractions should display, but the "Object gone!" messages should not appear.

6 Save the final program as **MYFRAC2.CPP**.

S U M M A R Y

- A constructor is a function that is called automatically each time an object is created.
- If you do not provide your own constructor, C++ provides one for class objects.
- When you want to initialize an object's data members immediately upon creation or perform other tasks when an object is created, you write your own constructor.
- You must give a constructor function the same name as the class for which it is a constructor.
- You cannot give a return type to a constructor function.
- A default constructor does not require any arguments, either because it receives no arguments or because all of its arguments have default values.
- You can override constructor default values for an object you are instantiating.
- If you override a constructor's default value, you must also override all parameters to the left of that value.
- If you omit any constructor argument when you instantiate an object, you must use default values for all parameters to the right of that argument.
- Constructors can be overloaded, allowing you to use the same function name for separate functions that have different argument lists.
- When the compiler cannot differentiate between two overloaded constructors, they are considered to be ambiguous.
- A destructor is a function that is called automatically each time an object is destroyed, either when it goes out of scope or when you delete it with the C++ keyword delete.
- As with constructors, C++ provides a destructor if you don't declare one.
- You must give a destructor function the same name as its class.
- You must preceed the destructor name with a tilde (~).
- As with constructors, you cannot give a return type to a destructor function.
- You cannot pass any values to a destructor.
- Unlike with constructors, only one destructor can exist for each class.
- The most common case in which code is needed in a destructor arises when an object contains a pointer to a member.

Q U E S T I O N S

1. A function that is called automatically each time an object is created is a(n) _____.
    a. constructor
    b. contractor
    c. builder
    d. architect

2. A variable w with a value 67 may be defined with _____.
    a. int w = 67;
    b. int w(67);
    c. int 67(w);
    d. both (a) and (b), but not (c)

3. A class Student has data members idNum, age, and creditHours. The code
    `Student sophomore(34);` results in _____.
    a. 34 being assigned to sophomore's idNum
    b. 34 being assigned to sophomore's age
    c. 34 being assigned to sophomore's creditHours
    d. impossible to tell

4. A constructor may be _____.
    a. provided automatically by C++
    b. written by you
    c. either (a) or (b)
    d. neither (a) nor (b)

5. A class named Student must have a constructor whose name is _____.
    a. Student
    b. ~Student
    c. constructor
    d. any legal C++ name

6. The return type you code for all constructors is _____.
    a. void
    b. the class type
    c. the same type as the first data member defined in the class
    d. no type

7. A default constructor _____.
    a. takes no arguments
    b. has default values for all its arguments
    c. either (a) or (b)
    d. neither (a) nor (b)

8. The constructor prototype in the form

```
Student(const int idNum=0, const int age=0; const int credits=60);
```

means all Student objects constructed with this constructor _____.
a. will have an idNum of 0
b. will have 60 credits
c. both (a) and (b)
d. neither (a) nor (b)

9. If you want to override constructor default values for an object you are instantiating, you must also override _____.
a. all other parameters to that constructor
b. all parameters to the left of that value
c. all parameters to the right of that value
d. no other parameters to that constructor

10. If you omit any constructor argument when you instantiate an object, you must use default values _____.
a. for all parameters to the constructor
b. for all parameters to the right of the argument
c. for all parameters to the left of the argument
d. for no other parameters

11. Student senior( ); is a(n) _____.
a. constructor call with no arguments
b. object instantiation
c. constructor call with all default arguments
d. prototype for a function that returns a student object

12. The prototype for the constructor for a Student class is

```
Student(const int idNum = 0, const double gpa = 4.0);
```

The definition Student Joshua; _____.
a. defines a student with idNum 0 and gpa 4.0
b. defines a student with no idNum and no gpa
c. defines a student with unknown idNum and unknown gpa
d. is illegal

13. The prototype for the constructor for a Student class is

```
Student(const int idNum = 0, const double gpa = 4.0);
```

The definition Student Keisha(3); _____.
a. defines a student with idNum 0 and gpa 4.0
b. defines a student with idNum 3 and gpa 4.0
c. defines a student with idNum 0 and gpa 3.0
d. is illegal

14. The prototype for the constructor for a Student class is

```
Student(const int idNum = 0, const double gpa = 4.0);
```

The definition `Student Lynette(1,2);` _____.
a. defines a student with idNum 0 and gpa 4.0
b. defines a student with idNum 0 and gpa 1.0
c. defines a student with idNum 1 and gpa 2.0
d. is illegal

15. The feature that allows you to use the same function name for separate functions that have different argument lists is called _____.
a. overriding
b. overloading
c. constructing
d. destructing

16. Providing two or more constructors for the same class _____.
a. requires different argument lists
b. requires different constructor names
c. requires different constructor types
d. is illegal

17. When the compiler cannot differentiate between two overloaded constructors, they are called _____.
a. overloaded
b. destructed
c. ambiguous
d. dubious

18. A function that is called automatically each time an object is destroyed is a _____.
a. constructor
b. destructor
c. destroyer
d. terminator

19. You must preceed the destructor name with a(n) _____.
a. exclamation point
b. octothorp
c. ampersand
d. tilde

20. The return type for all destructors is _____.
a. the class
b. void
c. the same as the first data member in the class
d. none

E X E R C I S E S

1. Write the class definition for dates that contain three integer data members: month, day, and year. (You may also use the code you created for exercise 1 in Lesson A of this tutorial.) Write the default constructor that assigns the date 1/1/2000 to any new object. Write a main() program that tests the constructor.

2. Modify the program in exercise 1 to create an array of 20 dates. Each date should be initialized to 1/1/2000. Test the constructor.

3. Remove the default constructor created for the date class in Exercise 1. Create an additional constructor for the date class created in exercise 1. Create a new constructor that will be called when you specify a month and a day only. The year for any date object for which you give only a month and a day is 1999. Test the constructor.

4. Remove the default constructor created for the date class in Exercise 1. Create a class for employee retirement accounts. Data members are employee ID, department, balance in account, and monthly contribution. Create constructors that allow you to define objects with no parameters, just an ID, or an ID and a department. Any data members not assigned should default to 0. Write a program to test the constructors.

debugging ▶ 5. Each of the following files in the TUT03 folder has syntax and/or logical errors. Determine the problem in each case, and fix the program.
   a. DEBUG3-1.CPP
   b. DEBUG3-2.CPP
   c. DEBUG3-3.CPP
   d. DEBUG3-4.CPP

Class Design Issues

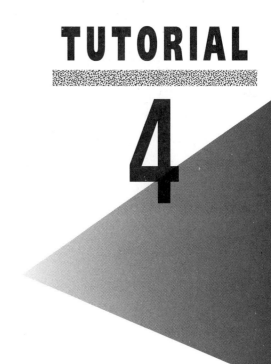

case ▶ You've designed and used your first class at Teacher's Pet Software. The fraction class you will use in educational programs includes a constructor, a destructor, and a few functions. You are now ready to add even more useful member functions to the class.

"You're doing great," your supervisor, Audrey Burns says, "but before you go any further you should do some thinking about exactly what constitutes a good class and a good member function, and how they should be stored."

"As always," you say, "I'm willing to learn."

Previewing the New FRACMORE Program

Before you begin this tutorial, take a look at the new FRACMORE program:

1 Load the **FRACMORE.CPP** program and execute it.

2 Examine the code. Notice that the class definition for the fraction class is not part of the file. The class also has new capabilities—you can invert or reduce a fraction. You will be creating this code in this tutorial.

LESSON A
objectives

In this lesson you will learn

- How to store your class components
- How to select and name member data and functions
- How to allocate and release memory for pointer data members

Working with Classes

Storing Class Components

When you start writing classes, they become lengthy very quickly. Even a small class with only two or three data members and two or three functions may require 20 or 30 lines of code. Add a main() program that uses the class (or a few classes), and you can easily have 60 or 70 lines of code in your program.

If you write a class definition and then store it in the file with the program that uses it, your program files become large (and hard to work with on a screen). In addition, when you define a useful class, you may want to use it in many programs. You can copy the class and function definitions from one file to another, but this method is both time-consuming and prone to error.

A better solution is to store your classes in a file of their own and then include that class file in any program that uses the class.

For example, consider a simple class called Item that has two private data members—item number and price—and three public functions—a constructor, a destructor, and a function to show the item.

You usually want to place a condition on the `#include<iostream.h>` statement at the beginning of a class definition. This step is described at the end of this section.

```cpp
#include<iostream.h>
class Item
  {
    private:
      int itemNum;
      double itemPrice;
    public:
      Item(const int i, const double p);  // constructor
      ~Item();  // destructor
      void showItem(void);
  };
Item::Item(const int i, const double p)
  {
    Item::itemNum = i;
    Item::itemPrice = p;
  }
Item::~Item()
  // empty destructor in place for future modification
  {
  }
void Item::showItem(void)
  {
    cout<<"Item "<<Item::itemNum<<" sells for "
        <<Item::itemPrice<<endl;
  }
```

Some programmers would prefer to save the Item class definition in a file named ITEM.H. No matter what you name this class file, it may still be referenced in an #include statement at the beginning of any program that needs access to the definition.

Rather than copy this class definition into every program that uses the Item class, you can save it in a file named ITEM.CPP and then include the ITEM.CPP file in your programs. A simple program to test including the class is as follows:

```cpp
#include"item.cpp"
void main()
  {
    Item pairPants(344, 39.95);
    pairPants.showItem();
  }
```

The output is Item 344 sells for 39.95.

When other programmers include a class that you have created, they are most interested in your public functions because they can use those functions in their own programs. To make the public functions easier to find in a lengthy class definition, many programmers list them first. If the class has many functions, you might also consider listing them in alphabetical order to make them easier to locate. Finally, don't forget to use comments liberally to explain the purpose of each function!

Many programmers divide the class into two separate files, one for the declarations and one for the implementation section. You may, for example, save the Item class declarations in a file called ITEM.H and the implementations in a file called ITEM.CPP. The ITEM.CPP file would then use #include to reference the ITEM.H file. In that case, you would include the ITEM.CPP file in the main() program.

The main() program can use the Item class because it includes the #include"item.cpp" directive. More importantly, any program or function you write later can also use the Item class if you specify an #include"item.cpp" directive. The effort you put into creating the item.cpp class is absorbed into future applications you write.

Storing the class definition in a separate file is an example of **implementation hiding**, or hiding the details of how the class works. The manner in which the class functions are implemented remains hidden from the main() program (as well as the main() programmer). We have used data hiding when we made class data members private so that they could not be inadvertently changed by nonmember functions. Similarly, implementation hiding keeps the methods hidden from programmers who are using your class. A programmer who cannot see your well-designed functions is more likely to use them exactly as they were intended and not start making adjustments in your code, thereby introducing errors. In fact, if you market your classes to others, you typically will not provide a copy of the function source code at all; instead, you will provide a compiled copy in object form.

Of course, to work with a class, a programmer who uses it must know the names and types of the public class members. Typically, you provide programmers who use your class with two items:

- written documentation of public data and functions, including the functions' return types, names, arguments, and purposes
- a source file with the public data members and function headers—in other words, the declarations in readable form, but not the implementations

In Tutorials 2 and 3, you created a Fraction class and a program to demonstrate this class. Now you can move the class definition into its own file.

1 Open the **MYFRAC2.CPP** program you completed in Tutorial 3, or open a similar completed version, **FRACPROG.CPP**, that contains a fraction class with a demonstration program. For reference, the program is listed here:

```cpp
#include<iostream.h>
class Fraction
{
    private:
        static char symbol;
        int numerator;
        int denominator;

        double floatingPoint;

        double convert(void);
    public:
        Fraction(const int n=0,const int d=1);

        Fraction(const int w, const int n, const int d);

        void getData(const int n,const int d);

        void showData(void);
    };
char Fraction::symbol = '/';

Fraction::Fraction(const int n, const int d)

    {
```

```
        Fraction::numerator=n;
        Fraction::denominator=d;
        Fraction::floatingPoint=convert();
    }
Fraction::Fraction(const int w, const int n, const int d)
    {
        Fraction::numerator = n + w * d;
        Fraction::denominator = d;
        Fraction::floatingPoint=convert();
    }
void Fraction::getData(const int n, const int d)
    {
        Fraction::numerator=n;
        Fraction::denominator=d;
        Fraction::floatingPoint = convert();
    }
double Fraction::convert(void)
    {
        double floating;
        floating = double(Fraction::numerator);
        floating = floating/ Fraction::denominator;
        return(floating);
    }
void Fraction::showData(void)
    {
        cout<<"Decimal is "<<Fraction::floatingpoint<<"  ";
        cout<<"Fraction is "<<Fraction::numerator
          <<Fraction::symbol<<Fraction::denominator<<endl;
    }
void main()
    {
        Fraction oneFraction,secondFraction,
          third Fraction(9),fourthFraction(4,7);
        oneFraction.getData(3,5);
        oneFraction.showData();
        Fraction nineFrac[9];
```

```
     for(int x = 0; x<2;++x)
       nineFrac[x].getData(x+1,10);
     for(x=0;x<9;++x)
       nineFrac[x].showData();
     secondFraction.showData();
     cout<<"third frac is ";
     thirdFraction.showData();
     fourthFraction.showData();
     Fraction fifthFraction(2,1,8);
     fifthFraction.showData();
   }
```

2   Save the program as **USEINCL.CPP**. You will be removing the class defini-
    tion from this file, leaving behind only the main() function, which will use
    an #include statement to obtain the class definition.

3   *Cut* (do not delete) the entire class definition, including both the definition
    and implementation sections, from the file. You should cut everything after
    `#include<iostream.h>` and before `void main()`.

4   In place of the lines you just cut, use the #include statement
    `#include"fraction.cpp"`.

5   Save the **USEINCL.CPP** file.

6   Open a new file and paste in the code you cut from **USEINCL.CPP**. Save
    this file as **FRACTION.CPP**.

7   Compile and run the **USEINCL.CPP** program. It works just as it did before,
    but it now obtains the class definition from the **FRACTION.CPP** file.

If you choose to separate a class definition into two or more files—for example,
putting the definitions in one file and the functions themselves in another—then the
file containing the functions must have an #include statement. The #include statement is needed to include the first file, which contains the function definitions.
Otherwise, C++ thinks you are creating functions without prototypes. Your main()
program will also use an #include statement for the header file. Thus, you end up
running a program that includes the header file more than once. As a result, you
define the same data members and functions more than once. C++ does not allow
you to define the same variables or functions multiple times, even if the definitions
are identical, so you will get a compiler error.

Additionally, once you have created several classes, each stored in its own file,
the identical #include statement might appear in several files. For example,
imagine that you create an Employee class definition with a member function that
produces output. The first statement in your EMPLOYEE.CPP file is
`#include<iostream.h>`. Next, you create a Client class that also has a member function that produces output. The first statement in the CLIENT.CPP file is
also `#include<iostream.h>`. If you write a program that uses both the
Employee and Client classes, your program contains `#include<iostream.h>`
at least twice. You will be defining the members of iostream.h more than once,
and the program will not run.

tip
· · · · · · · · · · · · · · ·

With the #define direc-
tive, some programmers
use the convention of capitalizing the filename and
adding an underscore and
an H or CPP, as in **ITEM_H**
or **ITEM_CPP**. Some programmers follow the con-
vention of beginning the
class name itself with an
underscore, as in **_ITEM_H**
or **_ITEM_CPP**. Actually,
any legal C++ identifier
will work correctly.

To resolve this problem, you can give the class definition section a #define name:

```
#define ITEM_CPP
// class definition goes here
```

Next, test to see whether the class has already been defined.

```
#ifndef ITEM_CPP
#define ITEM_CPP
// class definition goes here
#endif
```

The C++ directive #ifndef allows you to test whether a class has already been defined in a project. The #ifndef directive means "if not defined." If you place an #ifndef at the beginning of a class, and the class has not been defined, then the #define directive will be implemented. If the class has already been defined, everything up to the #endif directive will be ignored. So, even if you have more than one #include"item.cpp" statement in the same project, the definitions will be created only once.

Selecting Member Data and Functions

As you write larger and more complicated programs, the need for good planning and design becomes even more essential. Think of an application you use, such as a word processor or spreadsheet. The number and variety of user options is staggering. Not only would it be impossible for a single programmer to write such an application, but the components would never work together properly without thorough planning and design. Each class you design must be well thought-out. A great final project can be great only if each component is well designed—just ask anyone with a $30,000 car that leaks oil.

Usually, it is easier to select the data members you want in a class than it is to select the member functions. When you define a Fraction class, for example, you realize that the fraction will have a numerator and a denominator. (You might not predict you will want to store the decimal equivalent or the inverse of the fraction until you start thinking about the member functions, however.) Trying to imagine all of the different tasks you may want to perform on or with a fraction is much more difficult. Will you need to convert it to a decimal, or reduce it? Will you want to invert it, or do arithmetic with other fractions? Will you combine two functions to perform a single task, or require one function to perform several tasks?

When you begin to design a class and select its member functions, you need to consider the following questions:

■ Will special initialization tasks be necessary? Must I guarantee that class data members begin with specific values? If so, you should explicitly declare a constructor function.

- Will any special clean-up tasks be carried out when a class object goes out of scope? Must I ensure that a pointer is not left pointing to nothing? Must I free any memory that has been explicitly allocated during the life of the class object? If clean-up tasks are needed, you should explicitly declare a destructor function.
- Will class data members be assigned values after their construction? Will class data values need to be displayed? Will class data members need operations (such as arithmetic, sorting, or capitalizing) performed on them? These tasks will be performed by your other member functions.

When you know what data members and functions you will need, you may give them legal C++ identifiers. An often-overlooked element in class design is the selection of good data member and function names. Of course, C++ identifiers must not include spaces and cannot begin with a number, but other general guidelines apply as well:

tip

Some unprofessional programmers name functions or data members after their dogs or favorite vacation spots. Not only does this approach make their programs more difficult to understand, but it also marks them as amateurs.

- Use meaningful names. A data member named someData or a function named firstFunction() makes a program cryptic. You will forget the purpose of these identifiers within your own programs. All programmers occasionally use short nondescriptive names, such as x or val, in a short program written to test a function. In a professional class design, however, the names should be meaningful.
- Try to use pronounceable names. A data name like zbq is neither pronounceable nor meaningful. Sometimes, a name that looks meaningful when you write it, like goout(), may mean "go out" to you but "goot" to others. Very standard abbreviations do not have to be pronounceable. For example, anyone in business would interpret ssn as a Social Security number.
- Be judicious in your use of abbreviations. You may save a few keystrokes when creating a class function called getStat(), but is its purpose to output static variables, determine the status of flags, or print statistics?
- Try to avoid using digits in a name. Zero can be confused with "O" and "1" can be misread as "l". In a short test program it is sometimes convenient to name variables var1 and var2, but a final professional class design should use clearer names. The name budgetFor2001 probably will not be misinterpreted and is therefore acceptable.
- Use capitalization freely in multiword names. The goout() function would be better written as goOut(). A function name like initializeintegervalues() is far more readable as initializeIntegerValues(). Some C++ programmers prefer underscores, as in initialize_integer_values().
- Consider including a form of "to be," such as "is", or "are," in names for variables that are intended to hold a status. For example, whether the isOverdrawn variable is of type integer or boolean (a C++ type that holds true or false), the intent is clearer than if the variable is simply called Overdrawn. Using "is" or "are" can also help avoid confusion between data member names and function names. For example, isDone is probably a data member that indicates whether a procedure has finished; Done is more likely a function name.

When you begin to design a class, the process of determining which data members and functions are needed and what names they should receive may seem overwhelming. The design process is crucial, however. When you are given your first programming assignment, the design process may very well have already been completed. Most likely, your first assignment will be to write, or make modifications to, one small member function in a much larger class. The better the original design, the easier your job will be.

When you design your own classes as a professional, you should make all identifiers as clear as possible so that you may assign the individual functions to others for writing and, eventually, for maintenance. When you design your own classes as a student, you still need to make all identifiers as clear as possible, so that you can keep track of your work. You want to identify what needs to be done, choose names for those processes, and then write the code that makes up those processes.

Luckily, you do not have to write a C++ class or program completely before you can see whether the overall plan will work. Most programmers use stubs during the initial phases of a project. **Stubs** are simple routines that do nothing (or very little); you incorporate them into a program as "place holders."

In the following steps, you will create a stub for a function to be added to the fraction class. The function will invert a fraction—that is, it will replace the numerator with the denominator and replace the denominator with the numerator. This task isn't very difficult, but you might not have time to write the code at the moment.

1   Open the file **FRACTION.CPP**. In the public section of the Fraction class definition, add a function prototype for inverting a fraction:

```
void invertFraction(void);
```

2   In the implementation section, add a stub for a function that will invert a fraction:

```
void Fraction::invertFraction(void)
  {
  }
```

3   Compile and correct any syntax errors. Save the **FRACTION.CPP** file.

4   Open the **USEINCL.CPP** file that you created earlier in this lesson. It contains a small main() function that tests the inclusion of the **FRACTION.CPP** file. Compile and test the program, confirming that the inclusion of the invertFraction() function has not altered the functioning of the other members of the Fraction class.

5   Add two statements at the end of the main() function in **USEINCL.CPP** to call invertFraction(), and to display the inverted fraction:

```
oneFraction.invertFraction();
cout<<"Inverted: ";
oneFraction.showData();
cout<<endl;
```

6   Compile and test the program. Using invertFraction() should not change the execution of the program in any way. Although the "Inverted" message will display, oneFraction will not have been inverted.

7 To confirm that invertFraction() is actually called, open the **FRACTION.CPP** file and add an output statement to the invertFraction() function:

```
cout<<"Inside invert function"<<endl;
```

8 Compile the program, fix any syntax errors, and save the **FRACTION.CPP** file.

9 Run the program that is stored in **USEINCL.CPP** again. It should work as before, but now a message displays when the invertFraction() function is called, confirming that the function actually executes.

10 Now you can actually write the function body. Open the **FRACTION.CPP** file again. Remove the statement cout<<"Inside invert function"<<endl; from the invertFraction() function and replace it with statements that switch the values of the numerator and denominator:

```
int temp;
temp = Fraction::numerator;
Fraction::numerator = Fraction::denominator;
Fraction::denominator = temp;
```

11 Run the program in **USEINCL.CPP** again. This time, the invertFraction() function is not only called, but it also inverts the fraction. (Note that the floating point value is still the value for the original fraction.)

12 Save the **USEINCL.CPP** file.

tip

No fraction should ever have a denominator of 0, though a 0 numerator is acceptable. You might consider forcing a new 0 denominator to become 1, or at least displaying an error message if the denominator becomes 0.

Using Pointer Variables in Classes

Useful classes often have pointer members. When you design classes that contain pointer members, however, some new problems arise.

When you define a variable in a program or instantiate a class member containing data, sufficient memory is assigned from a store of memory that programmers term the **heap**. Once this memory is assigned, it remains unavailable for any other use while the variable continues to exist. Even if the program never uses the variable, it occupies reserved memory.

Unused memory frequently exists when you define an array as a class member. For example, a class defined for college professors might be named ClassList. The ClassList class may need to hold student IDs for each student enrolled in a section of a class. If some class sections in the college have 400 students, you can create a data member for the class—an array that can hold 400 student IDs.

```
class ClassList
  {
    private:
      int sectionNum;
      int studentID[400];
    public:
      // function prototypes will go here
  };
```

Instantiation of a class member with the statement `ClassList Speech100;` reserves memory for 400 student IDs. If the class has only 15 enrolled students, much memory will be wasted.

An alternative is to allocate memory dynamically. When you **dynamically allocate memory**, the computer determines the amount of memory to reserve during the run of the program, rather than during its compilation. The C++ operator used to allocate memory during the execution of a program is **new**.

When you use the new operator, you tell it how much memory to allocate from the heap. The computer selects the location, and new returns the starting address of the newly reserved memory. Because the new operator returns an address, you store new's return value in a pointer. For example, imagine that you have declared a double pointer as `double *doubPt;`. The statement `doubPt = new double;` would assign the beginning address in memory where enough storage for a double variable has just been allocated. To reserve storage for five adjacent doubles, you could write `doubPt = new double[5];`.

If you design a class with a pointer variable instead of a fixed array, you can dynamically allocate space for an array of the exact size you need. For example, in the ClassList class, instead of

```
class ClassList
  {
    private:
      int sectionNum;
      int studentID[400];
```

you can use a pointer variable for the student IDs:

```
class ClassList
  {
    private:
      int sectionNum;
      int *studentID;
```

tip

When class members contain pointers, problems arise when you assign one class member to another with the assignment operator =. You will learn how to handle this situation in Tutorial 6.

tip

....

▶ When you allocate memory
dynamically, it's possible
that enough memory won't
be available. This error situation will be resolved in
Tutorial 10.

Subsequently, you can allocate new memory with a statement such as

```
studentID = new int[numberOfEnrollees];
```

Whether a class section has 1 or 1000 students enrolled, the correct number of integers will be reserved.

In the following steps, you will create your own ClassList class so that you can observe dynamic memory allocation in action.

1 Open a new file. Type the #include statement #include<iostream.h> into this file.

2 Enter a class definition for ClassList. The data members will hold the section number and a pointer to the student ID list. Member functions include a constructor, a destructor, and functions to fill and display the class list.

```
class ClassList
  {
    private:
      int secNum;
      int *stuID;
    public:
      ClassList(int sec, int quan); // constructor receives
      //section number and enrollment figure
      ~ClassList(); // destructor
      void showClass(const int quan);
      void fillClass(int pos);
  };
```

3 Code the constructor that receives a section number and an enrollment figure:

```
ClassList::ClassList(int sec, int quan)
  {
    ClassList::secNum = sec;
    stuID = new int[quan];
    // allow enough memory depending on enrollment
  }
```

4 Code the destructor, which, for now, is a stub:

```
ClassList::~ClassList()
  {
  }
```

5 Write the fillClass() function, which allows the user to enter as many student IDs as necessary, based on enrollment:

```
void ClassList::fillClass(int pos)
  {
    cout<<"Enter student ID"<<endl;
    cin>> ClassList::stuID[pos];
  }
```

6 Write the showClass() function, which displays the section number along with the ID of each enrollee:

```
void ClassList::showClass(const int quan)
  {
    cout<<"Class section "<<ClassList::secNum<<endl;
    for(int x = 0; x <quan; ++x)
      cout<<ClassList::stuID[x]<<endl;
  }
```

7 Write a main() program to test the class:

```
void main()
  {
    int enrollment;
      cout<<"How many enrolled?"<<endl;  // of course, you
        //might want this step to be a function
      cin>>enrollment;
      ClassList Speech100(302, enrollment);
        // declare a class
      for(int x = 0; x<enrollment; ++x)
        Speech100.fillClass(x);  // fill the class with as
          // many students as needed
      Speech100.showClass(enrollment);
  }
```

8 Compile and test the program. Run the program several times, using different enrollment numbers. A typical run is shown in Figure 4-1.

```
How many enrolled?
3
Enter student ID
345
Enter student ID
456
Enter student ID
678
Class section 302
345
456
678
```

Figure 4-1: Output of DYNAM.CPP

9 Save the file as **DYNAM.CPP**.

You dynamically allocate memory to avoid reserving memory that you never use. Similarly, once you have finished using allocated memory, it should be returned to the heap.

You already know that when a class member goes out of scope, its destructor function is called, releasing the memory occupied by the object. When a class has a pointer data member, the destructor releases the memory occupied by all data members, including that occupied by the pointer variable. It doesn't release the memory *pointed to* by the pointer variable, however. Good programming practice requires you to release any allocated memory. The operator **delete** releases any block of memory previously allocated with new. You pass the beginning address of the allocated memory to delete.

In the following steps, you will add the statement to properly delete the memory allocated in the DYNAM.CPP program and then test this process.

1 Inside the currently empty destructor function, add the statement

```
delete (ClassList::stuID);
```

2 Compile and test the program, which should work as it did before. Save the program.

S U M M A R Y

- You can store a class in its own file and then include that class file in any program that uses the class. This approach makes classes easier to reuse.
- It is traditional to save class definitions in a header file with either a .H or a .CPP extension.
- Storing the class definition in a separate file is an example of implementation hiding, or hiding the details of how the class works.
- If you sell your classes to others, you typically do not provide buyers with a copy of the function source code; instead, you provide a compiled copy in object form.
- Many programmers separate the class into two separate files, one for the declarations and one for the implementation section.
- You provide programmers who use your class with written documentation and a source file containing the data member names and types and function headers.
- You can use the directives `#ifndef`, `#define`, and `#endif` to prevent duplicate declaration of header file members.
- Every class you design should be thoroughly planned.
- When you begin to design a class and select its member functions, you must consider whether special initialization tasks or special clean-up tasks will be necessary, and whether data members will be displayed or altered.
- General guidelines for naming data members and functions include using meaningful and pronounceable names, avoiding numbers, using capitalization appropriately, and making your intentions as clear as possible.
- Stubs are simple routines that do nothing (or very little); you incorporate them into a program as "place holders" while you are developing the program or class.
- When you define a variable in a program or instantiate a class member containing data, sufficient memory is assigned from a store of memory known as the heap.
- You can dynamically allocate memory so that the computer determines the amount of memory to reserve during the run of the program, rather than during its compilation.
- The new operator is used to allocate memory during the execution of a program. It returns a pointer to allocated memory.
- The delete operator releases any block of memory previously allocated with new. You pass the beginning address of the allocated memory to delete.

Q U E S T I O N S

1. In C++, class definitions are most often _____.
   a. stored with each program that uses them
   b. stored in a header file that is included in the programs that use them
   c. stored in a folder that you paste into every new project
   d. retyped for every new project

2. Header files often have the file extension _____.
   a. .H   c. .HEA
   b. .HE   d. .HEAD

3. Storing a class definition in a separate file is an example of _____.
   a. polymorphism   c. implementation hiding
   b. name mangling   d. inheritance

4. With commercial classes, the function source code is usually _____.
   - a. printed on high-quality paper
   - b. poorly written
   - c. provided on a disk
   - d. provided in object form

5. Many programmers separate a class into two files: _____.
   - a. one for the declarations and one for the implementations
   - b. one for the void functions and one for the other functions
   - c. one for the public data and one for the private data
   - d. one for the primary functions and one for the auxiliary functions

6. C++ allows you to define the same functions more than once in the same program _____.
   - a. if the definitions are identical
   - b. if the definitions are included in two separate #include files
   - c. if the definitions are located in a single #include file that is included more than once
   - d. C++ does not allow you to define the same functions more than once in the same program.

7. The #ifndef directive tests to see whether _____.
   - a. a class has been defined
   - b. a variable has been given a value
   - c. a class has no variable definitions
   - d. any objects of the class have been instantiated

8. If you design a class that needs special initialization tasks, you will want to design a(n) _____.
   - a. housekeeping routine
   - b. initializer
   - c. constructor
   - d. compiler

9. Which is a good guideline for creating function names?
   - a. Use all lowercase letters to identify the functions as C++ functions.
   - b. Use long names to reduce the likelihood of creating a duplicate function name.
   - c. Use abbreviations as much as possible to save both keystrokes and memory.
   - d. Avoid the use of digits because they are easily confused with letters.

10. A function's purpose is to print customer data. Which of the following is the best name for this function?
    - a. pcd(). It's short for "print customer data" and takes few keystrokes.
    - b. Printcustomerdata(). It states everything the function will do.
    - c. printCustomer(). It states the function's purpose and is easy to read.
    - d. lastFunction(). It is the final function called in most programs, and this name identifies the function's timing.

11. A data member holds a 1 or 0 depending on whether taxes have been paid. The best identifier for this member is _____.
    - a. taxes
    - b. paidTaxes
    - c. taxesArePaid
    - d. code

12. Simple routines that programmers use as place holders while a system is being tested are called _____.
    - a. stubs
    - b. stumps
    - c. holders
    - d. templates

13. The operator that allocates new memory is _____.
    a. allocate   c. new
    b. mem   d. next

14. The store of memory available to programs is the _____.
    a. store   c. pile
    b. stack   d. heap

15. Reserving memory during program execution is known as reserving it _____.
    a. dynamically   c. functionally
    b. statically   d. powerfully

16. If you create a class named SaleItem and each instantiation of the class requires 50 bytes, which of the following allocates enough memory for one SaleItem object, assuming that ptr is properly defined?
    a. ptr = new SaleItem;   c. either (a) or (b)
    b. ptr = new 50;   d. neither (a) nor (b)

17. If you create a class named SaleItem and each instantiation of the class requires 50 bytes, which of the following allocates enough memory for 50 SaleItem objects, assuming that ptr is properly defined?
    a. new 50[SaleItem];   c. either (a) or (b)
    b. new SaleItem[50];   d. neither (a) nor (b)

18. The operator that releases previously allocated memory is _____.
    a. release   c. delete
    b. return   d. destroy

EXERCISES

1. Create a class called Radio for objects that are radio stations. Define data members for frequency (such as 105.9) and call letters (such as WCKG). The class should have a constructor, destructor, and showData() function. Store the class definitions and implementations in a file named RADIO.CPP. Write a main() program that uses include to include the RADIO.CPP file and tests the functions.

2. Is each of the following a good C++ function name? Explain your answers.
    a. doIt()   d. empty()
    b. calculateGrossPay()   e. step3()
    c. determineinsurancepremium() f. changeGlobalSalarytoZero()

3. Create a customer class with the following data members: customer ID number, date of last purchase, credit limit, and balance due. Create a constructor, a destructor, and a showData() function. Create stubs for changeLastPurchDate(), changeCreditLimit(), and changeBalanceDue(). Write a main() function that tests these functions as stubs. Finally, implement at least one of the functions.

4. Create a class to keep track of softball performance. Data members include the player's number and an array to keep track of bases reached for each at-bat (0 through 4). Every player has a different number of at-bats; the array should be dynamically allocated. Write a program to test your class. The program should allow you to enter a player number, a number of at-bats, and the base performance at each at-bat. After data entry, display a record of the player's performance and the player's batting average (non-0 at-bats divided by total at-bats).

LESSON B
objectives

In this lesson you will learn

- How to identify types of coupling
- How to reduce coupling between your functions
- How to identify types of cohesion
- How to increase cohesion within your functions

Coupling and Cohesion

Reducing Coupling

Coupling is a measure of the strength of the connection between two functions; it is used to express the extent to which information is exchanged by functions. Coupling is either tight or loose, depending on how much one function depends upon information from another function. **Tight coupling**, which features much dependence between functions, makes programs more prone to errors; there are many data paths to manage, many chances for bad data to pass from one function to another, and many chances for one function to alter information needed by another function. **Loose coupling** occurs when functions do not depend on others. In general, you want to reduce coupling as much as possible because connections between functions make them more difficult to write, maintain, and reuse.

You can evaluate whether coupling between functions is loose or tight by looking at several characteristics:

- The intimacy between functions. The least intimate situation is one in which functions have access to the same global structures or variables; these functions have tight coupling. The most intimate way to share data is passing parameters by value—that is, by passing a copy of the variable from one function to another.
- The number of parameters that are passed between functions. The loosest (best) functions pass single parameters rather than entire structures, if possible.
- The visibility of accessed data in a function prototype. When you define a function, if you can state how it will receive and return values, it is highly visible and, therefore, loosely coupled. If a function will alter global values, you will not see them in a prototype, and the function is not loosely coupled.

Usually, you can determine that coupling is occurring at one of several levels. **Data coupling** is the loosest type of coupling and, therefore, the most desirable. This type of connection is also known as **simple data coupling** or **normal coupling**. Data coupling occurs when functions share a data item by passing parameters. For example, a class named Student might include a member function to determine eligibility for the dean's list.

```
class Student
  {
    private:
      int studentID;
      double gpa;
    public:
      void deansList(const double gpa);
  };
void Student::deansList(const double gpa)
  {
    if(gpa>=3.0)
      cout<<"Dean's List!"<<endl;
  }
```

The deansList() function receives a single data member, which it receives as a constant so the member's value cannot be altered by mistake. This approach represents data coupling and is good programming practice. Many of the functions you have written so far in this text have used data coupling.

Data-structured coupling is similar to data coupling, but an entire data structure is passed from one function to another. For example, consider an employee record class. You might write a function that compares one employee's record with another employee's record.

In the following steps, you will write a very simple class definition for an employee and a function that demonstrates data-structured coupling.

1   Open a new file.
2   Write a very simple class definition. The class will have two data members—idNum and salary—and two functions—a constructor and a compareEmployees() function.

```
class Employee
  {
    private:
      int idNum;
      double salary;
    public:
      Employee(const int id, const double sal);
      void compareEmployees(const Employee coWorker);
  };
```

3 The constructor assigns values; the compareEmployees() function compares the two employees:

```cpp
#include<iostream.h>
Employee::Employee(const int id, const double sal)
  {
    Employee::idNum = id;
    Employee::salary = sal;
  }
void Employee::compareEmployees(const Employee coWorker)
  {
    if(Employee::idNum==coWorker.idNum)
      cout<<"We have the same id number! ";
    if(Employee::salary>coWorker.salary)
      cout<<"but I make more"<<endl;
    else
      cout<<"but I don't make more"<<endl;
  }
```

tip

The compareEmployees() function in the program you are writing uses the this pointer without naming it.

4 Test the program by writing a short main() function:

```cpp
void main()
  {
    Employee me(678, 8.88), coWorker(678, 7.77);
    me.compareEmployees(coWorker);
  }
```

tip

The compareEmployees() function might more appropriately be used as a friend function. You will create friend functions in Tutorial 5.

5 Compile and test the program.
6 Save the program as **COMPARE.CPP**.
7 Change the value of me.salary to 5.55 and run the program again.

In the COMPARE program, an entire record—rather than a single data member—was passed to a function. The coupling could have been made looser by writing two separate functions, one to compare ID numbers and one to compare salaries. As every data member in each employee's record is needed, however, it is very appropriate to pass the entire structure in this case.

Control coupling occurs when one function passes a parameter to another function, controlling the other function or telling it what to do. For example,

```
void whatToDo(const int choice)
  {
    if (choice==1)
      functionOne();
    else
      if(choice==2)
        functionTwo();
      else
        functionThree();
  }
```

Of course, this kind of coupling is appropriate at certain times, but it implies that any function that calls whatToDo() is aware of how this function works, because an appropriate choice had to be made. This coupling is relatively tight. It can present a problem because, if you change the whatToDo() function, all functions that use whatToDo() must know about the change or they won't send the appropriate choice. Once you must keep track of all functions that might possibly call a second function, the opportunity for errors in a system increases dramatically.

External coupling and **common coupling** occur when two or more functions access the same global variable or global data structure, respectively. In either case, data can be modified by more than one function, which makes a program harder to write, read and modify.

Pathological coupling occurs when two or more functions change each other's data. An especially confusing case arises when functionOne() changes data in functionTwo(), functionTwo() changes data in functionThree(), and functionThree() changes data in functionOne(). This approach makes programs extremely difficult to follow and should be avoided at all costs.

Increasing Cohesion

Analyzing coupling allows you to see how functions connect externally with other functions. You also want to analyze how well the internal statements of a function accomplish the purposes of the function. **Cohesion** refers to how well the operations in a function relate to one another. In highly cohesive functions, all operations are related or "go together." Such functions are usually more reliable than those that have low cohesion. Such functions are considered "stronger," and they make programs easier to write, read, and maintain.

Functional Cohesion

Functional cohesion occurs when all of the operations in a function contribute to the performance of only one task. It is the highest level of cohesion; you should strive for functional cohesion in all functions you write. For example, consider this number class definition:

```
class Number
  {
    private:
      int number;
    public:
      Number();
      ~Number();
      int squareNumber(void);
  };
```

The squareNumber() function is straightforward. It squares a number:

```
int Number::squareNumber(void)
  {
    return(number*number);
  }
```

> It isn't just class member functions that should be cohesive; all functions should be designed so that they are cohesive.

> If you can write a sentence describing what a function does and use only two words, like "Cube value" or "Print answer," the function is probably functionally cohesive.

The function squareNumber() is highly cohesive; it performs one simple task, squaring a number. It is easiest to imagine mathematical functions as functionally cohesive because they often perform one simple task—adding two values or finding a square root, for example—but a function would also have high functional cohesion if the task was initializing the data members of a class or displaying a message. Because good functionally cohesive functions perform a single task, they tend to be short. The issue is not size, however. If it takes 20 statements to perform one task in a function, then the function is still cohesive.

In the following steps, you will add a new functionally cohesive function to the fraction class. This function will determine the greatest common denominator to the numerator and denominator of a fraction. The greatest common denominator is simply the largest whole number that divides evenly into both values.

> You may work in a programming environment with rules such as "No function will be longer than can be printed on one page" or "No function will have more than 30 lines of code." The rule-maker is trying to achieve more cohesion, but such rules represent an arbitrary way of going about it. It's possible for a two-line function to have low cohesion, and, although less likely, a 40-line function may possess high cohesion.

1　In the public declaration section of the Fraction class, in the **FRACTION.CPP** file, add a prototype for greatestCommonDenom(). This function will take no arguments; it accesses the private numerator and denominator of the class. It returns an integer, the largest whole number that divides evenly into both the numerator and denominator.

```
int greatestCommonDenom(void);
```

2 Add the function to the implementation section of the Fraction class. The function compares the numerator and denominator to determine which is smaller, and then stores the smaller value in x. For example, if the fraction is 10/35, the numerator is smaller and x = 10. The function then loops from this smaller value, integer by integer, down to zero. At any point, if x divides evenly into both the numerator and denominator (leaves a remainder of 0), then x is the greatest common denominator and the loop is exited. The return value is the greatest common denominator.

```
int Fraction::greatestCommonDenom()
  {
    int gcd;
    int smaller=(Fraction::numerator<Fraction::denominator)?
      Fraction::numerator: Fraction::denominator;
    for(int x = smaller; x>0; --x)
      if((Fraction::numerator % x == 0)
        && (Fraction::denominator % x == 0))
          {
            gcd = x;
            x = 0;
          }
    return(gcd);
  }
```

3 Compile the file. Save the **FRACTION.CPP** file.

4 Open a new file and write a short main() program to test the class.

```
#include<iostream.h>
#include"fraction.cpp"
void main()
  {
    Fraction one(10,35), two(6,18),three(1,4);
    cout<<one.greatestCommonDenom()<<" ";
    cout<<two.greatestCommonDenom()<<" ";
    cout<<three.greatestCommonDenom()<<endl;
  }
```

5 Compile and test the program. The output appears as in Figure 4-2.

```
5 6 1
```

Figure 4-2: Output showing greatest common denominators

6 Save the function header file. Note that even though the function greatestCommonDenom() has several lines of code, declares local variables, and contains a loop, it is still functionally cohesive because all steps in greatestCommonDenom() contribute to the same task—determining the greatest common denominator for the fraction.

Sequential Cohesion

Sequential cohesion arises when a function performs operations that must be carried out in a specific order, on the same data. It is a slightly weaker type of cohesion than functional cohesion because the function may perform a variety of tasks. The tasks are linked together because they use the same data, often transforming it in a series of steps. For example, this partially defined TheaterPatron class contains an ID number, name, address, and so on for each theater patron. It also contains a function that takes a ticket order.

tip
● ● ● ● ● ● ● ● ● ● ● ● ● ● ● ● ●
▶ If you write a sentence describing what a function does and you use words like "first," "next," or "finally," the function is probably not functionally cohesive, but probably is sequentially cohesive. Beware, though; it might only be temporally cohesive.

```
class TheaterPatron
  {
    private:
      int idNum;
      string firstName, lastName, address; // and so on
    public:
      double takeOrder(void);
  }
```

The takeOrder() function prompts for a quantity, and continues to prompt until the number entered is 12 or less. It then computes the price of the order at 12.50 per ticket and applies a 10% discount if the patron has ordered 10 or more tickets.

```
double TheaterPatron::takeOrder(void)
  {
    int quantity;
    double ticketPrice = 12.50,orderAmount;
    cout<<"Enter quantity you are ordering "<<endl;
    cin>>quantity;
    while(quantity>12)
      {
        cout<<"Invalid! No orders over a dozen!"<<endl;
        cin>>quantity;
      }
    orderAmount = ticketPrice * quantity;
    if (quantity > 9)
      orderAmount = orderAmount * .90;
    return(orderAmount);
  }
```

The steps in this function are sequentially cohesive because they operate in a specific order on the same data. Note that you must enter the quantity correctly before the orderAmount can be calculated or the discount taken. Very often, you can break a sequentially cohesive function down into more functionally cohesive units. For practical purposes, however, a sequentially cohesive function is an acceptable programming form.

In the following steps, you will write a new function for the Fraction class that is typical of functions with sequential cohesion. The function will reduce a fraction—for example, 10/35 can be reduced to 2/7.

1 To the public declaration section of the Fraction class, add the following prototype:

```
void reduceFraction(void);
```

2 The process to reduce a fraction involves finding the greatest common denominator for the numerator and denominator, and subsequently dividing each part of the fraction by this value. Assume we have not yet written the greatestCommonDenom() function. Add the following function to the implementation portion of the Fraction class.

```
void Fraction::reduceFraction(void)
  {
    int gcd;
    int smaller=(Fraction::numertor<Fraction::denominator)?
      Fraction::numerator : Fraction::denominator;
    for(int x = smaller; x>0; --x)
      if(Fraction::numerator % x == 0 &&
        Fraction::denominator % x == 0)
        {
          gcd = x;
          x = 0;
        }
    Fraction::numerator /= gcd;
    Fraction::denominator /= gcd;
  }
```

3 Compile the fraction class file and then save it.

4 Write a short main() program to test the new function:

```
#include<iostream.h>
#include"fraction.cpp"
void main()
  {
    Fraction oneFraction;
    oneFraction.getData(10,35);
    oneFraction.showData();
    oneFraction.reduceFraction();
    oneFraction.showData();
  }
```

5 Compile and test the main() program. This function performs several steps to produce a result. The sequence of events is very important. As you have previously created a greatestCommonDenom() function, you can probably see that the Fraction class would be even stronger if the reduceFraction() function was broken into separate functions, one of which would be greatestCommonDenom().

6 Save the program as **REDUCE.CPP**.

tip

. . . .

▶ If you write a sentence describing what a function does and you repeatedly use the same noun, the function is probably communicationally cohesive. A typical sentence would be "Input the year, make sure it is a valid year, determine if it is a leap year, and print the year."

Communicational Cohesion

Communicational cohesion occurs when functions contain statements that perform tasks that share data. The tasks are not related—just the data. It is considered a weaker form of cohesion than functional or sequential cohesion. For example, consider a ProspectiveClient class that contains a data member called prospectScore; this member stores a value based on the likelihood that the customer will buy your product. The partial class definition is as follows:

```
class ProspectiveClient
  {
    private:
      int prospectScore;
      int custNum;
      double annualIncome;
      int age;
      char maritalStatus;
    public:
      void determineScore(void);
  };
```

Assume that prospectScore is set to 0 upon its construction. The determineScore() function may add to the prospectScore based on criteria you have determined through experience and market research:

```
void ProspectiveClient::determineScore(void)
  {
  // our product is preferred by higher-income, older,
  // married people
    if(ProspectiveClient::annualIncome>30000)
      ProspectiveClient::prospectScore++;
    if(ProspectiveClient::age>40)
      ProspectiveClient::prospectScore++;
    if(ProspectiveClient::maritalStatus=='M')
      ProspectiveClient::prospectScore++;
  }
```

The determineScore() function is communicationally cohesive because its steps share data; the value prospectScore is adjusted repeatedly throughout the function. Other examples of functions that have communicational cohesion are ones that validate a value by performing several tests (Is the value positive? Is it less than 100? Is it a perfect square?) and functions that perform several different operations on the same data based on an input value. For example, the following class, CustRec, contains a function that takes a different action depending upon a transaction code:

```cpp
class CustRec
  {
    private:
       int acctNum;
       double balanceDue;
    public:
       void applyTransaction(void);
  };
void CustRec::applyTransaction(void)
  {
    char transCode;
    double transAmount;
    cout<<"Enter transaction code "<<endl;
    cin>>transCode;
    cout<<"Enter transaction amount "<<endl;
    cin>>transAmount;
    if (transCode = 'S')     // if sale transaction
      CustRec::balanceDue += transAmount;
    else
      if(transCode = 'P')     // if payment transaction
        CustRec::balanceDue -= transAmount;
  }
```

As the same information (balanceDue) is manipulated in different fashions, the applyTransaction() function is communicationally cohesive. Although balanceDue is shared, the actions performed on the data differ. More cohesion can be obtained by writing two functionally cohesive functions, addSaleToBalance() or subtractPaymentFromBalance().

Temporal, Procedural, Logical, and Coincidental Cohesion

Temporal cohesion arises when the tasks in a function are related by time. The prime examples of temporally cohesive functions in C++ classes are constructors and destructors. These functions may contain a variety of tasks that are unrelated to one another in any functional sense, but that must be performed upon the creation or destruction of an object—that is, at the same time.

Procedural cohesion arises when, as with sequential cohesion, the tasks of a function are performed in sequence. Unlike with sequential cohesion, however, the tasks do not share data with procedural cohesion. For example, main() functions are often procedurally cohesive. They consist of a list of tasks that must be performed in sequence but perform very different tasks, as in the following program:

```
void main()
  {
    getInput();
    validateData();
    computeResults();
    printResults();
  }
```

It is acceptable to use procedural cohesion in main() functions. The main() function in the above example can also be called a **dispatcher function**, because it sends messages to a sequence of (supposedly) more cohesive functions. If you sense a class member function has only procedural cohesion, you probably want to turn it into a dispatcher function.

Logical cohesion arises when a member function performs one or many tasks depending on a decision, whether the decision takes the form of a switch statement or a series of if statements. The actions performed may go together logically—that is, they may perform the same type of action—but they don't work on the same data. For example, one of three different error messages may print depending on an error code, or one of four different mathematical calculations may be carried out based on an operation symbol entered via the keyboard. Like a function that has procedural cohesion, a function that has only logical cohesion should probably be turned into a dispatcher function.

Coincidental cohesion, as the name implies, is based on coincidence. The operations in a function just happen to have been placed together. Obviously, this type of connection is the weakest form of cohesion and is considered undesirable. If you modify others' programs, you may see examples of coincidental cohesion. Perhaps the program designer did not plan well or perhaps an originally well-designed program was modified to reduce the number of modules in a program, leaving a number of unrelated statements grouped in a single function.

There is a time and a place for shortcuts. If you need a result from spreadsheet data in a hurry, you can type in two values and take a sum rather than creating a formula with proper cell references. If a memo must go out in five minutes, you don't have to change fonts or add clip art with your word processor. If you need a quick programming result, you might use cryptic variable names, tight coupling, and coincidental cohesion. When you create a professional application, however, you should keep professional guidelines in mind.

S U M M A R Y

- Coupling is a measure of the strength of the connection between two functions; it is used to express the extent to which information is exchanged by functions.
- Coupling is either tight or loose, depending on how much one function depends upon information from another function.
- Tight coupling makes programs more prone to errors.
- You can evaluate whether coupling between functions is loose or tight by examining the intimacy between functions, the number of parameters that are passed between them, and the visibility of accessed data in function prototypes.
- Data coupling, also known as simple data coupling or normal coupling, is the loosest type of coupling and, therefore, the most desirable. It occurs when functions share a data item by passing parameters.
- With data-structured coupling, an entire data structure is passed from one function to another.
- Control coupling occurs when one function passes a parameter to another function, controlling the other function or telling it what to do. The opportunity for errors in a system with control coupling increases dramatically.
- External coupling occurs when two or more functions access the same global variable.
- Common coupling occurs when two or more functions access the same global data structure.
- Pathological coupling occurs when two or more functions change each other's data.
- Cohesion refers to how well the operations in a function relate to one another.
- Highly cohesive functions are more reliable than those that have low cohesion; they make programs easier to write, read, and maintain.
- Functional cohesion, the highest level of cohesion, exists when all of the operations in a function contribute to the performance of only one task.
- Sequential cohesion operates when a function performs operations that must be carried out in a specific order, on the same data. It is a slightly weaker type of cohesion than functional cohesion.
- Communicational cohesion exists when functions contain statements that perform unrelated tasks on the same data.
- Temporal cohesion arises when the tasks in a function are related by time. Constructors and destructors are often temporally cohesive.
- Procedural cohesion describes functions in which the tasks of a function are performed in sequence, but the tasks do not share data.
- Logical cohesion is in effect when a member function performs one or many tasks, depending on a decision.
- Coincidental cohesion is based on coincidence; the operations in a function just happen to have been placed together. This weakest form of cohesion is not considered desirable.

Q U E S T I O N S

1. A measure of the strength of the connection between two functions is _____.
    a. cohesion
    b. coupling
    c. dependence
    d. subjection

2. The best form of coupling is _____.
    a. complete
    b. tight
    c. loose
    d. free

3   The loosest type of coupling is _____.
    a. data coupling
    b. control coupling
    c. external coupling
    d. pathological coupling

4. Which of the following statements is true?
    a. Data coupling is tighter than pathological coupling.
    b. Common coupling is looser than data coupling.
    c. Data-structured coupling is looser than control coupling.
    d. Control coupling is looser than data coupling.

5. The measure of how well the operations in a function relate to one another is _____.
    a. coupling
    b. cohesion
    c. adhesion
    d. conversion

6. The best functions have _____.
    a. high cohesion and tight coupling
    b. high cohesion and loose coupling
    c. low cohesion and tight coupling
    d. low cohesion and loose coupling

7. When all of the operations in a function contribute to the performance of only one task, a function has _____.
    a. singular cohesion
    b. tight cohesion
    c. functional cohesion
    d. sequential cohesion

8. The highest level of cohesion is _____.
    a. functional cohesion
    b. temporal cohesion
    c. logical cohesion
    d. sequential cohesion

9. Which is true?
    a. Sequential cohesion is slightly weaker than functional cohesion.
    b. Sequential cohesion is slightly stronger than functional cohesion.
    c. Sequential cohesion is much stronger than functional cohesion.
    d. Neither sequential cohesion nor functional cohesion is stronger than the other.

10. If the description of a function is "input the quantity, validate that the quantity is greater than 1, subtract 1 from the quantity, and print the quantity," the function is _____.

    a. sequentially cohesive
    b. logically cohesive
    c. communicationally cohesive
    d. functionally cohesive

11. With communicational cohesion _____.

    a. the tasks and the data are related
    b. the tasks are related; the data are not
    c. the data are related; the tasks are not
    d. the tasks and the data are unrelated

12. A constructor always has _____.

    a. communicational cohesion
    b. temporal cohesion
    c. logical cohesion
    d. no cohesion

13. Procedural cohesion is similar to sequential cohesion, except that with procedural cohesion _____.

    a. the tasks are not done in order
    b. the tasks are simpler
    c. the tasks share data
    d. the tasks do not share data

14. Which function is most likely to have procedural cohesion?

    a. main()
    b. findSquareRoot()
    c. getSaleSubtractDiscountAddTax()
    d. openFiles()

15. A function whose purpose is to send messages to other functions is known as a _____.

    a. dispatcher
    b. courier
    c. messenger
    d. sender

16. When a function performs tasks based on a decision, it has _____.

    a. functional cohesion
    b. coincidental cohesion
    c. logical cohesion
    d. no cohesion

17. The weakest form of cohesion is _____.

    a. coincidental
    b. functional
    c. logical
    d. communicational

18. Which is true?

   a. Coincidental cohesion is stronger than procedural cohesion.

   b. Logical cohesion is stronger than coincidental cohesion.

   c. Sequential cohesion is weaker than temporal cohesion.

   d. The weakest cohesion is functional.

E X E R C I S E S

1. Create a student record class with data members for ID number, numeric scores (up to 100) on four tests, and a final letter grade. Create a constructor that initializes all numeric data members to zero and the final letter grade to 'F'. Create three member functions:

   a. enterData(), which prompts the user for data for a student

   b. finalGrade(), which determines a student's final grade based on the following:

   ■ The student may drop the lowest test.

   ■ The highest test counts double.

   ■ A sum of 360 or better is an A, 320–359 is a B, 280–319 is a C, 240–279 is a D, and a total below 240 is an F.

   c. displayStudent(), which displays the ID number, test scores, and final letter grade for the student

   Write a main() program that declares an array of 10 students. Test your program, making sure each student receives the correct letter grade based on his or her test scores. Decide which type of cohesiveness is demonstrated by each of the three functions.

2. Rewrite the finalGrade() function from exercise 1 so that it becomes a dispatcher function, calling more cohesive functions to perform the subtasks involved in determining the student's grade. Decide which type of cohesiveness is demonstrated by each of your new functions.

3. Imagine a class named payrollRecord that contains data about an employee on our payroll, and functions that manipulate the data for paycheck and tax purposes. Give an example of a typical function name that might be a member of the PayrollRecord class that demonstrates:

   ■ functional cohesion

   ■ sequential cohesion

   ■ communicational cohesion

   ■ temporal cohesion

   ■ procedural cohesion

   ■ logical cohesion

   ■ coincidental cohesion

4. Each of the following files in the TUT04 folder has a function or functions with tight coupling or low cohesion. In each case, determine the problem, and rewrite the offending functions to improve their coupling or cohesion.

   a. DEBUG4-1.CPP

   b. DEBUG4-2.CPP

   c. DEBUG4-3.CPP

   d. DEBUG4-4.CPP

TUTORIAL

5

Friends

case ▶ You've been working hard to develop a fraction class for use in educational programs at Teacher's Pet software. The class has quite a few capabilities, but you've been thinking ahead. You plan to write programs that can perform arithmetic with fractions, so that, for example, a user could work with fraction addition problems.

"I'd really like to create functions that can use private data from two classes—so that I could add a member of the fraction class to a member of a whole-number class," you tell Audrey Burns, your supervisor. "I know the Accounts Receivable Department subtracts customer payment class data from customer balance class data. Those are different classes. How do they do it?"

Before Audrey can answer, you go on. "You know, I'd also like to use two instances of the same class, like adding two fractions together. I could then display the sum of two fractions for a user, or ask the user to type in the sum of two fractions after my program performs the calculation. If objects in programming should resemble real-world objects, then those operations should be possible."

"You are right on both counts," Audrey says. "Programming objects do resemble real-world objects, and you *can* do those things. All you need are friends."

Previewing the FRACFRND Program

1 Load the **FRACFRND.CPP** program and execute it. This program demonstrates the addition of two fractions.

2 Examine the code in both the **FRACFRND.CPP** program and the **FRACTION.CPP** header file. The fraction class now has a friend function. You will be creating this friend function and several others in this tutorial.

LESSON A
objectives

In this lesson you will learn

- What friends are
- How to declare a function as a friend
- How two classes can have the same friend function

Using Friends

What Are Friends?

Encapsulation and data hiding are two primary features of object-oriented programs. You use encapsulation when you place data and functions together in a "capsule," as objects. You use data hiding when you create private class members; they remain inaccessible to functions that are not part of the class.

In Tutorial 2, you learned the advantage of data hiding: once you create a class, including writing and debugging all of its member functions, no outside function can ever modify or use the private member data in your class. This approach means you can ensure that all data members are used correctly and in an appropriate fashion. Sometimes it may be convenient to allow an outside, non-member function to have access to a private data member, however.

For example, you may have two objects that belong to different classes, and you want a single function to use data members from each of the objects. If the function is a member of the first class, it doesn't have access to the data in the second class; if the function is a member of the second class, it doesn't have access to the data in the first class.

For instance, a class for customer data may include information such as the customer's number and balance due to the company. Another class may exist for each customer transaction, such as a purchase, payment, or return. Periodically, you wish to update the customer's record with transaction information.

tip

· · · · · · · · · · · · · · · · ·

A fully developed Customer
class would also include
data members for name,
address, telephone number,
and so on. A fully devel-
oped CustTransaction class
would permit transactions
other than payments.

Consider this partial customer class definition:

```
class Customer
  {
    private:
      int custNum;
      double balanceDue;
    public:
      Customer(const int num = 0, const double balance = 0.0);
          // prototype for constructor
  };
```

We also have a partial customer CustTransaction class definition:

```
class CustTransaction
  {
    private:
      int transNum;
      int custNum;
      double paymentAmount;
    public:
      CustTransaction(const int transNum = 0,
        const int num = 0, const double amt = 0.0);
          // prototype for constructor
  };
```

In a program that updates customer accounts, you match transactions to the appropriate customer and subtract payments from the customer's balance owed. In other words, you apply a paymentAmount from the CustTransaction class to the balanceDue from the Customer class. If you create a function that is a member of either the Customer or the CustTransaction class, however, the function will not have access to the private data in the other class.

A possible solution would be to make at least some of the private data in one of the classes public so that a nonmember function could access it. However, that strategy violates the concept of data hiding, which is essential to object-oriented programming. A better solution is to create a function that is a friend of each class.

A **friend function** can access private members of a class even though it is not a member of the class itself. In the example above, the function should be a friend to both the CustTransaction class and the Customer class, enabling the friend to use private data from the first class to alter private data in the second one.

Because friend functions can access private data, and the data members were made private for a reason, friend functions should be used only when absolutely necessary. Don't write friend functions simply to overcome data encapsulation—that approach violates the spirit of object-oriented programming.

A friend function can access private data from another class, but a friend function cannot be a friend on its own. That is, when you create a function, you cannot simply call it a friend function and declare it to be the friend of some class. The relationship is always one-sided; a class declaration must state which functions will be its friends. You can think of a class as *bestowing* friendship on a function. When you think about the principles of data hiding and encapsulation, this idea makes sense. Data hiding is used to make data members in a class private so that you can control access to them. Making data members private would be futile if any function could declare itself to be a friend of your class and then alter its private data. When creating a class, you must make a conscious decision whether any outside functions will have access to your private data, and you must explicitly bestow friendship on those functions.

How to Declare a Function as a Friend

A class may have any number of friends. The prototypes for all functions that are friends of a class are listed along with the other function prototypes in the class declaration section. The only difference is that the friend function prototypes are preceded by the keyword **friend.**

When a function tries to access an object's private data member, the compiler examines the list of function prototypes in the class declaration, and one of three things happens:

- The function is found to be a member function, and access is approved.
- The function is found to be a friend function, and access is approved.
- The function is not found to be a member or a friend, and access is denied; you receive an error message.

The function names memberDisplay() and friendDisplay() are not particularly good names to use when you design your own programs; they are included here simply to help you tell the member function from the friend function as you follow the discussion.

Recall the partial Customer class definition given earlier, to which we have added two function prototypes. The first prototype describes a function to display customer data. This member function is named memberDisplay(). The other prototype also describes a function to display customer data. This nonmember function is named friendDisplay().

```
class Customer
  {
    private:
      int custNum;
      double balanceDue;
    public:
      Customer(const int num = 0, const double balance = 0.0);
        // prototype for constructor
      void memberDisplay(void);
        // prototype for member function
      friend void friendDisplay(const Customer &oneCust);
        // prototype for friend function

  };
```

The member function memberDisplay() must be declared in the public section of the class definition, because your main() program or other functions will need to use memberDisplay() to access the private data members of the Customer class. The nonmember function, friendDisplay(), need not be declared in the public section. It is neither public nor private because it is not a member function; the words "public" and "private" do not pertain to the friend function. Therefore, you can prototype this function in any portion of the class declaration. Typically, programmers place this prototype wherever most of the other function prototypes are stored, which is usually the public section. Also, because a friend function is simply a nonmember function, it acts more like a public member than a private one.

The Customer class has two private data members and three functions—a constructor function and two display functions. The memberDisplay() function will return nothing and receive nothing, so it is prototyped as void. The complete function is shown below.

```
void Customer::memberDisplay(void)
  {
    cout<<"Customer "<<Customer::custNum<<"  Balance $"
       <<Customer::balanceDue<<endl;
  }
```

Except for its use of the word `friend`, the prototype of friendDisplay() contains nothing new. Nevertheless, it differs from the prototype for the member function.

```
friend void friendDisplay(const Customer &oneCust);
  // prototype for friend function
```

The `friend` keyword indicates that friendDisplay() is not a member of the Customer class. The friendDisplay() function returns no value, so its type is void. It takes one argument. Because the function will not change the argument, you use the keyword `const`. The type of argument that the function takes is a reference to Customer; that is, it will display data from one object whose type is Customer.

When you declare an instance of Customer, as in

```
Customer oneCustomer(812, 0.0);
```

you can use the memberDisplay() function:

```
oneCustomer.memberDisplay();
```

When you use the dot operator, the memberDisplay() function correctly displays the private data members of oneCustomer because of the this pointer received by memberDisplay(). As memberDisplay() is a member of Customer, the this pointer always points to the object used in the call to the function.

The friendDisplay() function is not a member of Customer; in fact, it is not a member of any class. Therefore, it does not have a this pointer. Instead, when you call friendDisplay(), you must pass it a copy of the object to be displayed. To call friendDisplay(), you must use

```
friendDisplay(oneCustomer);
```

The friendDisplay() function has the following structure:

```
void friendDisplay(const Customer oneCust)
  {
    cout<<"Customer "<<oneCust.custNum<<"  Balance $"
      <<oneCust.balanceDue<<endl;
  }
```

Two points must be made about this function. First, the word friend does *not* appear in the function header. (The function name friendDisplay() could be any legal C++ identifier.) This format makes sense if you remember that a function can never claim to be friend to a class; instead, the class must bestow friendship upon the function. Second, within the function, the friendDisplay() function cannot use the class name with the scope resolution operator when referring to a data member. The memberDisplay() function can refer to Customer::idNum and Customer::balanceDue because, as a member of the Customer class, the memberDisplay() function has a this pointer. The friendDisplay() function is not a member of the Customer class; it does not receive a this pointer, and Customer::custNum and Customer::balanceDue have no meaning. Instead, friendDisplay() receives the object oneCust, which is an instance of the Customer class, allowing the function to access the object's private data members using the dot operator.

In the following steps, you will create a friend function for the Fraction class. In Lesson B of this tutorial, you will modify this friend function so that it can add two fractions. For now, the friend function will simply display one fraction object.

1   Open the **FRACTION.CPP** header file you worked on in the previous tutorials or load the **FRACTION.CPP** file from the TUT05 folder. Immediately save the file as **FRAC5.CPP**. The file is fairly long now—you have been adding many useful members to the fraction class—and it looks intimidating. If you have been working through the tutorials, however, you realize that you can analyze each function as a separate entity. This tactic makes the class appear less overwhelming when the functions are all placed together. The **FRACTION.CPP** file is repeated here for your convenience:

```cpp
// declaration section
class Fraction
  {
    private:
      static char symbol;
      int numerator;
      int denominator;
      double floatingPoint;
      double convert(void);
    public:
      Fraction(const int n=0,const int d=1);
      Fraction(const int w, const int n, const int d);
      void getData(const int n,const int d);
      void showData(void);
      void invertFraction(void);
      void reduceFraction(void);
      int greatestCommonDenom(void);
  };
char Fraction::symbol = '/';
Fraction::Fraction(const int n, const int d)
  {
    Fraction::numerator=n;
    Fraction::denominator=d;
    Fraction::floatingPoint=convert();
  }
Fraction::Fraction(const int w, const int n, const int d)
  {
    Fraction::numerator = n + w * d;
    Fraction::denominator = d;
```

```
      Fraction::floatingPoint=convert();
  }
void Fraction::getData(const int n, const int d)
  {
    Fraction::numerator=n;
    Fraction::denominator=d;
    Fraction::floatingPoint = convert();
  }
double Fraction::convert(void)
  {
    double floating;
    floating = double(Fraction::numerator);
    floating = floating/Fraction::denominator;
    return(floating);
  }
void Fraction::showData(void)
  {
    cout<<"Decimal is "<<Fraction::floatingPoint<<"  ";
    cout<<"Fraction is "<<Fraction::numerator
      <<Fraction::symbol<<Fraction::denominator<<endl;
  }
void Fraction::invertFraction(void)
  {
    int temp;
    temp = Fraction::numerator;
    Fraction::numerator = Fraction::denominator;
    Fraction::denominator = temp;
  }
int Fraction::greatestCommonDenom()
  {
    int gcd;
    int smaller=
      (Fraction::numerator<Fraction::denominator)?
      Fraction::numerator : Fraction::denominator;
    for(int x = smaller; x>0; --x)
      if((Fraction::numerator % x == 0) &&
        (Fraction::denominator % x == 0))
```

```
        {
          gcd = x;
          x = 0;
        }
    return(gcd);
  }
void Fraction::reduceFraction(void)
  {
    int gcd;
    int smaller=
      (Fraction::numerator<Fraction::denominator)?
      Fraction::numerator : Fraction::denominator;
    for(int x = smaller; x>0; --x)
      if((Fraction::numerator % x == 0) &&
        (Fraction::denominator % x == 0))
        {
          gcd = x;
          x = 0;
        }
    Fraction::numerator /= gcd;
    Fraction::denominator /= gcd;
  }
```

2 Add a new friend function prototype in the public section of the class definition.

```
friend void fracFriend(const Fraction &aFrac);
```

3 Create the friend function. Notice that the Fraction class scope is not included in the function header because the fracFriend function is not a member of the Fraction class.

```
void fracFriend(const Fraction &aFrac)
  {
    cout<<"Fraction in friend function is "
      <<aFrac.numerator<<"/"<<aFrac.denominator<<endl;
  }
```

4 Save the file, which you have already named **FRAC5.CPP.**

5   Open a new file and write a short main() program to demonstrate the class:

```
#include<iostream.h>
#include"frac5.cpp"
void main()
  {
    Fraction oneFrac(3,5);  // create one Fraction object
    oneFrac.showData();
      // member function called with the dot operator
    fracFriend(oneFrac);
      // oneFrac passed to the friend function
  }
```

6   Compile and test the program. The output appears as in Figure 5-1.

```
Decimal is .6 Fraction is 3/5
Fraction in friend function is 3/5
```

Figure 5-1: Output of friend program

7   Save the file as **FRIEND.CPP**.

Two Classes with the Same Friend

When a nonmember function needs to refer to instances of two different classes, then both classes must grant friendship to the function. Consider a function that receives two objects: a customer record that includes a balance due, and a transaction record that includes a payment on account. The function uses the payment to update the customer balance. As a result, it needs access to private data from objects of both the Customer and CustTransaction class. The function prototype is

```
void updateCustomer(Customer &oneCust,
  const CustTransaction oneTrans);
```

> **tip**
> A complete CustTransaction class would not hold only payments. Customers participate in many other transactions, such as purchases and returns. For the sake of simplicity, however, we'll assume all transactions are payments.

The function, called updateCustomer(), is void because nothing is returned. It receives two arguments: a Customer object passed by reference (because its balance will change), and a CustTransaction object passed by value as a constant (because the transaction should not change).

Each class must place the updateCustomer() function in its friend list if updateCustomer() is to have access to private data belonging to objects of each type.

The Customer class has two data members, and it prototypes three functions: a constructor, a member function called memberDisplay(), and a friend function called updateCustomer(), whose purpose is to update a customer's record with CustTransaction data and display the results. The Customer class is

```
class Customer
  {
    private:
      int custNum;
      double balanceDue;
    public:
      Customer(const int num = 0,const double balance = 0.0);
          // prototype for constructor;
      void memberDisplay(void);
          // prototype for member function
      friend void updateCustomer(const Customer oneCust,
        const CustTransaction oneTrans);
  };
```

The CustTransaction class also has three data members and two functions—a constructor and the same friend function:

```
class CustTransaction
  {
    private:
      int transNum;
      int custNum;
      double paymentAmount;
    public:
      CustTransaction(const int transNum = 0,
        const int num = 0,const double amt = 0.0);
          // prototype for constructor
      friend void updateCustomer(const Customer oneCust,
        const CustTransaction oneTrans);
  };
```

tip

• • • • • • • • • • • • • • • • •

You must declare a variable
before you use it. You also
must declare, or prototype,
a function before you use
it. Similarly, a class must be
declared before you use it.

It makes sense that each class that wants updateCustomer() to be a friend must list this function as its friend. When you place these two class definitions in a file and try to compile it, however, error messages will indicate that some data members are inaccessible. If you place the Customer class definition first, when you later prototype the updateCustomer() friend function within the Customer class definition, the class CustTransaction has not yet been defined. If you place the CustTransaction definition first, when you later prototype the updateCustomer() friend function within the CustTransaction definition, the class Customer has not yet been defined. Either way, one of the class definitions makes reference to an undefined class.

The most common solution to this dilemma is to make a **forward reference** to one of the classes. This approach lets the compiler know that the class exists, and that the details will come later. The following header file allows the updateCustomer() function to be a friend to both Customer and CustTransaction, but does not produce any compiler errors:

```
class CustTransaction;    // a forward reference
class Customer
  {
    private:
      int custNum;
      double balanceDue;
    public:
      Customer(const int num = 0,const double balance = 0.0);
         // prototype for constructor
      void memberDisplay(void);  // prototype for member function
      friend void updateCustomer(const Customer oneCust,
        const CustTransaction oneTrans);
  };
class CustTransaction
  {
    private:
      int transNum;
      int custNum;
      double paymentAmount;
    public:
      CustTransaction(const int transNum = 0,
        const int num = 0, const double amt = 0.0);
         // prototype for constructor
      friend void updateCustomer(const Customer oneCust,
        const CustTransaction oneTrans);
  };
```

The same principle would hold true if three, four, or more classes had the same friend function. You would:

- forward declare all the classes except one
- define the class you *did not* forward declare, including the friend function prototype in the class definition
- define all classes that you *did* forward declare, which also contain the same friend function prototype
- define the friend function itself

In the previous section, you created a friend function for the Fraction class. Now you will create a WholeNum class to hold whole numbers. You will then modify the friend function that shows a fraction so that it includes a whole number.

1   Open the **FRAC5.CPP** file you created in the previous section. The file contains the class definition for Fraction, with the new friend function.

2   At the end of the file, begin a new class definition for a WholeNum. WholeNum will have one data member, an integer. It will also have a constructor.

```
class WholeNum
  {
    private:
      int whole;
    public:
      WholeNum(const int n);
  };
```

3   Write the WholeNum constructor:

```
WholeNum::WholeNum(const int n)
  {
    WholeNum::whole = n;
  }
```

4   Compile the file and correct any syntax errors.

5   A useful function is one that can compare a whole number with a fraction and determine which is larger. Create a friend function, named compareFracWhole(), that can access the private members of a fraction to obtain its numerator and denominator and that can access the private member of a WholeNum object for comparison. First, remove the fracFriend() prototype from the Fraction class and replace it with a prototype for compareFracWhole().

```
friend void compareFracWhole(Fraction aFrac, WholeNum aWhole);
```

6 Remove the actual function (both header and body) for fracFriend() because you will no longer use it.

7 Add a prototype for compareFracWhole() to the public section of the WholeNum class definition.

```
friend void compareFracWhole(Fraction aFrac, WholeNum aWhole);
```

8 At the top of the file, forward declare the WholeNum class. This approach avoids an error message when the compiler encounters a reference to WholeNum in the friend function prototype in Fraction.

```
class WholeNum;
```

9 At the end of the file, create the friend function. The function receives a fraction and a whole number and then converts the fraction to a whole part and a remainder part through integer division and modulus. If the whole part of the fraction is equal to the whole number and the remainder is 0, then the two values are equal.

```
void compareFracWhole(Fraction aFrac, WholeNum aWhole)
  {
    int fractionWhole, fractionLeft;
    fractionWhole = aFrac.numerator / aFrac.denominator;
    fractionLeft = aFrac.numerator % aFrac.denominator;
    if (fractionWhole == aWhole.whole && fractionLeft == 0)
      cout<<"The fraction and the whole number are equal"
        <<endl;
    else
      if (fractionWhole >= aWhole.whole)
        cout<<"The fraction is greater"<<endl;
      else
        cout<<"The fraction is less"<<endl;
  }
```

10 Save the file as **FRND2.CPP.**

11 Open a new file and create a main() program to demonstrate the new class and function:

```cpp
#include<iostream.h>
#include"frnd2.cpp"
void main()
  {
    Fraction fracSmall(1,3),fracSame(12,6),fracBig(9,2);
      // create three fractions
    WholeNum Two(2);
      // create a whole number with a value of 2
    compareFracWhole(fracSmall,Two);
    compareFracWhole(fracSame,Two);
    compareFracWhole(fracBig,Two);
  }
```

12 Compile and test the program. The results should resemble Figure 5-2.

```
The fraction is less
The fraction and the whole number are equal
The fraction is greater
```

Figure 5-2: Fraction member and friend output

13 Save the program as FRIEND2.CPP.

S U M M A R Y

- Despite the advantages of encapsulation and data hiding, sometimes it is convenient to allow an outside, nonmember function to have access to a private data member.
- A friend function can access private members of a class even though it is not a member of the class itself.
- A class declaration must state which functions will be its friends; that is, a class bestows friendship on a function.
- A class may have any number of friends.
- The prototypes for all functions that are friends of a class are listed with the other function prototypes in the class declaration section but are preceded with the keyword friend.
- Friend functions are neither public nor private; you can prototype a friend function in either the public or private portion of the class declaration.

- A friend function does not have a `this` pointer.
- When you write a friend function, the word `friend` does not appear in the function header. You also cannot use the class name with the scope resolution operator within the function when referring to a data member.
- When a nonmember function needs to refer to instances of two different classes, then both classes must grant friendship to the function.
- When two or more classes have the same friend, you must forward declare all of the classes except one. Then, you should define the class you *did not* forward declare, including the friend function prototype in the class definition. Next, define all classes you *did* forward declare, which also contain the same friend function prototype. Finally, define the friend function itself.

Q U E S T I O N S

1. You use data hiding when you create _____.
   a. inline functions
   b. private class members
   c. nonscalar types
   d. cryptic code

2. A function that can access private members of a class, even though it is not a member of the class itself, is _____.
   a. a friend
   b. an inline function
   c. a private function
   d. never allowed in object-oriented programming

3. Which is true?
   a. When you create a function, you can declare it to be a friend function.
   b. When you create a friend function, you must include the friend keyword in the function header.
   c. both (a) and (b)
   d. neither (a) nor (b)

4. Which is true?
   a. A class declaration must state which functions will be its friends.
   b. A friend function must declare to which classes it will be a friend.
   c. both (a) and (b)
   d. neither (a) nor (b)

5. A function can _____.
   a. be granted friendship by a class you create
   b. declare itself to be a friend of your class
   c. grant friendship to another function
   d. grant friendship to a class you create

6. A class may _____.
   a. not have friends
   b. have one friend
   c. have one friend function and one friend class
   d. have any number of friends

7. The prototypes for all functions that are friends of a class are listed with the other function prototypes _____.
   a. outside the class definition, in another file
   b. outside the class definition, but within the same file
   c. in the class declaration section
   d. in the class implementation section

8. The prototypes for friend functions must be listed in the _____.
   a. private declaration section
   b. public declaration section
   c. implementation section
   d. none of the above

9. The prototypes for friend functions are most often listed in the _____.
   a. private declaration section
   b. public declaration section
   c. implementation section
   d. none of the above

10. When a function tries to access an object's private data member, _____.
    a. if the function is a member function, then access is approved
    b. if the function is a friend function, then access is denied
    c. both (a) and (b)
    d. neither (a) nor (b)

11. A friend function is _____ member of the class that declares it to be a friend.
    a. a private
    b. a public
    c. an at-large
    d. not a

12. A friend function _____.
    a. receives a this pointer for the class that makes it a friend
    b. receives a this pointer for any class that uses it
    c. receives a this pointer for any class object passed to it
    d. does not have a this pointer for the class that makes it a friend

13. Consider this class:

```
class Item
   {
   private:
      int idNum;
   public:
      void showData(void);
      friend void displayData(const Item saleItem);
   };
```

Which is a legal statement within the showData() function?

a. cout<<Item.idNum;

b. cout<<Item::idNum;

c. cout<<saleItem.idNum;

d. cout<<saleItem::idNum;

14. Using the code from question 13, which is a legal statement within the displayData() function?

a. cout<<Item.idNum;

b. cout<<Item::idNum;

c. cout<<saleItem.idNum;

d. cout<<saleItem::idNum;

15. When a nonmember function needs to refer to instances of two different classes, then

a. only one class may grant friendship to the function

b. both classes must grant friendship to the function

c. either class may grant friendship to the function

d. neither class may grant friendship to the function

16. When a nonmember function needs to refer to instances of two different classes, then you must _____.

a. store the classes in separate files

b. make the classes friends of one another

c. make a forward reference to one of the classes

d. make a forward reference to both of the classes

17. A forward reference _____.

a. defines a class

b. eliminates the need to define a class

c. acknowledges the existence of a class

d. is illegal in object-oriented programming

18. If four classes had the same friend function, you would forward declare

a. nothing

b. one class

c. two classes

d. three classes

 # E X E R C I S E S

1. Create two classes. The first will hold sales transactions. Its data members include the date, amount of sale, and salesperson's ID number. The second class will hold salespeople, and data members include each person's ID number and name. Create a friend function that displays the date of sale, amount, and salesperson name for a sale. Write a short main() demonstration program to test your classes and function.

2. Create two classes. The first will hold customer data—specifically, a customer number and zip code. The second, a class for cities, will hold the city name, state, and zip code. Create a friend function that displays a customer number and the customer's city name. Write a brief main() program to test the classes and function.

LESSON B
o b j e c t i v e s

In this lesson you will learn

- How a friend can access two instances of a class
- How to bestow friendship upon a member function of another class
- How to bestow friendship upon another class

Using Friends with Multiple Classes

Two Instances of a Class Using a Friend

You have just used a friend function to access private data members from two objects that belong to two different classes. If you want a function to have access to two or more instances of the same class, you can use either a class member function or a friend function.

Consider a small CustTransaction class again:

```
class CustTransaction
  {
    private:
      int transNum;
      int custNum;
      double paymentAmount;
    public:
      CustTransaction(const int transNum = 0,
        const int num = 0,const double amt = 0.0);
          // prototype for constructor
  };
```

tip

You might not want to create a friend function to add two class members. You might prefer overloading an operator, a topic you will learn more about in Tutorial 6.

Often a customer has several transactions in a billing period, and you might choose to sum all of them before applying the total to the customer balance. In other words, you want to add two (or more) individual transactions to create a new object that holds the payment period's summary transaction that subsequently will be applied to the customer record. The new summary object will belong to the same class as an individual transaction; it will hold the numeric sum from more than one transaction. To distinguish a summary object from a regular transaction, you may use a predetermined transaction number, such as 999, to signal the presence of a summary record.

This summing task can be accomplished without a friend function. You simply create a member function for the CustTransaction class. The prototype is

```
CustTransaction addTrans(const CustTransaction aPayment);
```

The addTrans() function's return type is CustTransaction because it will return a new object that holds a total for the payment period. The function's name is addTrans(). The function receives one argument, a copy of a transaction. When you instantiate two CustTransaction objects, you will use one object's access to the addTrans() function to receive a copy of the other object and then produce a total.

When you instantiate three members of the CustTransaction class,

```
CustTransaction firstTrans(101, 888, 12.99),
  // customer 888 pays 12.99
  secondTrans(102, 888, 7.00), // customer 888 pays 7.00
  totalTrans;
```

the firstTrans and secondTrans can be combined into a totalTrans in two ways:

```
totalTrans = firstTrans.addTrans(secondTrans);
```

or

```
totalTrans = secondTrans.addTrans(firstTrans);
```

In other words, you can pass a copy of the second transaction to the first transaction's call to addTrans(), or you can just as easily pass a copy of the first transaction to the second's call to addTrans().

The member function addTrans() is

```
CustTransaction CustTransaction::
  addTrans(const CustTransaction aPayment)

    {
      CustTransaction billingSummary;// local, temporary object
      billingSummary.transNum = 999;
      billingSummary.custNum = CustTransaction::custNum;
      billingSummary.paymentAmount =
        CustTransaction::paymentAmount + aPayment.paymentAmount;
      return(billingSummary);

    }
```

The addTrans() function receives a copy of another transaction, called aPayment. It also creates a local temporary instantiation of CustTransaction called billingSummary. The billingSummary.transNum is set to 999, which is our code for summary records.

The billingSummary.custNum is set to the custNum of the object that called or invoked the addTrans() function—in other words, the custNum pointed to by the this pointer. The assignment of the custNum can just as easily be

```
billingSummary.custNum = aPayment.custNum;
```

because you wouldn't call this function to add two transactions unless they were for the same customer. You therefore assume (or add code to double-check) that the CustTransaction::custNum (custNum of calling object) is the same as the aPayment.custNum (that is, the custNum of the passed object).

Finally, the billingSummary.paymentAmount is set equal to the sum of the invoking object's (firstTrans) paymentAmount and the passed object's (secondTrans) payment amount. A copy of the entire newly constructed and defined billingSummary is returned to the calling function, where totalTrans receives it.

Making addTrans() become a member function of the CustTransaction class works perfectly well. If you think on a higher level, however, you usually will not think about adding transactions in this way. Making addTrans() into a member function requires that one instance of the class (firstTrans) invoke the function, and the other instance of the class (secondTrans) serve as an argument to the function. The second transaction "seems" to have a subsidiary role. Perhaps it should play such a role if it alters the first transaction, but it does not. In arithmetic, two numbers added to produce a total are treated equally; it doesn't matter which one comes first. In business, two paper and pencil transactions added to produce a summary record are treated "equally"; it shouldn't matter which one precedes the other. As a major principle of object-oriented programming is to better model real-world objects, making one transaction subsidiary to another violates the "spirit" of objects.

tip

You create a friend function to add two transactions for the same reason that you keep some class data members private. Although your programs would run if the transactions were added with a member function instead of a friend, or if the data members were public instead of private, the design of the class would no longer be object-oriented.

The solution is to create a friend function to the CustTransaction class. Each object to be added must be passed to the function, but the two objects will appear to be treated more equally. As the new function is a friend function, it will not have a this pointer. Thus, both transaction objects are passed, and neither of the transactions appears to have priority. Complete class declarations and a short demonstration program follow:

```cpp
#include<iostream.h>
// class declaration
class CustTransaction
   {
     private:
        int transNum;
        int custNum;
        double paymentAmount;
     public:
        CustTransaction(const int tNum = 0, const int cNum = 0,
           const double pAmt = 0.0);
        void displayTran(void);
        friend addTrans(const CustTransaction tran1,
           const CustTransaction tran2);
   };
// member function implementations
CustTransaction::CustTransaction(const int tNum,
   const int cNum, const double pAmt)
     {
        CustTransaction::transNum = tNum;
        CustTransaction::custNum = cNum;
        CustTransaction::paymentAmount = pAmt;
     }
void CustTransaction::displayTran(void)
   {
     cout<<"Transaction #"<<CustTransaction::transNum;
     cout<<" Customer #"<<CustTransaction::custNum;
     cout<<" Amount $"<<CustTransaction::paymentAmount<<endl;
   }
```

```
// nonmember friend function implementation
addTrans(const CustTransaction tran1,
  const CustTransaction tran2)
    {
      CustTransaction billingSummary;//local, temporary object
      billingSummary.transNum = 999;
      billingSummary.custNum = tran1.custNum;
      billingSummary.paymentAmount = tran1.paymentAmount +
        tran2.paymentAmount;
      return(billingSummary);
    }
// demonstration program
void main()
  {
    CustTransaction firstTran(101, 888, 12.99),
      secondTran(102, 888, 7.12),
      totalTran;
    totalTran = addTrans(firstTran, secondTran);
    firstTran.displayTran();
    secondTran.displayTran();
    totalTran.displayTran();
  }
```

The output appears as shown in Figure 5-3.

```
Transaction#101 Customer#888 Amount $12.99
Transaction#101 Customer#888 Amount $7.12
Transaction#999 Customer#888 Amount $20.11
```

Figure 5-3: Fraction and WholeNum comparison

In the following steps, you will create a friend function to add two Fraction class objects together.

1   Open the **FRND2.CPP** file, which contains the Fraction class definition. Save the file as **FRND3.CPP**.

2   In the public section of the class definition, add a prototype for a friend function that will eventually be used to add two fractions. The function returns a new fraction that is the sum of the two fractions passed to it.

```
friend Fraction addFrac(const Fraction a, const Fraction b);
```

3   At the end of the **FRND2.CPP** file, add the friend function. To add two fractions, such as 3/8 and 1/6, you can do the following:

- Multiply both the numerator and denominator of 3/8 by 6, the denominator of 1/6. This operation results in 18/48.
- Multiply both the numerator and denominator of 1/6 by 8, the denominator of 3/8. This operation results in 8/48.
- Add the numerators of the two results, resulting in 26/48.
- Reduce the fraction by dividing 26 and 48 by their greatest common denominator, 2, resulting in 13/24.

The addFrac() function follows these steps, using two local fractions, a and b, to hold the temporary values of the two fractions being summed.

```
Fraction addFrac(const Fraction a, const Fraction b)
  {
    int numA, denomA, numB, denomB, numNew, denomNew;

    numA = a.numerator * b.denominator;

    denomA = a.denominator * b.denominator;

    numB = b.numerator * a.denominator;

    numNew = numA + numB;

    denomNew = denomA;

    Fraction newFrac(numNew, denomNew);

    newFrac.reduceFraction();
        // this function is already part of the fraction.cpp file
    return(newFrac);
  }
```

4   Compile the file, correcting any syntax errors, and save it.

5 Open a new file and write a short demonstration program to test the friend function.

```cpp
#include<iostream.h>
#include"frnd3.cpp"
void main()
  {
    Fraction firstFrac, secondFrac, totalFrac;
    firstFrac.getData(3,8);
    secondFrac.getData(1,6);
    totalFrac = addFrac(firstFrac, secondFrac);
    totalFrac.showData();
  }
```

6 Compile the program. Correct any syntax errors and save the program as **TESTADD.CPP.**

7 Run the program. Confirm that the addition works correctly. Change the values for firstFrac and secondFrac several times, and confirm that the addition remains correct.

Making a Friend of a Member of Another Class

Classes can bestow friendship on nonmember functions; they can also bestow friendship on functions that are members of other classes.

Consider two classes developed for a college registration system. One class is named StudentRequest; it holds a student idNum and a section in which the student is requesting enrollment. The other class, named ClassRec, holds information about one section of a class, including a section number, enrollment limit, and current enrollment.

When a student requests to enroll in a specific section, you want to access the current enrollment figure for the class and determine whether the class has enough room based on the class size limit. In other words, a StudentRequest function needs access to a ClassRec private data member.

A possible solution is to create a function named grantEnrollment() that belongs to the StudentRequest class; the ClassRec class may then bestow friend status on this function. The grantEnrollment() function can be used to compare the current enrollment and the enrollment limit, thereby determining whether the class has space for the student making the request.

Creating the class definitions requires three operations:

■ Forward declare the class that is granting friendship, because the class that holds the friend will use this class name.
■ Declare the class that contains the function that will be a friend.
■ Define the class that is granting friendship. When you name the function that is a friend, you must use the class name of the class where the function is a member as well as the scope resolution operator.

tip

This example shows a class granting friendship to a single function that is a member of another class. You may, however, grant friendship to as many member functions of other classes as appropriate.

Examine the following class definitions for ClassRec and StudentRequest. Notice the sequence of the forward declaration of ClassRec, the declaration of StudentRequest with the grantEnrollment() prototype, and the ClassRec declaration, which makes a friend of grantEnrollment().

```cpp
#include<iostream.h>
class ClassRec;   // forward declaration of ClassRec so
    //StudentRequest can refer to it
class StudentRequest

  {
    private:
      int idNum;

      int secRequest;

    public:

      StudentRequest(const int id, const int req); // constructor

      void grantEnrollment(ClassRec &oneClass);
        // member function to grant enrollment in class

  };
class ClassRec
  {
    private:
      int sectionNum;
      int enrollLimit;
      int enrollCurrent;
    public:
      ClassRec(const int sec, const int lim, const int curr); // constructor
      friend void StudentRequest::grantEnrollment(ClassRec &oneClass);
        // grantEnrollment is a friend

  };
```

The constructors for the two classes contain nothing unusual:

```cpp
ClassRec::ClassRec(const int sec, const int lim, const int curr)
  {
    ClassRec::sectionNum = sec;
    ClassRec::enrollLimit = lim;

    ClassRec::enrollCurrent = curr;

  }
StudentRequest::StudentRequest(const int id, const int req)

  {

    StudentRequest::idNum = id;

    StudentRequest::secRequest = req;

  }
```

The grantEnrollment() function is a member of the StudentRequest class. When grantEnrollment is called, it receives a reference variable containing the class requested by the student. The body of the function compares current enrollment with the class limit. If not enough room is available, a message, "Enrollment denied—class full", is displayed. If there is enough room, not only does an "Enrollment accepted" message display, but the class section's current enrollment is also increased.

```
void StudentRequest::grantEnrollment(ClassRec &oneClass)
  {
    if(oneClass.enrollCurrent >= oneClass.enrollLimit)
      cout<<StudentRequest::idNum
        <<" Enrollment denied --class full"<<endl;
    else
      {
        cout<<StudentRequest::idNum
          <<" Enrollment accepted"<<endl;
        ++oneClass.enrollCurrent;
      }
  }
```

The grantEnrollment() function is able to access and even alter a member of the ClassRec class because grantEnrollment() is a friend of ClassRec.

Consider a short demonstration program. Three student objects are instantiated, each requesting class section 101. One ClassRec is instantiated for Psych section 101, which has a current enrollment of 28 and a limit of 30—that is, room for two more students.

```
void main()
  {
    StudentRequest Molly(334, 101),
      Alfonso(488,101),
      Eric(599, 101);
      // three students
    ClassRec Psych(101, 30, 28);
    Molly.grantEnrollment(Psych);
    Alfonso.grantEnrollment(Psych);
    Eric.grantEnrollment(Psych);
  }
```

Upon requests by Molly and Alfonso, their enrollments are accepted. The class limit is then reached. When Eric makes a request, his enrollment is denied. The output is as follows:

```
334 Enrollment accepted
488 Enrollment accepted
599 Enrollment denied -- class full
```

tip
. . . .

For this classroom-scheduling example, we assume that once a room is scheduled for a section, no other sections may be held there at any other time during the week. A more complicated scheduling program would also take into account the day of the week and the time of day. In addition, we assume a single-building campus in our example. Obviously, a full-fledged scheduling program is more complicated than the task we are tackling here.

For classroom scheduling, two classes of objects are needed: sections and rooms. When a section is scheduled, a search is made for a room that will hold the number of students that may be enrolled. You can create a room assignment function that is not only a member of the class that holds class sections, but also a friend of the room class; the latter characteristic means that it can access seat limit data that are private to the room class.

1   Open a new file and enter the code for a class section similar to the one used in this tutorial. For the purposes of this exercise, your ClassRec will need only a section number, an enrollment limit, and a room number as private data members. The class has a constructor in which values are received for section number and enrollment limit, but the room number is set to 0 until a room assignment is made. The program also includes a display function.

```cpp
#include<iostream.h>
class ClassRec
   {
     private:
        int sectionNum;
        int enrollLimit;
        int roomNum;
     public:
        ClassRec(const int sec, const int lim);
          // constructor
        void showClassRoom(void);
          // function to display class and room data
   };
```

2   You must also create a class for room records. RoomRec will contain data members for the room number and seat limit. It also has a data member, roomIsOccupied, which stores a 1 or 0, respectively, indicating whether the room is already scheduled or free. A member function, roomData(), allows values to be assigned to the room number, seat limit, and occupied status for any room.

```cpp
class RoomRec
   {
     private:
        int roomNum;
        int seatLimit;
        int roomIsOccupied;
     public:
        void roomData(const int rm, const int seats,
          const int  occ);
   };
```

3 Add a function prototype to make a room assignment. In the public section of the ClassRec class, add

```
void roomAssign(RoomRec &aRoom);
```

4 In the public section of the RoomRec class, add a declaration for the friend function:

```
friend void ClassRec::roomAssign(RoomRec &aRoom);
```

5 Forward declare the RoomRec class at the top of the file, just before the beginning of the declaration for ClassRec:

```
class RoomRec;
```

6 Add the constructor functions for ClassRec, forcing all new class sections to have room 0:

```
ClassRec::ClassRec(const int sec, const int lim)
  {
    ClassRec::sectionNum = sec;
    ClassRec::enrollLimit = lim;
    ClassRec::roomNum = 0;
  }
```

7 Add the function to show the class section data:

```
void ClassRec:: showClassRoom(void)
  {
    cout<<ClassRec::sectionNum<<" is assigned to "
      <<ClassRec::roomNum<<endl;
    if(ClassRec::roomNum ==0)
      cout<<"No assignment made for "
        <<ClassRec::sectionNum<<endl;
  }
```

8 Add a function that assigns values to rooms:

```
void Roomrec::RoomData(const int rm, const int seats,
  const int occ)

  {

    RoomRec::roomNum = rm;

    RoomRec::seatLimit = seats;

    RoomRec::roomIsOccupied = occ;

  }
```

9 Write the room assignment function. The room assignment function checks to see whether a class section has not been assigned a room (roomNum is still 0) and whether a room is both unoccupied and has enough seats. If the class has not been scheduled and the room meets the class conditions, the room's status is changed to occupied, and the section is assigned the room number.

tip

••••••••••••••••

In C++, the statement `if (!aRoom.roomIsOccupied)` is interpreted as "if not aRoom.roomIsOccupied." It could also be coded as `if(roomIsOccupied==0)`.

```
void ClassRec::roomAssign(RoomRec &aRoom)

  {

    if (ClassRec::roomNum == 0)

      if(!aRoom.roomIsOccupied &&
        aRoom.seatLimit >= ClassRec::enrollLimit)

        {

          aRoom.roomIsOccupied = 1;

          ClassRec::roomNum = aRoom.roomNum;

        }

  }
```

10 Write a short demonstration program that declares three classes and five rooms. The program tries to find a room for each class by passing each room in the array, one at a time, to the roomAssign() function.

```
void main()
  {
    ClassRec English(801,25);
       // English section 801 has 25 students
    ClassRec Accounting(802,15);
       // Accounting section 802 has 15 students
    ClassRec Biology(803,40);
       //Biology section 803 has 40 students
    RoomRec rm[5];
    // some typical room data
    rm[0].roomData(101,20,1); // room holds 20; occupied
    rm[1].roomData(102,20,0); // room holds 20; available
    rm[2].roomData(103,30,0); // room holds 30; available
    rm[3].roomData(104,30,1); // room holds 30; occupied
    rm[4].roomData(105,20,0); // room holds 20; available
    for(int x=0;x<5;++x)
      {
        English.roomAssign(rm[x]);
        Accounting.roomAssign(rm[x]);
        Biology.roomAssign(rm[x]);
      }
    English.showClassRoom();
    Accounting.showClassRoom();
    Biology.showClassRoom();
  }
```

11 Compile the program and correct any syntax errors.

12 Test the program. During program execution, the first room (rm[0], which is room 101) is passed to each section. It's not a suitable room because it's occupied. The second room (rm[1], room 102) is passed to the English section, but the English section needs seats for 25. So, the second room is passed to the Accounting section. This section needs only 15 seats, so the room assignment is made. The second room is passed to the Biology section, but the Accounting class already occupies it. The third room (room 103) is acceptable to the English class. Even after five loops, Biology has not been assigned to a room because no room can handle an enrollment of 40. The final output looks like Figure 5-4.

```
801 is assigned to 103
802 is assigned to 102
803 is assigned to 0
No assignment made for 803
```

Figure 5-4: Room assignment output

13 Change room capacities and class section requirements to confirm that room assignment is taking place correctly.

14 Save the program as **ROOMASSN.CPP**.

Making a Friend of Another Class

You can bestow friendship on a function that is a member of another class. You can also bestow friendship on several functions that are members of another class. In addition, you can bestow friendship on all functions that are members of another class, either by making each function a friend or by making a friend of the entire class.

To grant friendship to an entire class, when constructing the class definition, simply write the keyword `friend` followed by `class` and the name of the class.

For example, in the previous section, a ClassRec class granted friendship to the grantEnrollment() function with the following statement:

```
friend void StudentRequest::grantEnrollment(ClassRec &oneClass);
```

Alternatively, friendship can be granted to the entire StudentReqest class with the statement

```
friend class StudentRequest;
```

This approach makes every function that is a member of StudentRequest become a friend of the granting class.

When you make a class like StudentRequest become a friend of ClassRec, it does not mean ClassRec is a friend of StudentRequest. ClassRec *can* be a friend of StudentRequest, but only if you declare it to be so within the StudentRequest definition.

S U M M A R Y

- If you want a function to have access to two or more instances of the same class, you have the choice of using either a class member function or a friend function.
- Creating a friend function is often preferable to creating a member function because the former strategy better models the actions of real-world objects.
- When you create a friend function that uses two instances of the same class, you usually want to pass both objects to the function so that neither object appears to have priority.
- Classes can bestow friendship on functions that are members of other classes.
- Creating the class definitions in which one class function is named as a friend to another class requires that you forward declare the class that is granting friendship, declare the class that contains the friend function, and finally define the class granting friendship.
- You can bestow friendship on all functions that are members of another class, either by making each function a friend or by making a friend of the entire class, as in `friend class friendlyClass;`. This statement makes every function that is a member of friendlyClass become a friend of the granting class.

Q U E S T I O N S

1. If you need a function to access two or more instances of the same class, you can use _____.
   a. a class member function
   b. a friend function
   c. either (a) or (b)
   d. neither (a) nor (b)

2. Consider this prototype declared within the Item class:

```
Item addItems(const Item anItem);
```

   This function returns _____.
   a. nothing
   b. void
   c. an object of the Item class
   d. a pointer to an object of the Item class

3. Consider the same function as in question 2. The function receives _____.
   a. nothing
   b. a copy of a member of the Item class
   c. an address of a member of the Item class
   d. a copy of the Item class

4. Consider the same function as in question 2, and assume these declarations are made: `Item oneItem, twoItem, threeItem;`. Which of the following is correct?
   a. threeItem = oneItem.addItems(twoItem);
   b. threeItem = twoItem.addItems(oneItem);
   c. both (a) and (b)
   d. neither (a) nor (b)

5. You need to multiply two private data members of two separate objects that are of the same class. You would _____.
   a. create a member function because it is easiest
   b. create a friend function because it is easiest
   c. create a member function because the objects should be treated equally
   d. create a friend function because the objects should be treated equally

6. You need to display two private data members from one object of a class. You would _____.
   a. create a member function to preserve data hiding
   b. create a friend function to implement object-oriented programming
   c. create both friend and member functions to give the programmer a choice
   d. not create a function, but just display the data members directly

7. You need to multiply two private data members of two separate objects that are of the same class. You have created a friend function to do the multiplication. You will _____.
   a. use the this pointer for both objects within the function
   b. use the this pointer for one of the objects within the function and pass the other object
   c. pass both objects to the function
   d. call the function twice, passing one object each time

8. Classes can bestow friendship on _____.
   a. nonmember functions
   b. functions that are members of other classes
   c. both (a) and (b)
   d. neither (a) nor (b)

9. You may grant friendship to _____.
   a. no member functions of other classes
   b. one member function from one other class
   c. one member function each from as many classes as appropriate
   d. as many member functions of other classes as appropriate.

10. Creating a class definition when one class is granting friendship to a function that is a member of another class requires first _____.
    a. a forward declaration of the class that holds the member function being granted friendship
    b. a forward declaration of the class that is granting friendship
    c. the definition of the class that contains the function that will be a friend
    d. the definition of the class that is granting friendship

11. When you declare a member of another class to be a friend, you must use _____.
    a. the keyword friend
    b. the scope resolution operator
    c. both (a) and (b)
    d. neither (a) nor (b)

12. You can bestow friendship on _____.
    a. a function that is a member of another class
    b. several functions that are members of another class
    c. all functions that are members of another class
    d. any of these

13. You can bestow friendship on all members of another class by _____.
    a. making each function a friend
    b. making a friend of the entire class
    c. either (a) or (b)
    d. neither (a) nor (b)

14. Which grants friendship to the class Student?
   a. friend Student;
   b. friend class Student;
   c. either (a) or (b)
   d. neither (a) nor (b)

15. If MyClass is a friend of YourClass, which is true?
   a. YourClass is a friend of MyClass
   b. YourClass is not a friend of MyClass
   c. YourClass may or may not be a friend of MyClass
   d. YourClass cannot be a friend of MyClass

16. If MyClass is a friend of YourClass, and YourClass is a friend of MonicasClass, which is true?
   a. MyClass is a friend of MonicasClass
   b. YourClass is a friend of MyClass
   c. MonicasClass is a friend of MyClass
   d. MonicasClass may or may not be a friend of MyClass

17. If MissysClass is a friend of HarrysClass, then which is true?
   a. all members of MissysClass are friends of HarrysClass
   b. all members of HarrysClass are friends of MissysClass
   c. both (a) and (b)
   d. neither (a) nor (b)

E X E R C I S E S

1. Create a class to hold a daily weather report with data members such as dayOfMonth, highTemp, lowTemp, amountRain, and amountSnow. Instantiate 30 objects and initialize them with sample data. At month-end, a monthly object is created. Its date is 99 and it stores the high temperature, low temperature, and rain and snow totals for the month. Write a program to create the month-end weather report from the 30 daily reports.

2. Create a class to hold data for apartments you rent, such as apartment number and monthly rent. Create a second class for tenants with data members such as name, phone number, and apartment number. Create a member function for the tenant class that can access and display the tenant's name and monthly rent amount. Write a demonstration program for your classes.

debugging ▶ Each of the following files in the TUT05 folder has a class with a friend function or functions, and each has syntax and/or logical errors. Determine the problem in each case, and fix the program.
   a. DEBUG5-1.CPP
   b. DEBUG5-2.CPP
   c. DEBUG5-3.CPP
   d. DEBUG5-4.CPP

Overloading

case ▶ You've been working on the Fraction class for quite a while, but you're getting impatient. "My programs aren't doing much yet," you say, "and the syntax involved in the function calling is very awkward. If I want to add two fractions, I'd like to just throw a plus sign between them!"

Audrey Burns, your supervisor, provides some reassurance. "As soon as you overload some operators," she explains, "you'll have programs that are much easier to understand."

Previewing the OVERLOAD Program

1 Load the **OVERLOAD.CPP** program in the TUT06 folder and execute it. This program is a child's game that will ask you to input a fraction and then test your knowledge of how much more is needed to make a whole number.

2 Examine the code. Notice how the fractions can be input, output, subtracted, and compared as if they were a built-in variable type instead of class objects. In this tutorial, you will create the overloaded functions to perform these tasks.

In this lesson you will learn

- How the concepts of overloading and polymorphism can be extended
- What rules are associated with overloading operators
- How to overload math operators
- How to work with multiple operations in a statement

Overloading Operators

Overloading and Polymorphism

You are already familiar with overloading:

- You overload your vocabulary when you distinguish between opening a door, opening a bank account, opening your eyes, and opening a computer file.
- You overloaded functions in Tutorial 1 when you gave two functions the same name, but different argument types.
- You overloaded constructors in Tutorial 3 by creating two constructors for the same class, which, by definition, must have the same name.

The benefit of having more than one function with the same name lies in the fact that you can use one easy-to-understand function name without paying attention to the data types involved.

You are already familiar with the concept of polymorphism, meaning "many forms." Polymorphism allows the same operation to be carried out differently depending on the object. When you overload a verb such as "open," the verb is said to be polymorphic; when you overload a function, the function name is polymorphic.

For purists, a subtle difference exists between overloading and polymorphism. Some reserve the term "polymorphism" (or **"pure polymorphism"**) for situations in which one function can be used with a variety of arguments (for example, a constructor that can take one, two, or three arguments). The term "overloading" is applied to situations where multiple functions are defined with a single name (for example, three functions that square integers, floats, and doubles). Certainly, the two terms are related; both refer to the ability to use a single name to communicate multiple meanings. For now, you can think of overloading as a primitive type of polymorphism. You will be able to distinguish between overloading and polymorphism more precisely after completing Tutorial 9.

The situation in which two totally separate actions result from what seems to be the same operation or command occurs frequently in all computer programming languages—not just object-oriented languages. For example, in most programming languages and applications such as spreadsheets and databases, the plus sign has a variety of meanings:

- Alone before a value (called **unary form**), + indicates a positive value, as in the expression +7.
- Between two integers (called **binary form**), + indicates integer addition, as in the expression 5 + 9.
- Between two floating-point numbers (also called binary form), + indicates floating-point addition, as in the expression 6.4 + 2.1.

tip

Polymorphism will be discussed in even greater detail in Tutorial 7, which discusses inheritance.

tip

The use of functions that are distinguished by their number or types of arguments is sometimes called **parametric overloading**.

Expressing a value as positive is very different from performing arithmetic, so the + is polymorphic in that it can take one or two arguments and have a different meaning in each case. In addition, the code that is generated by the compiler for integer addition often differs dramatically from the code created for floating-point addition, so the + is overloaded; that is, distinct procedures are carried out based on the arguments. Even though the two types of addition force the computer to perform two separate procedures, spreadsheet and database users (as well as programmers) do not concern themselves with the multiple object code routines. They think of the + operation as a single operation: addition.

The creators of C++ (and other languages) were not required to overload the + symbol. This tactic would be unnecessary if separate symbols were used for integer addition and floating-point addition—perhaps I+ and F+, for example. However, not only would the expressions that programmers write look confusing and unnatural, it would also take longer to learn a programming language. Likewise, separate symbols would be needed for integer and floating-point subtraction, multiplication, and division, not to mention many other operations, such as greater than and less than. Just as others can understand "open" correctly when we provide the context of "door" or "eyes," the plus sign is understood in context by the compiler. Of course, overhead (time and memory) is involved when the compiler must determine *which* type of action to initiate when it encounters a +. Nevertheless, using the computer's time and memory to perform this task is preferable to using the programmer's time and memory to keep track of unnatural symbols.

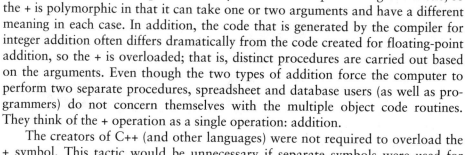

In addition to overloading, compilers often need to perform **coercion** when the + symbol is used with mixed arithmetic. Depending on the programming language, when an integer and floating-point number are added, the integer may be coerced into a floating-point number before the appropriate addition code executes.

Overloading Operators—The Rules

Just as the +, -, *, and / symbols make it easy to work with built-in data types such as int and double, you might find it convenient to use the same symbols with your classes. When you add two integer values, it is clear what should be added. Classes, however, contain a variety of data members. As a result, if you want the compiler to perform arithmetic with two class objects, you must tell the compiler what you mean.

For example, an Employee class might contain a name, department number, and salary. You would never need to add two employees' names or department numbers, but if you have 100 instances of Employee, you might want to obtain a total salary figure.

As another example, you might have a Salesperson class that contains a data member for annual sales, and a Client class that contains a data member for annual revenue. You might wish to perform division with these two dissimilar classes to determine a particular Client's percentage contribution to a particular Salesperson's annual sales total.

Operator overloading is the process by which you apply operators to your own abstract data types. You overload an operator by making it a function; subsequently, it may be used just like any other function. In the same way that the modulus operator, %, is not defined for use with floating-point values, you don't overload every available operator for each class defined. Rather, you choose the operators that you need and that make sense for your class.

C++ operators are classified as unary or binary, depending on whether they take one or two arguments, respectively. Table 6-1 lists the unary C++ operators that you may overload; Table 6-2 lists the binary operators that may be overloaded. If an operator is normally defined to be unary, then you cannot overload it to be binary, and vice versa. Of course, if an operator is either binary or unary, such as +, you may overload it in either context.

If a unary operator is allowed to be placed only in front of objects with built-in C++ types, then the same holds true for your classes when you overload the operator. In other words, the expression !Employee is allowed; the expression Employee! is not.

Operator	Usual use	Associativity
->	member	left to right
->*	indirect pointer to member	left to right
!	not	right to left
&	address of	right to left
*	indirection (dereference)	right to left
+	positive value	right to left
–	negative value	right to left
++	increment	right to left
--	decrement	right to left
~	complement	right to left

Table 6-1: Unary operators that may be overloaded

Operator	Usual use	Associativity
*	multiplication	left to right
/	division	left to right
%	remainder (modulus)	left to right
+	addition	left to right
-	subtraction	left to right
<<	shift bits left	left to right
>>	shift bits right	left to right
>	greater than	left to right
<	less than	left to right
>=	greater than or equal to	left to right
<=	less than or equal to	left to right
==	equal to	left to right
!=	not equal to	left to right
&&	logical AND	left to right
||	logical OR	left to right
&	bitwise AND	left to right
|	bitwise inclusive OR	left to right
^	bitwise exclusive OR	left to right
=	assignment	right to left

Table 6-2: Binary operators that may be overloaded

Operator	Usual use	Associativity
+=	add and assign	right to left
-=	subtract and assign	right to left
*=	multiply and assign	right to left
/=	divide and assign	right to left
%=	modulus and assign	right to left
&=	bitwise AND and assign	right to left
|=	bitwise OR and assign	right to left
^=	bitwise OR and assign	right to left
<<=	shift left and assign	right to left
>>=	shift right and assign	right to left
()	function call	left to right
[]	array element subscript	left to right
->	structure pointer reference	left to right
new	allocate memory	right to left
delete	deallocate memory	right to left
,	comma	left to right

Table 6-2 (continued)

Tables 6-1 and 6-2 list the usual use for each operator that may be overloaded. When you overload any of these operators to use with your classes, C++ does not require you to use the operator for the usual purpose. For example, you may legally overload the + symbol to mean subtraction, although it would obviously be poor programming practice.

In addition, the tables list the normal associativity for each operator. **Associativity** refers to the order in which actions within an expression are carried out. You may not change associativity when you overload operators. For example, assignment takes place from right to left, as in int x = 8;. You may not change assignment for your classes to take place from left to right, as in 2376 = Employee;.

You also cannot change the normal precedence of any operator. For example, you cannot cause addition to take place prior to multiplication in an expression such as Item + increase * discount;.

Specifically, four operators cannot be overloaded. They are listed in Table 6-3.

Operator	Usual use
.	member
.*	pointer to member
::	scope resolution
?:	conditional

Table 6-3: Operators that cannot be overloaded

In addition to the prohibited operators listed in Table 6-3, you cannot overload operators that you invent. For example, because C++ does not include a $ operator, you may not define this symbol as an operator.

Overloading Math Operators

When you code an expression such as 4 + 7, C++ understands that you intend to carry out binary integer addition because of the context in which you have placed the + symbol. When you code an expression such as regularSal + bonus, if C++ can recognize regularSal and bonus as declared double variables, then floating-point addition will take place. Similarly, when you code Clerk + Secretary, if C++ can recognize Clerk and Secretary as two instances of a class, then it will try to find an overloaded operator function that you have written for the + symbol. The name of the operator function that overloads the + symbol is **operator+()**.

Assume that you have an Employee class with two data members (idNum and salary) and three member functions (a constructor, a member function that adds two employees' salaries, and an overloaded + operator that adds two employees' salaries). The class definition is as follows:

```
class Employee
  {
    private:
      int idNum;
      double salary;
    public:
      Employee(const int id, const double salary);
        //constructor
      double addTwo(const Employee &emp);
        //member function
      double operator+(const Employee &emp);
        //overloaded operator +
  };
```

The syntax of the addTwo() function contains nothing new; you have been writing functions like it since Tutorial 2. This member function takes a constant Employee object argument and returns a double. As you will recall, the function is written as follows:

```
double Employee::addTwo(const Employee &emp)
  {
    double total;
    total  = salary + emp.salary;
    return (total);
  }
```

tip
....
salary **can also be referred to as** Employee::salary.

A main() function that declares two objects of Employee type—Clerk and Driver, for example—could use either of the following statements to sum the salaries of the two Employee objects:

```
double sum;
sum = Clerk.addTwo(Driver);    // use one or the other
sum = Driver.addTwo(Clerk);
```

Using the operator+() function can work in the same way as using any other member function. If you simply substitute operator+ for each instance of addTwo in the code above, you will achieve identical results. The function becomes

```
double Employee::operator+(const Employee &emp)
  {
    double total;
    total  = salary + emp.salary;
    return (total);
  }
```

and the operator+() function could be used as follows:

```
sum = Clerk.operator+(Driver);    // use one or the other
sum = Driver.operator+(Clerk);
```

If the operator+() function works in exactly the same manner as the addTwo() function, why not just use the addTwo() function? The answer, as you may have guessed, is that, instead of the awkward sum = Clerk.operator+(Driver);, the operator+() function allows you to code:

```
sum = Clerk + Driver;    // use one or the other
sum = Driver + Clerk;
```

This syntax is more natural and easier to remember than the member-dot-function call syntax.

In the following steps, you will overload the + operator for the Fraction class that you have created in previous tutorials. The operator+() function will sum two Fraction objects and give a Fraction as the result.

1   Open the **FRACTION.CPP** file that you have been creating, or open the very similar file **FRAC6.CPP** in the TUT06 folder. The declaration section is

```
//declaration section
class Fraction
  {
    private:
        static char symbol;
        int numerator;
        double floatingPoint;
        int denominator;
        double convert(void);
    public:
        Fraction(const int n=0,const int d=1);
        Fraction(const int w, const int n, const int d);
        void getData(const int n,const int d);
        void showData(void);
        void invertFraction(void);
        int greatestCommonDenom(void);
        void reduceFraction(void);
        friend Fraction addFrac(const Fraction a,
          const Fraction b);
  };
```

The class currently contains data members for a fraction's numerator, denominator, symbol (the slash), and equivalent floating-point value. In addition to two constructors, functions are available to assign values to a fraction, invert a fraction, and so on. Save this file as **FRAC_OP.CPP**.

2 Add the prototype for the operator+() function to the other member functions in the public section of the class declaration. Note that the function will accept a reference to a Fraction object and return a copy of a Fraction object. The logic used to add two fractions in this function is the same as that used with the friend function named addFrac() that you created in Tutorial 5.

```
Fraction Fraction::operator+(Fraction &secondFraction);
```

3 In the implementation section of the class definition, code the function:

```
Fraction Fraction::operator+(Fraction &secondFraction)
  {
    Fraction result;
    int tempNum, tempDenom;
    tempNum = Fraction::numerator *
      secondFraction.denominator + secondFraction.numerator *
        Fraction::denominator;
    tempDenom = Fraction::denominator *
      secondFraction.denominator;
    result.getData(tempNum, tempDenom);
    result.reduceFraction();
    return(result);
  }
```

4 Compile the file and correct any syntax errors. Save the file.

5 Open a new file and write a program to test the overloaded + operator:

To compile FRAC_OP.CPP without any errors, you may add #include<iostream.h> as the first line in the file. You need this statement because some of the functions use cout, which is defined in iostream.h. After compiling FRAC_OP.CPP and clearing up all syntax errors, you can remove the #include line because your main() programs that use FRAC_OP.CPP will include both iostream.h and FRAC_OP.CPP.

```
#include<iostream.h>
#include"frac_op.cpp"
void main()
  {
    Fraction firstFrac(1,8), secondFrac(2,7), sum;
    sum = firstFrac + secondFrac;
    sum.showData();
  }
```

6   Compile and test the program.   Save it as **TESTOP.CPP**. The output appears as in Figure 6-1.

```
Decimal is 0.410714 Fraction is 23/56
```

Figure 6-1: Output showing Fraction class addition

7   You can also add overloaded operators for subtraction, multiplication, and division. Add three prototypes to the class definition in FRAC_OP.CPP:

```
Fraction Fraction::operator-(Fraction &secondFraction);

Fraction Fraction::operator*(Fraction &secondFraction);

Fraction Fraction::operator/(Fraction &secondFraction);
```

8   With subtraction, the likelihood of producing negative fractions increases. In Tutorial 3, you were advised that negative fractions would display in a clearer format if you added the following code to the beginning of the getData() member function. If you did not add this code to getData() at that time, you should do so now. Change the getData() function prototype so that the numerator and denominator are no longer constants.

```
Fraction(int n=0, int d=1);
```

Remove the two instances of the keyword const from the getData() header and add the following code to the beginning of getData():

```
void Fraction::getData(int n, int d)
  {
    if(d<0)     // if the denominator is negative
      {
        d = -d;
        // reverse the sign on both the denominator
        n = -n;    // and the numerator
      }
```

Make the same change to the Fraction constructors.

9 Code the operator-() function in the implementation section. The only difference between this function and the operator+() function is the minus sign in the third line of the function body. Note that the order of the numerators you are subtracting is crucial. When you add, 2 + 4 is the same as 4 + 2; the same is not true of subtraction. The object to the left of the minus is the object represented by the this pointer in the operator-() function; the object to the right of the minus is the passed parameter.

```
Fraction Fraction::operator-(Fraction &secondFraction)
  {
    Fraction result;
    int tempNum, tempDenom;
    tempNum = Fraction::numerator *
      secondFraction.denominator -
        secondFraction.numerator * Fraction::denominator;
    tempDenom = Fraction::denominator *
      secondFraction.denominator;
    result.getData(tempNum, tempDenom);
    result.reduceFraction();
    return(result);
  }
```

10 Code the operator*() function in the implementation section.

```
Fraction Fraction::operator*(Fraction &secondFraction)
  {
    Fraction result;
    int tempNum, tempDenom;
    tempNum = Fraction::numerator *
      secondFraction.numerator;
    tempDenom = Fraction::denominator *
      secondFraction.denominator;
    result.getData(tempNum, tempDenom);
    result.reduceFraction();
    return(result);
  }
```

11 Code the operator/() function in the implementation section.

```
Fraction Fraction::operator/(Fraction &secondFraction)

   {

     Fraction result;

     int tempNum, tempDenom;

     tempNum = Fraction::numerator *
       secondFraction.denominator;

     tempDenom = Fraction::denominator *
       secondFraction.numerator;

     result.getData(tempNum, tempDenom);

     result.reduceFraction();

     return(result);

   }
```

tip
• • • • • • • • • • • • • • • • •
The same concerns about
which fraction serves as
the calling fraction that
applied to the operator-()
function also apply to the
operator/() function.

12 Compile the file and correct any syntax errors. Save the file.

13 Modify the **TESTOP.CPP** program to test all of the overloaded operators:

```
#include<iostream.h>

#include<frac_op.cpp>

void main()

   {

     Fraction firstFrac(3,8), secondFrac(1,7),
       sum, difference, product, dividend;

     sum = firstFrac + secondFrac;

     difference = firstFrac — secondFrac;

     product = firstFrac * secondFrac;

     dividend = firstFrac / secondFrac;

     sum.showData();

     difference.showData();

     product.showData();

     dividend.showData();

   }
```

14 Compile, test, and save the program. The output appears as in Figure 6-2.

```
Decimal is 0.517857 Fraction is 29/56
Decimal is 0.232857 Fraction is 13/56
Decimal is 0.053571 Fraction is 3/56
Decimal is 2.625 Fraction is 21/8
```

Figure 6-2: Output using overloaded operators

Multiple Operations in a Statement

One notable exception to allowing several operators in the same statement involves the RPG language. To add three values in RPG, you must first add two values, producing a temporary total. Then, in a separate statement, you add the third value to that total.

Most modern programming languages allow several operators to be used in the same statement. For example, to add three values in C++, you write a statement like total = a + b + c;. Because one purpose of operator overloading is to create class operators that work "naturally" like built-in operators, your class operators should have the same capability.

Recall the overloaded operator+() function that adds two employee salaries:

```
double Employee::operator+(const Employee &emp)
  {
    double total;
    total  = salary + emp.salary;
    return(total);
  }
```

If you want to add salaries for three Employee objects, it would be convenient to use natural addition syntax:

```
void main()
  {
    Employee Clerk(115, 20000.00), Driver(256, 15500.55),
      Secretary(567, 34200.00);
    double sum;
    sum = Clerk + Driver + Secretary;
    cout<<"Sum is "<<sum;
      // Output should be "Sum is 69700.55"
  }
```

When you run this program, you may receive an error message similar to "Illegal structure operation." Because the associativity of addition occurs from left to right, the attempt to execute the addition follows this sequence:

- The leftmost + operator is encountered, and C++ recognizes an Employee on each side of the + symbol. The overloaded operator+() function is called, and salaries for Clerk and Driver are added. A double is returned.
- The next + operator is encountered. An Employee object is located to the right of the +, but a double value to the left. You have not created a function that can handle this situation, nor does a built-in + operation, so an error message appears.

If you wanted to add only a class object's salary and a double, in that order, you could create a new Employee class function that accepted a double as an argument, allowing a function call such as sum = Secretary + sum;. Because you cannot overload operators that work with C++'s built-in data types, however, you can't overload the + associated with a double. Thus, you could never code sum = sum + Secretary;, using the double sum on the left side of the + operator. If you want the + operator to work in as natural a way as possible, this limitation is unacceptable.

The best solution is to modify the operator+() function so that it does not return a double, but rather an object of Employee type. It makes sense that when two integers are added, the result should be an integer. It should likewise make sense that when two Employees are added, the result is an Employee.

If the overloaded operator+() function is modified to create a temporary Employee object and store the sum of two Employee salaries there, then the function can return an Employee object instead of a double.

tip

It is important that the operator+() function returns an Employee object rather than a reference to an Employee object. If operator+() returned a pointer to total, then the returned pointer would be meaningless. When the operator+() function ends, the local variable total would go out of scope.

```
Employee Employee::operator+(const Employee &emp)
  {
    Employee total(999,0);
      // use a "dummy" value like 999 for empNum,
      // as it isn't actually an Employee
    total.salary = Employee::salary + emp.salary;
    return(total);
  }
```

To add salaries for three Employee objects, you can use natural addition syntax:

```
void main()
  {
    Employee Clerk(115, 20000.00), Driver(256, 15500.55),
      Secretary(567, 34200.00);
    Employee sum(0,0);
    sum = Clerk + Driver + Secretary;
    cout<<"Sum is ";
    sum.showData();        // Output is "Sum is 69700.55"
  }
```

The sequence of events now occurs as follows:

- The leftmost + operator is encountered, and C++ recognizes an Employee on each side of the + symbol. The overloaded operator+() function is called, and salaries for Clerk and Driver are added. A temporary Employee object with the total salary (35500.55) is returned.
- The next + operator is encountered. An Employee object is now found on each side of the +, so the overloaded operator+() function is called again. Salaries for the temporary object and the Secretary are added, and a new temporary Employee object with the total salary (69700.55) is returned.
- The temporary object is assigned to the sum Employee object. Assuming you have written a simple showData() function for the Employee class, sum.showData() can be used to access the total salary figure for display purposes.

Because of the nature of fractions, it was a natural step to design the operator+() function for the Fraction class so that it returns a Fraction object. To confirm that addition of several Fractions operates correctly, write a small demonstration program.

1   Open a new file and begin to write a new program with two include files:

```
#include<iostream.h>
#include"frac_op.cpp"
```

2   Write a short program that adds several fractions:

```
void main()
  {
    Fraction a(1,10),b(2,10),c(4,10),d(2,20),result;
    result = a + b + c;
    result.showData();
    result = a + b + c + d;
    result.showData();
  }
```

3   Confirm that 1/10 + 2/10 + 4/10 equals 7/10, and that 1/10 + 2/10 + 4/10 + 2/20 equals 4/5. Save the program as **TESTADD.CPP**.

S U M M A R Y

- Overloading functions is helpful because you can use one easy-to-understand function name for several functions without paying attention to the data types involved.
- Polymorphism is the feature that allows the same operation to be carried out differently depending on the object.
- Specifically, polymorphism occurs when one function can be used with a variety of arguments (for example, a constructor that can take one, two, or three arguments). In contrast, overloading occurs in situations where multiple functions are defined with a single name (for example, three functions that square integers, floats, and doubles).
- Without operator overloading, programmers would need separate symbols for integer and floating-point arithmetic; this requirement would make programs look confusing and it would take longer to learn a programming language.
- Operator overloading is the process by which you apply operators to your own abstract data types.
- You overload an operator by making it a function; subsequently, it may be overloaded like any other function.
- C++ operators are classified as unary or binary, depending on whether they take one or two arguments, respectively.
- If an operator is normally defined to be unary, then you cannot overload it to be binary, and vice versa.
- C++ does not require you to use any overloaded operator for the usual purpose; good programming practice, however, dictates that you follow this convention.
- Associativity—the order in which actions within an expression are carried out—may not change when you overload operators.
- You cannot change the normal precedence of any overloaded operator.
- Operators that may not be overloaded are . (member), .* (pointer to member), :: (scope resolution), and ?: (conditional).
- You cannot overload operators that you invent.
- When C++ encounters instances of a class using an operator, it will try to find an overloaded operator function that you have written for that operator.

- The name of any overloaded operator function consists of the keyword operator followed by the symbol—for example, `operator+()`.
- The syntax of using an overloaded operator is more natural and easier to remember than the member-dot-function call syntax of an ordinary function.
- Because one purpose of operator overloading is to create class operators that work "naturally" like built-in operators, you should be able to use more than one overloaded class operator in the same statement. This approach involves making an overloaded operator function's return type a class member.

Q U E S T I O N S

1. The programming language feature that allows the same operation to be carried out differently depending on the object is _____.
   a. polymorphism
   b. inheritance
   c. allocation
   d. mangling

2. Specifically, overloading involves _____.
   a. one function with a variety of arguments
   b. multiple functions defined with the same name
   c. one function with multiple names
   d. multiple functions with different names

3. When an operator is used alone with a single variable argument, the operator is said to be _____.
   a. unique
   b. unary
   c. alone
   d. allocated

4. Forcing a variable type to become another type before accessing an appropriate function is known as _____.
   a. regression
   b. recursion
   c. conversion
   d. coercion

5. Without overloading of the + operator, _____.
   a. addition could not be performed on built-in types
   b. addition could not be performed on class objects
   c. class objects could not be added to one another
   d. programs would be harder to read and understand

6. C++ "knows" to call an overloaded operator function instead of a built-in operator function based on the _____.
   a. syntax
   b. language
   c. context
   d. symbol

7. You overload an operator by making it a _____.
   a. variable
   b. built-in type
   c. function
   d. class

8. You should overload _____.
    a. every available operator for each class you define
    b. only one operator for each class you define
    c. the operators that make sense for a specific class
    d. new operators you invent

9. If an operator is normally defined to be only unary, then you _____.
    a. may overload it to be binary
    b. must overload it to be binary
    c. may not overload it to be binary
    d. may not overload it

10. When you overload an operator for use with your classes, you _____.
    a. must use the overloaded operator for the usual purpose
    b. should use the overloaded operator for the usual purpose
    c. may not use the overloaded operator for the usual purpose
    d. may not overload operators that have a usual purpose

11. Associativity refers to _____.
    a. mathematical precedence
    b. how variables interact
    c. how the compiler determines which overloaded operator to use
    d. the order in which actions within an expression are carried out

12. When you overload operators, you may change _____.
    a. associativity
    b. precedence
    c. binary operators to unary ones
    d. none of the above

13. Which of the following operators may be overloaded?
    a. . (member)
    b. :: (scope resolution)
    c. % (modulus)
    d. ?: (conditional)

14. Which of the following may be overloaded as an operator?
    a. \
    b. @
    c. &
    d. >

15. The name of the operator function that overloads the * symbol is _____.
    a. operator*()
    b. *operator()
    c. op*()
    d. *op()

16. Assuming you have properly overloaded the / operator for a Number class, and that a and b are two members of the Number class, which expression is legal?
    a. a/b
    b. a.operator/(b)
    c. both (a) and (b)
    d. neither (a) nor (b)

17. Assuming you have properly overloaded the ! operator for a Number class, and that a and b are two members of the Number class, which expression is legal?
    a. !a
    b. b!
    c. a!b
    d. all of these are legal

18. Assuming you have properly overloaded the * operator to perform multiplication for a Number class, and that a, b, and c are three members of the Number class, which expression is legal?
    a. a*b
    b. a*b*c
    c. both (a) and (b)
    d. neither (a) nor (b)

19. To perform multiple arithmetic operations in a single statement, overloaded operator functions should return _____.
    a. void
    b. a copy of the values passed to them
    c. an object of the class type
    d. the address of the function

20. Which of the following is the best function prototype for an overloaded - for a Number class?
    a. Number operator-(const Number &num);
    b. Number& operator-(int num);
    c. int Number(operator-());
    d. void operator-(Number &num);

E X E R C I S E S

1. Create a class definition for bank accounts. Data members include the account number and balance. Member functions should include a constructor and a function to display account data. Overload the + operator to add balances from two separate accounts, returning a dummy account object with account number 9999. Write a short demonstration program to test your class.

2. Create a class definition for airline flights. Data members include the flight number, departure city code (example: LAX), destination city code (example: ORD), and number of passengers. Write member functions to assign values and display data. Overload the + operator to add one passenger to the flight each time a ticket is sold. Write a short demonstration program to test your class.

3. Create a class definition for student examinations. Data members include a student ID and exam score. As a member function, include a data entry function, a display function, and overloaded += and \= operators. Write a program that declares an array for 10 student examinations. Enter data, and then display the class average. Computing the average involves adding all scores to a total before dividing by the number of scores.

LESSON B
objectives

In this lesson you will learn

- How to overload the output operator
- How to overload the input operator
- How to overload ++ and --
- How to overload ==
- How to overload =
- How to overload [] and ()

Overloading Output, Input, and Other Operators

tip

You do not need to understand the use of << as a bitwise left-shift operator to understand that it is overloaded or how to use it with cout. If you're curious, however, bitwise left-shift simply means that each bit in a given byte takes the value of the bit to the right. Thus, 00010100 becomes 00101000. The leftmost bit is lost, and the new rightmost bit becomes a 0. Incidentally, the binary number 00010100 is 20 and 00101000 is 40; left-shifting is actually just a tricky way of multiplying by 2.

Overloading Output

You already know that C++ automatically overloads several of its operators. The + operator is understood differently in unary and binary contexts. The << operator is also overloaded by C++. It is both a bitwise left-shift operator and an output operator. It acts as an output operator only when cout appears on the left side.

When you use cout in a program, you must include #include<iostream.h>. The iostream.h file defines the cout object. The cout object is actually a member of a class named ostream. The iostream.h file overloads << with functions that output each of C++'s built-in data types. For example, the overloaded << shown below can output an integer:

```
ostream& operator<<(ostream &out, int n);
```

tip

Tutorial 8 will discuss input and output in greater detail.

This function, called operator<<(), returns a reference to ostream. It accepts two arguments: a reference to ostream and an integer. In other words, the function receives an address where output will go and a value to output. Recall how we created Employee addition to return an Employee object so that more than one addition operation could be carried out by the same statement. Similarly, cout's operator<<() function returns the next address for output, ensuring that a statement with multiple outputs like cout<<22<<33; will work. The statement cout<<22 returns a reference to an object that 33 can use.

You may also overload the << operator to work with your classes. Instead of a showData() function for an Employee that requires the statement

```
Clerk.showData();
```

tip

The reason that cout's overloaded << operator needs to receive a reference to ostream is because << is a friend function, which you will recall, has no this pointer (unlike a member function).

you may prefer a more natural form:

```
cout<<Clerk;
```

To overload the << operator so that it can work with an Employee object, you must add the overloaded operator<<() function to the Employee class. The prototype is

```
friend ostream& operator<<(ostream &out, const Employee&emp);
```

This function is a friend to the ostream class. It receives a reference to an ostream object, called out within the function, and a reference to an Employee, called emp within the function. The Employee reference is const because the output should not alter the Employee's data. The contents of the function body may display an Employee with any desired text and in whatever format you wish. For example:

```
ostream& operator<<(ostream &out, const Employee &emp)
{
    out<<"Employee number is "<<emp.empNum;
    out<<"  Salary is "<<emp.salary<<endl;
    return (out);
}
```

Any program that includes an Employee declaration such as Employee aWorker; may subsequently use a statement such as cout<<aWorker; to display the aWorker's data. The cout code is only a few characters shorter than aWorker.showData();, but it makes Employee appear to be a built-in data type. Using the overloaded << operator allows the use of simpler program statements; the class takes care of all the details.

In the following steps, you will modify the FRAC_OP.CPP header file that contains the Fraction class definitions to overload the << operator.

1   Open the **FRAC_OP.CPP** file, if necessary.

2   Add a prototype for the operator<<() function in the public section of the class declarations, with the other function prototypes. The prototype is

```
friend ostream& operator<<(ostream &out, const Fraction&frac);
```

tip

Programmers sometimes refer to the ability to use multiple calls to the same operator function (as in cout<<22<<33;) as **stacking** or **chaining**.

tip

The "out" in this function is not a keyword. It is a programmer-chosen local name for the reference to ostream.

tip

The function name is not Employee::operator<<(). The operator << is not a member of Employee; it is a friend.

3   In the class implementation section, add the operator<<() function:

```
ostream& operator<<(ostream &out, const Fraction &frac)
  {
    out<<frac.numerator<<frac.symbol<<frac.denominator;
    return(out);
  }
```

4   Save the header file.

5   Open a new file to write a short demonstration program that tests the operator<<() function. Write the program.

```
#include<iostream.h>
#include"frac_op.cpp"
void main()
  {
    Fraction a(1,10), b(3,4);
    cout<<a<<endl;
    cout<<b<<endl;
    cout<<"The two fractions are "<<a<<" and "<<b<<endl;
  }
```

6   Each cout statement should now work correctly. Save the program as **TESTOUT.CPP.**

Overloading Input

If the << operator can be overloaded for output, it makes sense that the >> operator can also be overloaded for input. The advantage, once again, comes from cleaner, easy-to-read programs.

Consider an Employee class that contains an idNum and a salary. You can create an operator>>() function that uses istream (which is defined in iostream.h, along with ostream). Within the function, the name in is used to hold an ostream object:

Unlike with the operator<<()
function, the Employee
object cannot be passed as a
constant. That's because this
function needs to change
Employee's data values.

```
istream& operator>>(istream &in, Employee &emp)
  {
    cout<<endl;    // to clear the buffer
    cout<<"Enter employee number ";
    in>>emp.empNum;
    cout<<"Enter the salary ";
    in>>emp.salary;
    cout<<"       Thank you!"<<endl;
    return(in);
  }
```

You could improve this operator>>() function even more by adding code that verifies valid employee numbers and salaries. No matter how many instructions you place within the operator>>() function, however, when you write a program that uses an Employee class member such as Clerk, you need only the following code:

```
cin>>Clerk;
```

In the following steps, you will add an overloaded operator>>() function for the Fraction class.

1   Open the **FRAC_OP.CPP** file, if necessary.
2   To the public class declaration area of the Fraction class, add the following prototype:

```
friend istream& operator>>(istream &in, Fraction &frac);
```

3 In the implementation section, add the following function:

```
istream& operator>>(istream &in, Fraction &frac)
 {
   cout<<endl;
   cout<<"Enter a numerator for a fraction ";
   in>>frac.numerator;
   cout<<"Enter a denominator ";
   in>>frac.denominator;
   frac.reduceFraction();
   return(in);
 }
```

4 Compile and save **FRAC_OP.CPP.**

5 Open a new file and write a short demonstration program to test your operator>>() function.

```
#include<iostream.h>
#include"frac_op.cpp"
void main()
  {
    Fraction aFrac;
    cin>>aFrac;
    cout<<aFrac;
  }
```

6 Compile and test the program. For any numerator and denominator you supply, the fraction should display. Save the program as **TESTIN.CPP.**

Overloading ++ and --

With C++, you use ++ and -- to increment and decrement variables. An important difference arises in how expressions are evaluated when the ++ or -- is placed before a variable rather than after it.

When a prefix operator like ++ is used in an expression, the mathematical operation takes place before the expression is evaluated.

```
num = 3;
result = ++num;
cout<<result;      // displays 4
cout<<num;         // displays 4


num = 3;
result = num++;
cout<<result;      // displays 3
cout<<num;         // displays 4
```

With the prefix operator, the variable is increased, then evaluated, and finally assigned to the result. With the postfix operator, however, the variable is evaluated, then assigned, and finally increased.

You can use the prefix ++ or -- with your classes, just like any other overloaded operator. Consider an Inventory class definition with data members for a stock number and a quantity sold. Its three member functions are a constructor, an overloaded operator<<() function for output, and an overloaded operator++() function for incrementing the quantity sold each time that a sale occurs.

```
class Inventory
  {
    private:
      int stockNum;
      int numSold;
    public:
      Inventory(const int stknum, const int sold);
      friend ostream& operator<<
        (ostream &out, const Inventory &item);
      Inventory& operator++();
  };
```

This program will execute without the line `return(*this)` **because the this pointer is returned automatically. It's clearer, however, if you explicitly return the this pointer.**

Overloading the prefix operator ++ does not involve learning anything new. The function returns a reference to an Inventory object, and it takes no arguments. Because the function is a member function of the Inventory class, it will receive a this pointer to the object that calls it; therefore, no information need be passed to the operator++() function. The reference to the Inventory object returned is a reference to the this object—that is, a reference to the (newly incremented) object that was passed to the function. The operator++() function is as follows:

```
Inventory& Inventory::operator++()
  {
    ++Inventory::numSold;
    return(*this);
  }
```

With the operator++() member function, a prefix ++ applied to an Inventory object means to increase the numSold by 1:

```
Inventory someItem(789, 84);
  // someItem has stockNum 789,
  //and we've sold 84
++someItem;
cout<<someItem;     // output will show we've sold 85
```

A problem arises if you want to use a postfix ++ operator as well. C++ needs a method for distinguishing between the two. You need to code a separate function prototype,

```
Inventory& operator++(int);
```

and a separate function,

```
Inventory& Inventory::operator++(int)
  {
    Inventory::numSold++;
    return(*this);
  }
```

The int argument to operator++() is a dummy argument. You do not pass an integer to the operator++() function when you want to overload the postfix ++. The int is present only to help C++ tell the difference between the prefix and postfix operators, and subsequently distinguish the two functions. In other words, if you call the prefix ++ operator function with a statement such as ++someItem, the function with no dummy argument will be called; if you call the postfix operator function with a statement such as someItem++, the function with the dummy argument will be called.

In the following steps, you will add a prefix ++ operator to the Fraction class. When a fraction is incremented, you simply add the denominator value to the numerator. For example, when incremented, 1/4 becomes (4 + 1)/4 or 5/4.

1   To the **FRAC_OP.CPP** file, add a prototype for the ++ operator:

```cpp
Fraction& operator++();
```

2   Add the following function:

```cpp
Fraction& Fraction::operator++()
  {
    Fraction::numerator = Fraction::numerator
    + Fraction::denominator;
    return(*this);
  }
```

3   Save the class definition file. Open a new file to write a short demonstration program:

```cpp
#include<iostream.h>
#include"frac_op.cpp"
void main()
  {
    Fraction aFrac(1,4);
    ++aFrac;
    cout<<aFrac;    // output is 5/4
  }
```

4   Compile and test the program. Save it as **TESTOP4.CPP**.

Overloading ==

tip

As the Fraction class creator, you can decide exactly what == means. If you want to ensure that a fraction like 2/8 is evaluated as being equivalent to 1/4, then remove the const from the operator==() function header and add two calls to the reduceFraction function prior to the comparison. One call will use the Fraction class scope operator; the second call will use a dot operator. If you want == to mean the fractions have the same numerator and denominator before reduction, omit those statements.

At this point, writing an operator==() function should be an easy task. You simply decide what will constitute equality in class members. Must every data member be equivalent, or only key data members? The operator==() function may return either an integer or a boolean variable representing true or false.

In the following steps, you will create an operator==() for the Fraction class.

1   To the **FRAC_OP.CPP** file, add the following prototype:

```cpp
int operator==(Fraction const &secondFrac);
```

2   In the implementation section, add the following function:

```cpp
int Fraction::operator==(Fraction const &secondFraction)
  {
    if (Fraction::numerator == secondFraction.numerator
      &&
        Fraction::denominator == secondFraction.denominator)
      return(1);
    else
        return(0);
```

3   Compile and save the file. (You may encounter problems if you don't include iostream.h.)

4   Write a new demonstration program:

```cpp
#include<iostream.h>
#include"frac_op.cpp"
void main()
  {
    Fraction oneFrac(2,5), sameValFrac(2,5),
      diffValFrac (3,5);
    if(oneFrac==sameValFrac)
      cout<<"First comparison is Same"<<endl;
    if (oneFrac == diffValFrac)
      cout<<"Second comparison is Same"<<endl;
  }
```

5 Compile and run the demonstration program. Only the first comparison should produce output. Save the file as **TESTCOMP.CPP**.

tip
· · · · · · · · · · · · · · · · ·
A similar situation occurs
when you create a new
object and make an assignment, as in Employee
Clerk = Driver;. Clerk
is constructed with a
default copy constructor
provided by the compiler.

Overloading =

Like + and -, the operator = may be overloaded for use with your own classes. Unlike with + or -, if you don't define the = operator, C++ provides a definition for you. You have already used = with your classes in statements such as

```
Employee Clerk(115, 20000.00), Driver;
Driver = Clerk;    // assigns 115 and 20000.00 to Driver
```

and

```
Employee Clerk(115, 20000.00), Driver(256, 15500.55),
  Secretary(567, 34200.00);
Employee sum;
sum = Clerk + Driver + Secretary;
  // assigns a temporary Employee object that
  // is the result of addition to sum
```

If the class being assigned does not include pointer data members, and if you intend to use the = operator to assign the value of every member of the class object on the right of the = operator to each member of the class object on its left, then you do not need to write an overloaded = operator. Obviously, if you want the = operator to do something other than assign each member, you must create a custom operator=() function. In addition, if the class contains pointers, you should create a custom function.

If a class contains a pointer and one member object is copied to another, then two objects will contain pointers to the same memory. This overlap may not pose a problem until one of the objects is deleted or goes out of scope. When the destructor function is called for the first object, it releases the memory to which that object points. Now the second object contains a pointer to deallocated memory.

Consider a class for the videos owned by a video rental store. Class data members for each video include a title and the number of copies owned. Functions include a constructor, destructor, and showMovie() function.

```
class Movie
  {
    private:
      char *title;
      int copies;
    public:
      Movie(const char *name, const int c);
      ~Movie();
      void showMovie(void);
  };
```

Because the length of the video titles varies widely, you might want to allocate memory dynamically during construction, based on the exact amount of storage needed.

```
Movie::Movie(const char *name = '\0',const int c = 0)
  {
    Movie::title = new char[strlen(name)+1];
      // include  string.h to use strlen function
      // allocates enough memory to hold the title
      // plus one more character for a NULL
    strcpy(Movie::title,name);
      // copy name to movie title
    Movie::copies = c;
  }
```

For a review of new and delete, see Lesson A in Tutorial 4.

You have already learned that you should delete any memory you allocate. Because the Movie title is allocated with the new operator, the destructor is coded as follows:

```
Movie::~Movie()
  {
    delete Movie::title;  // delete memory that was
      // allocated upon construction
  }
```

When you use the Movie class within a program, you can make statements like

```
Movie film1("ET",2);
Movie film2("Wizard of Oz",5);
Movie film3("Honey, I Shrunk the Kids",1);
```

Each film title will be allocated exactly as much storage as it needs. If you make an assignment using the default = operator, such as

```
film1 = film2;
```

a problem arises when the class objects go out of scope. The assignment copies all of the members of film2 to film1. The title pointers are copied, so both film1.title and film2.title now point to the same memory (which holds "Wizard of Oz"). Eventually the program ends, and both film1 and film2 go out of scope. When the destructor is called for one film, it releases the memory that was allocated for its title. When the destructor is called for the other film, you receive an error message, "Null pointer assignment," because the title pointer now points to deallocated memory.

You can avoid this problem by overloading the = operator so that the two video title pointers don't point to the same memory. When film2 is copied to film1, you deallocate the memory with film2's title, allocate new memory for film2's title, and copy film1's title to film2.

```
void Movie::operator=(Movie &otherMovie)
  {
    if (Movie::title!=NULL)
      delete(Movie::title);
        // if a title exists, delete it
    Movie::title = new char[strlen(otherMovie.title) + 1];
      // allocate new memory for the copied title
    strcpy(Movie::title, otherMovie.title);
      // copy the title to the new memory
    Movie::copies = otherMovie.copies;
  }
```

Overloading [ ] and ( )

C++ provides two special operators that can be used as adjuncts to the more conventional operators: the subscript operator and the parentheses operator.

The subscript operator, operator[ ], is declared like any other function, but called in a manner similar to accessing an array element. As with every other operator, you can include instructions within an operator[ ] function. Typically, you use this function to perform some task that requires an argument and does not quite fit into another operator's usual meaning.

Consider an Inventory class with data members stockNum, price, and quantity. If the price changes frequently, it might be convenient to create a function that assigns a new price. You might not want to use the operator=( ) function for this purpose because you have already developed this function to change every data member of an Inventory object. Of course, you could create a standard member function with a name like changeItemPrice(), but you may also use an operator[ ] function.

The function prototype might be

```
void operator[](double newPrice);
```

The function returns nothing and receives a double. As a member function, it also receives a this pointer to the calling object. The implementation is as follows:

```
void Inventory::operator[](double newPrice)
  {
    Inventory::price = newPrice;
  }
```

To use the function with an Inventory object named oneItem, simply write a program statement like

```
oneItem[14.99];
```

Even though the 14.99 within the brackets looks similar to a subscript, it obviously is not. It simply represents an easy way to assign a value to one data member of the class.

In the following steps, you will add an overloaded operator[ ] to the Fraction class. You have already created operator++( ) to add 1 to a fraction. Write operator[ ] to add a value to only the numerator of a fraction.

1 Open the **FRAC_OP.CPP** file, if necessary.

2 The operator[ ] function will receive an integer argument and return a Fraction object for which the numerator has been increased. Add the following prototype:

```
Fraction operator[](int increaseVal);
```

3 Add the function that creates a new Fraction object with the same denominator as the calling Fraction, but an increased numerator:

```
Fraction Fraction::operator[](int increaseVal)
  {
    Fraction temp;
    temp.numerator = Fraction::numerator + increaseVal;
    temp.denominator = Fraction::denominator;
    return(temp);
  }
```

4 Save the **FRAC_OP.CPP** file.

5 Write a short demonstration program:

```
#include<iostream.h>
#include"frac_op.cpp"
void main()
  {
    Fraction a(0,6);// create a Fraction with value 0/6
    for(int x = 1; x <6; ++x)
      {
        a = a[1];
        cout<<"Next fraction in series is "<<a<<endl;
      }
  }
```

6 Compile and test the program. The output displays the series 1/6, 2/6, 3/6, 4/6, 5/6.

7 Save the file as **TESTSUB.CPP**.

In a very similar manner, operator()—the parentheses operator—can be used to make multiple assignments within a class. To overload this operator to assign both a price and a quantity to a member of the Inventory class, code the following prototype:

```
void operator()(double newPrice, int newQuan);
```

The function is

```
void Inventory::operator()(double newPrice, int newQuan)
  {
    Inventory::price = newPrice;
    Inventory::quantity = newQuan;
  }
```

and the function call with an Inventory item is

```
oneItem(3.99, 1000);
```

At first glance, oneItem appears to be a function, but oneItem is an object and the function is the parentheses operator function.

The availability of the subscript and parentheses operator functions allows the programmer to create specialized functions in addition to, or that don't seem appropriate for, the other operator symbols.

Now that the Fraction class includes so many useful member functions, writing an educational program that uses the class is a relatively simple task. Your main() program can be short because the class does the work.

1   Open **TESTIN.CPP**, which you wrote earlier in this lesson. It declares a fraction named aFrac, accepts values for this variable, and displays the fraction.

2   Add a declaration for two more Fractions: bFrac, initialized to a value of 1, and answer.

```
Fraction bFrac(1,1),answer;
```

3   Before the statement that inputs aFrac, add an explanation:

If the player doesn't enter a larger denominator, the result will be negative. If you do not want to rely on the player giving the desired input, add a function to check the denominator and continue prompting until a larger denominator is entered.

```
cout<<"This program will test your knowledge of fractions."
  <<endl;
cout<<"Enter a numerator, then a larger denominator."
  <<endl;
```

4   After the statement that inputs aFrac, compute the difference between 1 and aFrac, using the overloaded operator-() function.

```
bFrac = bFrac - aFrac;
```

5   Prompt the student:

```
cout<<endl<<endl;
cout<<"With the fraction "<<aFrac
  <<", how much more does it take to make a whole?"
    <<endl;
cin>>answer;
```

6   Finally, make the comparison using the overloaded==() function:

```
if (answer == bFrac)
  cout<<"Good job!"<<endl;
else
  cout<<"Sorry -- the answer was "<<bFrac<<endl;
```

7   Remove or comment out the line cout<<aFrac;.

8   Compile and test the program. Output from a typical game is shown below:

```
This program will test your knowledge of fractions.
Enter a numerator, then a larger denominator.


Enter a numerator for a fraction 5

Enter a denominator 7


With the fraction 5/7, how much more does it take to make a
whole?

Enter a numerator for a fraction 2

Enter a denominator 7

Good job!
```

Figure 6-3: Typical fraction game

9   Save the program as **GAMEOP.CPP**.

S U M M A R Y

- When you use cout in a program, you include `<iostream.h>`, which defines the cout object. The cout object is actually a member of a class named ostream.

- The iostream.h file overloads << with functions that output each of C++'s built-in data types. In addition, cout's operator<<() function returns the next address to output so that a statement with multiple stacked outputs will work.

- When a prefix operator such as ++ is used in an expression, the mathematical operation takes place before the expression is evaluated. With the postfix operator, the variable is evaluated and then incremented.

- You can use the prefix ++ or -- with your classes, just like any other overloaded operator.

- For a prefix increment, the operator++() function returns a reference to an object of its class, and it takes no arguments. Its prototype takes the form `ClassName& operator++()`.

- For a postfix increment, you must code a separate function whose prototype takes the form `ClassName& operator++(int)`. The int argument to operator++() is a dummy argument; it exists to enable C++ to distinguish between the prefix and postfix operators.

- The = operator may be overloaded. If you don't provide a definition for this operator, C++ defines it for you.

- The subscript operator may be overloaded to accept one value to pass to a function; the parentheses operator may be overloaded to take multiple arguments.

QUESTIONS

1. The << operator is used for output only when _____.
   a. it is used as a binary operator
   b. it is used as a unary operator
   c. cout is to the left
   d. you write a function to overload it

2. The built-in << operator returns _____.
   a. void
   b. the same type as the data passed to it
   c. a reference to the ostream
   d. a copy of the ostream

3. If the << operator has been overloaded appropriately for the class Number, and a and b are members of the Number class, then which statement is legal?
   a. cout<<a;   c. both (a) and (b)
   b. cout<<a<<b;   d. neither (a) nor (b)

4. Assume the class Number has one integer data member, named val. Further assume that a is a member of Number and that a.val has been assigned a value of 649. If the << operator has been overloaded for the Number class, what will be produced by cout<<a;?
   a. 6   c. the value is 649
   b. 649   d. it is impossible to tell

5. Using an overloaded << operator for a class _____.
   a. is the only way to display values of data members of a class
   b. works correctly only if all data members are private
   c. allows output statements within a program that uses the class to become simpler
   d. is possible only if the >> operator is overloaded as well

6. Which is the best prototype to overload the << operator for a Number class?
   a. ostream& operator<<(ostream &out, const Number &num);
   b. friend ostream& operator<<(ostream &out, const Number &num);
   c. Number& operator<<(ostream &out, const Number &num);
   d. friend ostream operator<<(const Number &num);

7. The >> operator _____.
   a. may be overloaded for input
   b. must be overloaded if there will be input to classes
   c. must be overloaded if the << operator is overloaded
   d. may be overloaded for input, but not for shifting bits

8. When the >> operator is overloaded for input, one parameter that should be passed to the function is a _____.
   a. reference to istream   c. copy of istream
   b. reference to ostream   d. copy of ostream

9. A usable function header for an overloaded >> operator for a Number class is

_____.

    a. Number operator>>(istream &in, Number &num)

    b. istream& operator>>(istream &in, const Number &num)

    c. friend istream& operator>>(istream &in, Number &num)

    d. istream& operator>>(istream &in, Number &num)

10. If the >> operator is overloaded properly for use for input with a Number class, and a
and b are members of the Number class, which of the following statements is allowed?

    a. cin>>a;   c. both (a) and (b)

    b. cin>>a,b;   d. neither (a) nor (b)

11. The difference between the expressions ++x and x++ is _____.

    a. nothing

    b. how they are evaluated

    c. whether x is incremented

    d. whether x may be assigned to another variable

12. Assume num = 8;. The value of the expression num++ is _____.

    a. 7   c. 9

    b. 8   d. impossible to tell

13. If the ++ operator is overloaded properly, the operator++() function returns

_____.

    a. a copy of an incremented member of a class

    b. a copy of an incremented data item

    c. a reference to a class member data item

    d. the this pointer

14. To overload a prefix ++ for a Number class, an appropriate function header is

_____.

    a. Number& Number::operator++(Number &num)

    b. Number& Number::operator++(int)

    c. Number& Number::operator++()

    d. this Number::operator++(Number &num)

15. To overload a postfix ++ for a Number class, an appropriate function header is

_____.

    a. Number& Number::operator++(Number &num)

    b. Number& Number::operator++(int)

    c. Number& Number::operator++()

    d. this Number::operator++(Number &num)

16. If you use a + operator with a class and receive no error messages, then _____.

    a. you must have overloaded it

    b. you may have overloaded it

    c. you must not have overloaded it

    d. + cannot be used with classes

17. If you use an = operator with classes, then _____.
   a. you must have overloaded it
   b. you may have overloaded it
   c. you must not have overloaded it
   d. = cannot be used with classes

18. If a class named Number has one private data member, val, and a and b are objects of type Number, then to copy b.val to a.val in a main() program you code _____.
   a. a.val = b.val, if you have overloaded =
   b. a.val = b.val, if you have not overloaded =
   c. a = b; regardless of whether you have overloaded =
   d. private data members may not be copied

19. If the subscript operator has been correctly overloaded for a Number class to accept an integer value, and num is a member of the number class, which of the following statements is correct?
   a. [num]44;   c. num=[44];
   b. num[44];   d. num44;

20. Which of the following statements is true?
   a. The subscript operator may take only one argument.
   b. The parentheses operator may take only one argument.
   c. The subscript operator may take multiple arguments.
   d. none of the above

E X E R C I S E S

1. Add some functions to the bank account class created in exercise 1 in Lesson A. Overload the >> and << operators for use with the bank account class. Test the functions.

2. Overload the [ ] operator to add a passed dollar amount to a bank account balance. Write a short program to test the function.

3. Create a class definition for symphony concert performances. Data members include the concert number, month, day, and year of the concert, and tickets sold. Create a constructor and functions that overload the >> and << operators. Overload the ++ operator to add 1 to tickets sold each time that a ticket is purchased. Overload the -- operator to subtract 1 from tickets sold when a ticket is returned. Overload the () operator to change the month, day, and year of the concert. Write a program to test your class.

debugging ▶   4. Each of the following files in the TUT06 folder has overloaded operators, and each contains syntax and/or logical errors. Determine the problem in each case, and fix the program.
   a. DEBUG6-1.CPP
   b. DEBUG6-2.CPP
   c. DEBUG6-3.CPP
   d. DEBUG6-4.CPP

TUTORIAL

7

Inheritance

case ▶ You are becoming comfortable with creating classes, and terms like "constructor" and "overloading" no longer seem mysterious. During a well-deserved break at Teacher's Pet, you finish your soft drink and toss the aluminum can into the recycle bin.

"You know, Audrey," you say to your supervisor, who is also taking a break, "I'm glad that Teacher's Pet is into recycling. I like knowing that my can isn't going into a landfill, and I'm glad that my trial program listings are printed on recycled paper."

"Then you'll like the concept of inheritance," Audrey says. "It's one of the building blocks of object-oriented programming. It allows you to build on classes that you've already developed, rather than starting each new class from scratch. I'll show you how it's done after our break."

Previewing the INHERIT program

The file INHERIT.CPP contains a brief example of inheritance.

1 Open **INHERIT.CPP** in the TUT07 folder. Compile and run the program.

2 Examine the code. A new class for mixed numbers inherits the attributes of the Fraction class. You will be writing similar programs in this tutorial.

LESSON A
objectives

In this lesson you will learn

■ What inheritance is

■ How to create a derived class

■ How to choose the class access specifier

■ How to override parent class functions

Understanding Inheritance

tip

• • • • • • • • • • • • • •

▶ When you organize a hard disk, you use a form of inheritance. Your C drive probably contains a number of folders, each of which contains more individual folders, and so on. You can picture class inheritance as being similar.

What Is Inheritance?

Inheritance is the principle that knowledge of a general category can be applied to more specific objects. You are familiar with the concept of inheritance from all sorts of nonprogramming situations.

When you hear the term "inheritance," you are apt to think of genetic inheritance. You know that your hair and eye color have been inherited. You may have selected a pet to own or a variety of plant to grow on the basis of its parent's genetic traits. With genetic inheritance, you often think about hierarchies of classifications—your Siamese is a member of the cat family, which is a mammal, which is an animal, and so on. With any subject matter, your knowledge of existing hierarchies makes it easier to understand new information. If a friend tells you he's getting an item that belongs to the "Carmello" category, you may be uncertain what he means. If he tells you that the item is a variety of tomato, you understand many of a Carmello's traits without ever having seen one—that is, you know a Carmello tomato has the general traits of a tomato (but possibly different traits than a "Beefsteak" tomato). If you had not heard of the tomato category, your friend can explain that a tomato is a member of the fruit category, and you will at least have an idea that a Carmello must grow, have seeds, and probably be edible.

Objects used in computer programs are also easier to understand if you can place them within a hierarchy of inheritance. Suppose you have written several programs with a class named Inventory. You have learned the names of the data items, and you understand what the various member functions do. If you need to write a program using a new class named BackOrder, the job will become easier if BackOrder has been inherited from Inventory. BackOrder may have some additional data members and functions, but it will also have the members with which you are already familiar. You will need to master only the new members. The BackOrder class is inherited from the Inventory class, or **derived** from it. The Inventory class is called a **parent class**, **base class**, or **superclass**; the BackOrder class is called a **child class**, **derived class**, or **subclass**.

In many cases, a derived class may not possess all of its parent's traits. You may be the only redhead in your family; some fruits should not be eaten. Members of the BackOrder class may require a different display format than members of the Inventory class. Thus, a useful feature of inheritance is that the descendant class can override those attributes from the parent that are inappropriate.

In some object-oriented programming languages, such as Java and SmallTalk, every new class *must* inherit from an existing class. C++ is sometimes called a **hybrid** object-oriented programming language because you may create original base classes without deriving them from some other class. You have been creating new classes without inheritance throughout this text.

In the Overview of this book, you learned that inheritance is considered a basic building block of object-oriented programming. To be truly "object-oriented," a programming language must allow inheritance. One major feature of object-oriented programming is its ability to create new classes from ones that already exist. Programs in which you create classes that are derived from existing classes offer several advantages:

- You save time because much of the code needed for your class is already written.
- You save additional time because the existing code has already been tested—that is, it is **reliable**.
- You save even more time because you already understand how the base class works and can concentrate on only the new complexity added with your extensions to the class.
- In a derived class, you can extend and revise a parent class without corrupting its existing class features.
- If other classes have been derived from the parent class, the parent class is even more reliable because the more situations in which the code has been used, the more likely that logical errors have already been found and fixed.

Despite its advantages, inheritance is not used as often as it could be. In many companies, a program is needed to solve a particular problem quickly. Developing good general-purpose software from which more specific classes can be inherited is more difficult and takes more time than writing a "quick and dirty" program to solve the immediate problem. Because the benefits of creating a good reusable base class are usually not realized in one project, programmers often have little incentive to design good software from which future programs can create derived classes. If programmers take the time to develop good, reliable base classes, however, future programming projects will go much more smoothly.

Creating a Derived Class

Consider a class originally developed by a company to hold customer information, such as an ID number and name. Member functions include a constructor and destructor, and member functions to input and output the data.

With C++, you cannot inherit regular functions and variables, only classes.

A NameAndNumber class that is fully developed most likely would contain address information, a phone number, and other personal data. For simplicity, this NameAndNumber class is short.

```
class NameAndNumber
  {
    private:
      int idNum;
      char lastName[20];
      char firstName[15];
    public:
      NameAndNumber();
      ~NameAndNumber();
      void inputData(const int num, const char *last,
          const char *first);
      void outputData(void);
  };
```

The company soon realizes that the NameAndNumber class can be used for more than customers. Full-time employees, part-time employees, and suppliers all have names and numbers as well. The NameAndNumber class appears to be a good candidate to be inherited by new classes. A major problem exists, however.

When a class serves as a base class to others, all of its members are inherited, *except* for any private members. When you think about data hiding and encapsulation, this restriction makes sense. You make class data members private so that they cannot be accessed or altered by nonmember functions. If anyone could access your private data members by simply inheriting your class, then using the private keyword would really be pointless. While having private members is a good idea, there really is no point in inheriting the NameAndNumber class if it includes a private name and number that can't be inherited.

Fortunately, C++ provides an alternative to private and public specifiers. The specifier **protected** allows members to be used by class member functions *and* by derived classes, but not by other parts of a program. Thus, the following rewritten NameAndNumber class represents a good candidate for an inheritable base class:

```
class NameAndNumber
  {
    protected:
      int idNum;
      char lastName[20];
      char firstName[15];
    public:
      NameAndNumber();
      ~NameAndNumber();
      void inputData(const int num, const char *last,
        const char *first);
      void outputData(void);
  };
```

Information on how to choose among the three class access specifiers is provided in the next section.

To create a derived class, you include the following elements in the order listed:

- the keyword `class`
- the derived class name
- a colon
- a class access specifier, either `public`, `private`, or `protected`
- the base class name
- an opening bracket
- the class definition statements
- a closing bracket
- a semicolon

A common programmer error is to place two colons after the derived class name. C++ will then display an error message because two colons indicate class scope, and the class has yet to be completely declared. Declaring a derived class requires using a single colon following the new class name.

For example, to create a Customer class that inherits the members of the NameAndNumber class, you could code

```
class Customer : public NameAndNumber
  {
    // other statements here
  };
```

The Customer class contains all of the members of NameAndNumber because it inherits them. If it also includes an additional data member, balanceDue, and two more functions, inputBalDue() and outputBalDue(), then a complete class definition is as follows:

```
class Customer : public NameAndNumber
  {
    private:
      double balanceDue;
    public:
      void inputBalDue(const double bal);
      void outputBalDue(void);
  };
```

After the Customer class is defined, a program can contain statements like the following:

```
Customer cust;
cust.inputData(215,"Santini","Linda");
cust.outputData();
  //these two functions are defined in the base class NameAndNumber
cust.inputBalDue(147.95);
cust.outputBalDue();
  // these two functions are defined in the derived class Customer
```

Of course, the Customer object can use its own member functions, inputBalDue() and outputBalDue(). Additionally, it can use the NameAndNumber functions, inputData() and outputData(), as if they were its own. On the other hand, the Customer object cannot use the base class constructor or destructor.

The following are never inherited:

- constructor functions
- destructor functions
- friend functions
- static data members
- static member functions
- overloaded new operators
- overloaded = operators

If a derived class requires any of these items, they must be explicitly defined within the derived class definition.

In Tutorial 3, you overloaded the Fraction constructor to accept a mixed number that has both a whole and a fractional part. In the following steps, you will define a class named MixedNum that inherits all attributes of the Fraction class, but also includes a whole-number part.

1 Open the **FRAC_OP.CPP** header file you have been creating, or use the file named **FRAC_OP.CPP** in the TUT07 folder.

2 Change the specifier at the beginning of the class from `private` to `protected`. The derived mixed-number class will then be able to inherit the previously private data members of Fraction. Save the file as **FRAC7.CPP** for use in this tutorial.

3 Open a new file. Type the two include statements for this file:

```
#include<iostream.h>
#include"frac7.cpp"
```

4 Create the MixedNum class. It will inherit Fraction with public access. The class will have one new data member to hold the whole-number part of a mixed number, and two new functions that get and show data.

```
class MixedNum : public Fraction
  {
    private:
      int whole;
    public:
      void getMix(const int w,const int n,const int d);
      void showMix(void);
  };
```

5 Code the getMix() function, which performs three assignments: to the whole-number part of MixedNum, and to the numerator and denominator of the Fraction part of MixedNum.

```
void MixedNum::getMix(const int w,const int n,const int d)
  {
    MixedNum::whole = w;
    MixedNum::numerator = n;
    MixedNum::denominator = d;
  }
```

6 Code the showMix() function.

```
void MixedNum::showMix(void)
  {
    cout<<MixedNum::whole<<" "<<MixedNum::numerator<<"/"
      <<MixedNum::denominator<<endl;
  }
```

7 Write a main() program to test the inheritance.

```
void main()
{
  MixedNum mNumber;
  mNumber.getMix(4,1,2);
  mNumber.showMix();
}
```

8 Compile and test the program. The output should be the number 4 1/2. Save the program as **INHER1.CPP**.

Choosing the Class Access Specifier

When you define a derived class, you may insert one of the three class access specifiers (public, private, or protected) just prior to the base class name. For example, you can write

```
class Customer : public NameAndNumber
```

Using the public access specifier, as in the example above, is the most common technique. If a derived class uses the public access specifier, then the following statements are true:

■ Base class members that are public remain public in the derived class.
■ Base class members that are protected remain protected in the derived class.
■ Base class members that are private are inaccessible in the derived class.

If a derived class uses the protected access specifier, then the following statements are true:

■ Base class members that are public become protected in the derived class.
■ Base class members that are protected remain protected in the derived class.
■ Base class members that are private are inaccessible in the derived class.

If a derived class uses the private access specifier, then the following statements are true:

■ Base class members that are public become private in the derived class.
■ Base class members that are protected become private in the derived class.
■ Base class members that are private are inaccessible in the derived class.

In other words, any private base class members are always inaccessible in any classes derived from them. With private inheritance, both public and protected base class members become private. With protected inheritance, both public and protected base class members become protected. With public inheritance, both public and protected base class members retain their original access status.

Consider a class named Person with three data members, each with one of the access specifiers:

```
class Person
  {
  private:
    double salary;
  protected:
    int age;
  public:
    char initial;
    void showPerson(void);
  };
```

tip

No matter which access specifier you use when creating a child class, access to parent class members never becomes more lenient than originally coded.

tip

If you do not use any access specifier when creating a derived class, access is private by default.

The showPerson() function can refer to salary, age, and initial. A main() program that uses the Person class can use showPerson() to access any of the three data members. Although it is unusual to make a class data member public, initial is public in this case so a main() program can also refer to initial directly, without using a member function. For example,

```
void main()
  {
    Person Carmen;
    cout<<Carmen.initial;
  }
```

Assume you create three derived classes from the Person class: Introvert, SomewhatShy, and Extrovert. Introvert inherits privately:

```
class Introvert : private Person
  {
    private:
      int idNum;
    public:
      void showIntrovert(void);
  };
```

The Introvert class has four data members: salary, age, initial, and idNum. The showIntrovert() function may use idNum because both are members of the same class. This function may also access initial and age, which are private to the Introvert class. It may not use salary; because it was private in Person, salary remains inaccessible to the showIntrovert() function. The showIntrovert() function may call the showPerson() function, which is private to Introvert, and the showPerson() function may then access salary. A main() program that instantiates an Introvert object may not access any of the four data items directly.

The SomewhatShy class inherits with protected access:

```
class SomewhatShy : protected Person
  {
    private:
       int idNum;
    public:
       void showShy(void);
  };
```

Like Introvert, the SomewhatShy class also has four data members. Of course, the function showShy() may reference idNum, but it may also reference age and initial, both of which are protected in the SomewhatShy class. When a SomewhatShy object is instantiated in the main() program, it may use the showShy() function to access idNum, initial, or age; the showShy() function, however, may not access salary directly. The showShy() function has access to the showPerson() function, which is inherited as protected. The showShy() function can call showPerson(), which can then use salary.

The Extrovert class inherits with public access:

```
class Extrovert : public Person
  {
    private:
       int idNum;
    public:
       void showExtrovert(void);
  };
```

When you instantiate an Extrovert object in a main() program, it may use the showExtrovert() function to display any of the four data members (salary, age, initial, or idNum). The main() program cannot access salary directly—even though Extrovert inherits with public access, salary remains private to Person. Additionally, a main() program that uses the Extrovert class may call the showPerson() function to access salary, age, or initial. The main() program can even access the initial variable directly.

The following statements describe this situation:

- If a class has private data members, they can be used only by member functions of that class.
- If a class has protected data members, they can be used by member functions of that class and by member functions of derived classes.
- If a class has public data members, they can be used by member functions of that class, by member functions of derived classes, and by the main() program.

Nine combinations are possible here. Remember that private data can be accessed only by member functions (or friend functions) and not by any functions in derived classes. If a class serves as a base class, most often its data members are protected and its member functions are public. Data members are made protected so that only member functions or child class member functions can access them. The access specifier in derived classes is most often public, so that the derived class may refer to all nonprivate data and functions of the base class.

As with genetic inheritance, class inheritance may continue for more than one generation. Interestingly, when a class is derived from another derived class, the newly derived class never has any more liberal access to a base class member than its immediate predecessor.

Consider this simple GrandParent class:

```
class GrandParent
  {
    public:
      int x;
  };
```

If you define a Parent class with private access, x becomes private in Parent:

```
class Parent : private GrandParent
  {
  };
```

If you then define a Child class with public access to Parent,

```
class Child : public Parent
  {
  };
```

then x is still private in Child, even though Child uses the public specifier. This situation arises because x was private in Parent. Even though x was public in Grandparent, it is private in Parent, and Child cannot have more lenient access to x than Parent has.

Overriding Parent Class Functions

When a new class is derived from an existing class, the derived class has access to nonprivate member functions in the base class. The new class may also have its own member functions. Those functions may have names that are identical to the function names in the base class.

Consider the NameAndNumber class again:

```
class NameAndNumber
  {
    protected:
      int idNum;
      char lastName[20];
      char firstName[15];
    public:
      NameAndNumber();
      ~NameAndNumber();
      void inputData(const int num, const char *last,
        const char *first);
      void outputData(void);
  };
```

The inputData() and outputData() functions are straightforward, and may be coded as follows:

```
void NameAndNumber::inputData(const int num,
  const char*last, const char *first)
  {
    NameAndNumber::idNum = num;
    strcpy(NameAndNumber::lastName,last);
    strcpy(NameAndNumber::firstName,first);
  }
void NameAndNumber::outputData(void)
  {
    cout<<"ID #"<<NameAndNumber::idNum;
    cout<<" "<<NameAndNumber::firstName<<" ",
      <<NameAndNumber::lastName<<endl;
  }
```

You might create a derived class from NameAndNumber. An Employee class could inherit the members of NameAndNumber and include a department number and an hourly salary. It also includes new inputData() and outputData() functions because the Employee class has additional data members to be accommodated.

```
class Employee:public NameAndNumber
  {
    private:
      int dept;
      double hourlySalary;
    public:
      void inputData(const int id, const char *last,
        const char *first, const int dep, const double sal);
      void outputData(void);
  };
```

The Employee inputData() function receives data defined in NameAndNumber as well as data defined in Employee. Employee::inputData() could assign values to idNum, lastName, and firstName directly, but you can also call NameAndNumber's inputData() function, which has already coded these operations.

```
void Employee::inputData(const int id, const char *last,
  const char *first, const int dep, const double sal)

  {

    NameAndNumber::inputData(id,last,first);
      // note the class scope

    Employee::dept = dep;

    Employee::hourlySalary = sal;

  }
```

Employee can also have its own outputData() function, which differs from the generic NameAndNumber outputData() function:

```
void Employee::outputData(void)

  {

    cout<<"Employee ID #"<<Employee::idNum<<endl;

    cout<<" Employee is "<<Employee::lastName<<", ";
      // last name plus a comma and space

    cout<<Employee::firstName[0]<<"."<<endl;
      // first initial

    cout<<" Salary: "<<Employee::hourlySalary
      <<" Department "<<Employee::dept<<endl;

  }
```

tip

● ● ● ● ● ● ● ● ● ● ● ● ● ● ●

▶ **A derived class object can be assigned to a base class object, as in** person = worker;**. The assignment causes each data member to be copied from worker to person, leaving off any data for which the base class doesn't have members. The reverse assignment cannot take place without writing a specialized function.**

In the following program, two objects are created: a NameAndNumber object named person, and an Employee object named worker.

```
void main()

  {

    NameAndNumber person;

    person.inputData(123,"Kroening","Ginny");

    person.outputData();

    cout<<endl<<endl; // double space

    Employee worker;

    worker.inputData(987,"Lewis","Kathy",6,23.55);

    worker.outputData();

  }
```

This program produces the following output:

```
ID# 123 Ginny Kroening


Employee ID #987
  Employee is Lewis, K.
  Salary: 23.55 Department 6
```

Figure 7-1: Output from NameAndNumber and Employee classes

The different output formats demonstrate that the outputData() function called using the person object differs from the outputData() function called using the worker object. Likewise, the inputData() functions are separate. Any NameAndNumber object calls the NameAndNumber functions. If a class derived from NameAndNumber has functions with the same name, the new class functions override the base class functions. The exception occurs when you use a class specifier, as in the following:

```
worker.NameAndNumber::inputData(id,last,first);
  // note the class scope
```

Use of the class name NameAndNumber serves to indicate precisely which class inputData() function should be called.

The functions used by members of the Employee class remain separate from those used by members of the NameAndNumber class. These functions are not overloaded. Overloaded functions, you will recall, require different parameter lists, and the outputData() functions in NameAndNumber and Employee have identical parameter lists. Instead, Employee's outputData() function overrides the outputData() function defined in NameAndNumber.

When any class member function is called, the following steps take place:

- The compiler looks for a matching function name in the class of the object using the function name (also called the class of the object invoking the method).
- If no match is found in this class, the compiler looks for a matching function name in the parent class.
- If no match is found in the parent class, the compiler continues up the inheritance hierarchy until the base class is reached.
- If no match is found in any class, an error message is issued.

tip

If a base class contains a function that the derived class should not have, you can create a dummy, or empty, function with the same name in the derived class. If a derived class object uses this function name, no statements will be executed.

In the following steps, you will add a function to the MixedNum class that will override a function in the Fraction class.

1 Open the **FRAC7.CPP** file, which contains the current Fraction class definitions.

2 To the public declaration section of the Fraction class, add a prototype for an explain() function:

```
void explain(void);
```

3 Add the explain() function in the implementation section of the **FRAC7.CPP** file:

```
void Fraction::explain(void)
  {
    cout<<"A fraction is a representation"<<endl;
    cout<<"indicating the quotient of two numbers."<<endl;
    cout<<"It is often used to express a part of a whole."
      <<endl;
  }
```

4 Save the file.

5 Open the **INHER1.CPP** file, which contains the MixedNum definition.

6 Add a prototype for an explain() function to the public section of the MixedNum declarations:

```
void explain(void);
```

7 Add the function to the implementation section:

```
void MixedNum::explain(void)
  {
    cout<<"A mixed number has a whole part ";
    cout<<"and a fraction part."<<endl;
  }
```

8 Add a new declaration to the short main() program, which already displays the MixedNum object named mNumber. This new declaration will instantiate a Fraction object.

```
Fraction aFrac;
```

9 At the end of the main() function, add two function calls that will demonstrate that the two explain() functions are accessed by the appropriate objects:

```
cout<<"Fraction explanation follows:"<<endl;
aFrac.explain();
cout<<"Mixed number explanation follows: "<<endl;
mNumber.explain();
```

10 Compile and test the program. The output appears as in Figure 7-2.

```
Fraction explanation follows:
A fraction is a representation
indicating the quotient of two numbers.
It is often used to express a part of a whole.
Mixed number explanation follows:
A mixed number has a whole part and a fraction part.
```

Figure 7-2: Explanations

11 Save the program.

Overriding a base class member function with a derived member function demonstrates the concept of polymorphism. Polymorphism permits the same function name to take many forms. When you inherit functions and then override them with identically named functions in a subclass, the same message can be carried out appropriately by different objects. Just as the command "Play!" invokes different responses in a CD player and a baseball player, a program command such as showData() or explain() can invoke different responses in different objects. This ability models the way things work in the real world, and is a basic feature—and advantage—of object-oriented programming.

S U M M A R Y

- Inheritance is the principle that knowledge of a general category can be applied to more specific objects.

- When you inherit a class in C++, the new class has all of the original class's members. The new class may have additional data members and functions as well.

- A new class is derived from a parent class, base class, or superclass. The derived class may also be called a child class or subclass.

- A derived class can override inappropriate attributes from the parent.

- For a programming language to be considered object-oriented, it must allow inheritance.

- Inheritance offers an advantage in that much of the code needed for a derived class is already written and is reliable, allowing you to concentrate on only the new complexity added with your extensions to the class.

- Despite its advantages, inheritance is not used as often as it could be because developing good general-purpose base classes is a time-consuming task.

- When a class serves as a base class to others, all of its members are inherited, except for any private members.

- The protected access specifier allows members to be used by class member functions and derived classes, but not by other parts of a program.

- To create a derived class, type the keyword `class`, the derived class name, a colon, a class access specifier, the base class name, an opening bracket, the class definition statements, a closing bracket, and a semicolon.

- The following are never inherited: constructor functions, destructor functions, friend functions, static data members, static member functions, overloaded new operators, and overloaded = operators.

- When you define a derived class, you may insert one of the three class access specifiers (public, private, or protected) just prior to the base class name.

- The public access specifier is the most commonly used approach.

- If a derived class uses the public access specifier, then public base class members remain public in the derived class, protected base class members remain protected in the derived class, and private base class members are inaccessible in the derived class.

- If a derived class uses the protected access specifier, then public or protected base class members are protected in the derived class. Private base class members are inaccessible in the derived class.

- If a derived class uses the private access specifier, then public or protected base class members become private in the derived class, and private base class members are inaccessible in the derived class.

- If you do not use any access specifier when creating a derived class, access is private by default.

- If a class has private data members, they can be used only by member functions of that class.

- If a class has protected data members, they can be used by member functions of that class and by member functions of derived classes.

- If a class has public data members, they can be used by member functions of that class, by member functions of derived classes, and by the main() program.

- When a class is derived from another derived class, the newly derived class never has any more liberal access to its ancestor class members than its parent does.

- A derived class may include a function with the same name as a function in the parent class. The function in the derived class overrides the function in the base class.
- When a class member function is called, the compiler looks for a matching function name in the class of the object using the function name (also called the class of the object invoking the method). If no match is found, it looks for a matching function name in the parent class, continuing up the inheritance hierarchy until it reaches the base class. If no match is found, an error message is issued.

QUESTIONS

1. Inheritance is the principle that _____.
    a. classes with the same name must be derived from one another
    b. knowledge of a general category can be applied to more specific objects
    c. C++ functions may be used only if they have logical predecessors
    d. one function name may invoke different methods

2. Compared with the classes from which they are derived, inherited classes may have _____.
    a. additional data members
    b. additional member functions
    c. both (a) and (b)
    d. neither (a) nor (b)

3. A base class may also be called a _____.
    a. child class
    b. subclass
    c. derived class
    d. parent class

4. A derived class may also be called a _____.
    a. subclass
    b. superclass
    c. parent class
    d. base class

5. A derived class _____ override attributes of a parent class.
    a. may
    b. may if the two classes have the same name
    c. must
    d. must not

6. To be called object-oriented, a programming language must allow _____.
    a. functions that return only a single value
    b. #include files
    c. inheritance
    d. all of the above

7. Code that has already been tested is said to be _____.
    a. inherited
    b. reusable
    c. reliable
    d. polymorphic

8. When a class serves as a base class to others, _____.
   a. all of its members are inherited
   b. all of its members are inherited, except for any private members
   c. all of its members are inherited, except for any protected members
   d. none of its members is inherited unless specifically listed

9. You separate a derived class name from its access specifier with _____.
   a. a colon
   b. two colons
   c. at least one space
   d. a semicolon

10. Which of the following are never inherited?
    a. public data members
    b. constructor functions
    c. void functions
    d. overloaded + operators

11. If a derived class uses the public access specifier, then _____.
    a. public base class members remain public in the derived class
    b. protected base class members become public in the derived class
    c. both (a) and (b)
    d. neither (a) nor (b)

12. If a base class member is private, then _____.
    a. if a derived class uses the public access specifier, the data member becomes public
    b. if a derived class uses the protected access specifier, the data member becomes protected
    c. both (a) and (b)
    d. neither (a) nor (b)

13. Private data can be accessed by _____.
    a. class member functions
    b. functions in derived classes
    c. both (a) and (b)
    d. neither (a) nor (b)

14. If a class will serve as a base class, most often the base class data members are _____.
    a. private
    b. protected
    c. public
    d. polymorphic

15. When a class is derived from another derived class, the newly derived class _____.
    a. may have more liberal access to a base class member than its immediate predecessor
    b. may have the same type of access to a base class member as its immediate predecessor
    c. may have more limited access to a base class member than its immediate predecessor
    d. both (b) and (c)

16. When a new class is derived from an existing class, the derived class member functions _____ have names that differ from base class function names.
    a. may
    b. may if the two classes have the same name
    c. must
    d. must not

17. A function in a derived class that has the same name as a function in the parent class
_____.

    a. will cause an error message to display

    b. will override the base class function

    c. will be overridden by the base class function

    d. will execute immediately after the base class function executes

18. When a child class function is called, the compiler looks first for a matching function name in the _____.

    a. class of the object using the function name

    b. immediate ancestor class

    c. base class

    d. descendant class

E X E R C I S E S

1. Create a base class named Rectangle that includes data members for length and width, as well as functions to assign and display those values. Derive a class named Block that contains an additional data member to store height, and functions to assign and display the height. Write a main() program that demonstrates the classes by instantiating and displaying the values for both a Rectangle and a Block.

2. Add a member function to the Rectangle class created in exercise 1 that computes the area of a Rectangle (length multiplied by width). Add a member function to Block that has the same name, but overrides the computation with a volume calculation (length by width by height). Write a main() program that demonstrates the classes.

3. Create a base class for books for a library. Data members include title and author. Derive two classes: Fiction, which also contains a numeric grade reading level, and NonFiction, which contains a variable to hold the number of pages. Write a main() program to demonstrate the classes.

LESSON B
objectives

In this lesson you will learn

- How to use constructor initialization lists
- How to inherit from base classes with constructors
- How to override inherited access
- How to use multiple inheritance

Inheritance Techniques

Constructor Initialization Lists

Many constructor functions consist of a series of assignment statements. For example, consider an Inventory class with two data members and a constructor:

```cpp
class Inventory
  {
    protected:
      int itemNum;
      double itemPrice;
    public:
      Inventory(int n, double p);
  };
```

The constructor for the Inventory class may be written as follows:

```cpp
Inventory::Inventory(int n, double p)
  {
    Inventory::itemNum = n;
    Inventory::itemPrice = p;
  }
```

The constructor can just as easily be implemented in the declaration section for the class, eliminating the need for a separate function body:

```cpp
class Inventory
  {
    protected:
      int itemNum;
      double itemPrice;
    public:
      Inventory (int n,double p){itemNum = n,itemPrice =p;};
  };
```

As an alternative, you can replace the assignment statements within a constructor body with a **constructor initialization list.** The constructor initialization list is inserted after the argument list for the constructor function, preceded by a single colon. For example, the Inventory class can be rewritten as follows:

```cpp
class Inventory
  {
    protected:
      int itemNum;
      double itemPrice;
    public:
      Inventory(int n,double p):itemNum(n),itemPrice(p) { };
  };
```

This constructor initialization list initializes itemNum with n and itemPrice with p. As a result, itemNum and itemPrice are given the correct values just as with the original constructor. The curly brackets following the list remain empty because you no longer need any assignment statements in the body of the function. (The brackets could contain other statements if needed.)

The difference between assignment and initialization is often very subtle, and programmers may mingle the two terms rather casually. When you declare a simple scalar variable and give it a value, you can declare and assign:

```cpp
int z;
z = 100;
```

tip

You can also initialize with `int z(100);`

Alternatively, you can initialize:

```
int z = 100;
```

In the first example, z is created and then given a value. In the second example, z receives a value at its creation. This subtle difference applies to class objects just as it does to scalar variables: constructor initialization lists provide values for class members upon construction.

There are four reasons to understand the use of constructor initialization lists:

- Many C++ programmers prefer this method, so it is used in many programs.
- Technically, a constructor *should* initialize rather than assign values.
- Reference variables and constant class members cannot be assigned values; they must be initialized.
- When you create a derived class and instantiate an object, a parent class object must be constructed first. You add a constructor initialization list to a derived class constructor to construct the parent class.

Base Class Construction

tip

If a base class constructor requires arguments, you must create a constructor for any derived class—even if the derived class does not need a constructor for any other reason.

When you instantiate an object in a C++ program, its constructor is called. This pattern holds true whether you write a custom constructor or use a default constructor. When you instantiate a derived class object, a constructor for its base class is called first, followed by the derived class constructor. This format is followed even if both the base and derived classes have only default constructors. If a base class constructor is not a default constructor—that is, if the base class constructor requires arguments—then you must provide a constructor for the derived class.

For example, consider a class developed for all items sold by a pet store. A fully developed PetInven class might contain data members for species, breed, medical and diet information, and so on. For purposes of this example, however, we'll use a very limited class. Its data members include a stock number and price.

```
class PetInven
   {
     protected:
        int stockNum;
        double price;
     public:
        PetInven(const int stk, const double pr) :
        stockNum(stk), price(pr) {};
           // a constructor with an initialization list
           // a constructor with assignments
           // in the body could also be used
   };
```

Several derived classes may exist—one for animals sold in the store, and others for accessories, food, training classes, and so on. You can create a derived Animal class that contains all members of PetInven, plus a data member for age and a constructor.

```
class Animal: public PetInven
   {
      protected: // private would work here as well
        int petAge;
      public:
        Animal(const int age);    // constructor -- not complete yet
   }
```

If Animal were merely a base class, its constructor could have the following format:

```
Animal::Animal(const int age)
  // constructor function -- not complete yet
  {
    Animal::petAge = age;
  }
```

tip

If you fail to call a needed base class constructor in the initialization list for a derived class (for example, not calling the PetInven constructor when constructing an Animal), you will receive an error message such as "Cannot find default constructor to initialize base class."

As a simple base class, the Animal class constructor requires an integer argument that initializes petAge. Because Animal is derived from PetInven, however, when an Animal object is constructed, the PetInven class will also be constructed. The PetInven constructor requires arguments for stockNum and price.

The prototype for the Animal class constructor must include arguments for the stock number and price (so PetInven can be constructed) as well as the age of the animal:

```
class Animal : public PetInven
   {
      protected:    // private would work here as well
        int petAge;
      public:
        Animal(const int stk,const double price,const int age);
          // constructor
   };
```

The Animal constructor may then be coded as follows:

```
Animal::Animal(const int stk, const double price, const int age) :
  PetInven (stk, price)
    {
       Animal::petAge = age;
    }
```

tip

· · · · · · · · · · · · · · · ·

When you construct a derived class object, the base class constructor is called first. When a derived class object is destroyed, the child class destructor is called first and the base class destructor is called last.

Just as a simple scalar variable may be initialized in a constructor initialization list, so may a class object. The PetInven constructor is called in the Animal constructor header, initializing the members of PetInven. The PetInven constructor is placed in the constructor initialization list for the Animal constructor, as PetInven must receive values for stockNum and price before an Animal object can be instantiated completely. The PetInven constructor must be called, because an Animal object is incomplete without PetInven. A child class cannot exist if no parent class exists.

The Animal class could also be coded as follows:

```
class Animal : public PetInven
  {
    protected:    //private would work here as well
      int petAge;
    public:
      Animal(const int stk, const double price,
        const int age) : PetInven(stk,price),
          petAge(age) { };
  };
```

In this example, the constructor initialization list initializes both PetInven and petAge.

The Fraction class currently contains a default constructor. To demonstrate base class construction, you will temporarily eliminate it.

1   Open the **FRAC7.CPP** file. Either cut or comment out the two existing Fraction constructor prototypes and the two existing Fraction constructor functions. Because you will want only a default constructor to demonstrate base class construction here, cut or comment out all functions in the Fraction class that instantiate a Fraction without assigning initial values. The Fraction class should contain at least the following statements:

```
class Fraction
  {
    protected:
      int numerator;
      int denominator;
    public:
      // constructor prototype created in step 2
      // will go here
  };
```

2   Create a new constructor prototype in the public declaration section:

```
Fraction(const int n, const int d);
```

3   In the implementation section, write the new constructor function:

```
Fraction::Fraction(const int n, const int d)
  {
    Fraction::numerator = n;
    Fraction::denominator = d;
  }
```

4   Save the file as **FRAC7NEW.CPP**.

5   Open a new file and type in the two include statements:

```
#include<iostream.h>
#include"frac7new.cpp"
```

tip

· · · · · · · · · · · · · · · ·

▶ If a default base class constructor exists, then no compiler error will arise if you omit the call to the base class constructor when deriving a class. Because the Fraction class has a default constructor as well as a newly created constructor, you could also create a MixedClass constructor that does not call the Fraction constructor.

6 Create a new MixedClass class that is derived from Fraction. MixedClass will have an integer wholeNum and its own constructor and display functions. The constructor will create a Fraction and assign a value to the wholeNum part.

```
class MixedClass : public Fraction
  {
    private:
      int wholeNum;
    public:
      MixedClass(const int w, const int n, const int d) :
        Fraction(n,d), wholeNum(w) { };
      void showMix(void);
  };
```

7 Write the showMix() function:

```
void MixedClass::showMix(void)
  {
    cout<<"Mixed number is "<<MixedClass::wholeNum;
    cout<<" "<<MixedClass::numerator<<"/"
      <<MixedClass::denominator<<endl;
  }
```

8 Add a main() program to demonstrate the classes:

```
void main()
  {
    MixedClass aValue(8,1,7);
    aValue.showMix();
  }
```

9 Compile and test the program. The output appears as in Figure 7-3.

```
Mixed number is 8 1/7
```

Figure 7-3: MixedClass output

10 Save the program as **BASECON.CPP**.

Overriding Inherited Access

Nine inheritance access specifier combinations are possible: class members that are private, protected, or public any be inherited with private, protected, or public access. In addition, you may override the class access specifier for any specific class members. For example, consider the Person base class with members of all three types:

```
class Person
  {
    private:
      double salary;
    protected:
      int age;
    public:
      char initial;
      void showPerson(void);
  };
```

If a derived class, SomewhatShy, uses the protected access specifier when inheriting from Person, then the following statements hold true:

- salary, which is private in Person, is inaccessible in the derived class.
- age, which is protected in the base class, remains protected in the derived class.
- initial, which is public in the base class, becomes protected in the derived class.
- showPerson(), which is public in Person, becomes protected in the derived class.

If you want initial to remain protected in SomewhatShy, but you want showPerson() to be public in SomewhatShy, you can override the access specifier for showPerson(). In the SomewhatShy class definition, you write the following code:

```
class SomewhatShy : protected Person
  // inheritance is still protected
  {
    // other members that are private or protected
    // can be coded here with the proper specifier
    public:
      Person::showPerson;
        // showPerson() is public in the SomewhatShy class
        // other public members can be placed here
        // along with showPerson()
  };
```

The showPerson() member function may now be used in the main() program with any Person object or any SomewhatShy object. [If showPerson() remained protected, only members of Person or SomewhatShy could use it.] Within the SomewhatShy class, the protected access specifier is overridden for the showPerson() function.

In the above example, showPerson() was allowed more liberal access. You can also override the inherited access to make an individual member's access more conservative. For example, you can define SomewhatShy as follows:

```
class SomewhatShy : protected Person
  // inheritance is still protected
  {
    private:
      Person::initial;
    public:
      Person::showPerson;
        // showPerson() is public in the SomewhatShy class
  };
```

In addition to overriding showPerson()'s protected access so as to make it public, you are overriding initial's protected access and making it private. Of course, you still can't access members that were private in the base class.

Multiple Inheritance

A base class may have many child classes. Earlier in this tutorial, for example, we created a Person class and then derived Introvert, SomewhatShy, and Extrovert from it. A company may create an Employee base class and derive Salaried, Hourly, and Contract classes from it. A college may use a superclass named Student and derive UnderGrad and Grad subclasses from it.

A derived class may also derive from more than one base class. For example, a company may have two classes: Inventory and Employee. Inventory has data members such as itemNumber and itemPrice. Employee contains empNumber and empSalary. Perhaps when the company obtains a patent, objects of a new class, Patent, are instantiated. The company wants Patent objects to contain data about both the item in Inventory and the Employee who developed the product. The two base classes are defined as follows:

tip

You already use multiple inheritance each time you include iostream.h in a program. The cin and cout objects are each derived from other classes. See Tutorial 8 for more details.

```cpp
class Inventory
  {
    protected:
      int itemNumber;
      double itemPrice;
    public:
      Inventory(void);
      ~Inventory(void);
      void showData(void);
  };
class Employee
  {
    protected:
      int empNumber;
      double empSalary;
    public:
      Employee(void);
      ~Employee(void);
      void showData(void);
  };
```

The new Patent class inherits from both Inventory and Employee:

```
class Patent: public Inventory, public Employee
  {
    private:
      int patentNum;
    public:
      void showAll(void);
  };
```

The Patent class includes all members of both the Inventory and Employee classes. The showAll() function may be used to display the data members directly or it may call the Inventory and Employee showData() functions individually, as shown below:

```
void Patent::showAll(void)
  {
    cout<<Patent::patentNum<<endl;
    Inventory::showData();
    Employee::showData();
  }
```

When you instantiate a Patent object,

```
Patent newInvention;
```

you may then call the showAll() function with the following statement:

```
newInvention.showAll();
```

A problem arises, however, if you attempt to call showData():

```
newInvention.showData(); // ambiguous call
```

The Patent subclass inherits from both Inventory and Employee, and both base classes have a showData() function. When the newInvention object is used, the C++ compiler does not know whether to call the showData() function that is a member of Inventory or the showData() function that is a member of Employee.

This conflict can be resolved using the scope resolution operator, as in

```
newInvention.Inventory::showData();
```

or

```
newInvention.Employee::showData();
```

Even though the dilemma of identically named functions in two parent classes is resolved fairly easily, many programmers avoid multiple inheritance because of this type of problem. You have already learned that a derived class must often call its parent class constructor with an initialization list. A derived class with more than one parent must provide for the constructors of all parents, so the syntax can become quite complicated. The Patent class could have been developed using single inheritance from either the Inventory or Employee class alone, with the necessary additional data members being declared as part of the Patent class. The resulting class definition would be easier to understand and less prone to error than the one that inherits from two base classes.

In previous examples, you have created mixed numbers through inheritance, using the Fraction class as a base and adding a whole-number part. An alternative approach is to create a new base class for whole numbers and a derived Mixed class that inherits from both Fraction and WholeNum.

1   Open **FRAC7.CPP**, which contains the Fraction class definition. Create a new member function that simply shows a fraction without advancing to a new line. In the protected section, place the following prototype:

```
void showFrac(void);
```

2   In the implementation section, write the new function:

```
void Fraction::showFrac(void)
  {
    cout<<Fraction::numerator<<"/"
      <<Fraction::denominator;
  }
```

3   Save the file.
4   Open a new file. Enter the first two lines:

```
#include<iostream.h>
#include"frac7.cpp"
```

5   Create a new WholeNum base class:

```cpp
class WholeNum
  {
    protected:
      int wholeNum;
    public:
      void getWhole(const int w);
      void showWhole(void);
  };
void WholeNum::getWhole(const int w)
  {
    WholeNum::wholeNum = w;
  }
void WholeNum::showWhole(void)
  {
    cout<<WholeNum::wholeNum;
  }
```

6   Create the derived class named Mixed:

```cpp
class Mixed : public Fraction, public WholeNum
  {
    public:
      void showMixed(void);
  };
void Mixed::showMixed(void)
  {
    cout<<"New mixed number is ";
    WholeNum::showWhole();
    cout<<" ";
    Fraction::showFrac();
    cout<<endl;
  }
```

7   Write a main() program to test the Mixed class:

```
void main()
  {
    Mixed aMixedNumber;
    aMixedNumber.getData(3,5); // uses base class function
    aMixedNumber.getWhole(9); // uses base class function
    aMixedNumber.showMixed(); // uses derived class function
  }
```

8   Compile and test the program.
9   Save the file as **BASE.CPP.**

Virtual Base Classes

You already know that a base class may have many descendants through single inheritance. A PetInven base class, for example, may have child classes Animal and Accessory that hold data for two different types of pet store inventory items. You also know that a class may inherit from two other classes through multiple inheritance. For example, a Sale class might inherit from both Animal and Accessory, as Sale objects might need data from either type of item. The class definition for Sale would begin as follows:

```
class Sale: public Animal, public Accessory
  {
  };
```

Sale inherits from both Animal and Accessory, and both Animal and Accessory inherit from PetInven. Thus, Sale ends up with two copies of PetInven. To avoid this duplicate inheritance, you use the keyword **virtual,** which indicates that the base class should be used only once:

```
class Animal : virtual public PetInven
  {
  };
```

and

```
class Accessory : virtual public PetInven
  {
  };
```

Now when Sale is defined as

```
class Sale: public Animal, public Accessory
  {
  };
```

the members of PetInven are included just once in Sale.

An additional problem arises with the constructor functions in this situation. When a Sale object is constructed, it needs to construct its base classes. If its base classes, Animal and Accessory, are both constructed, then PetInven will be constructed twice. Therefore, when you write the Sale class constructor, it must handle the construction needs of Animal, Accessory, *and* PetInven. For example, if PetInven requires values for stock number and price, Animal requires age, Accessory requires size, and Sale requires date, then the Sale constructor might take the following form:

```
Sale(int stk, double price, int age, char size, int date):
  saleDate(date), PetInven(stk, price), Animal(age),Accessory(size) { };
```

Because the virtual keyword is used when Animal and Accessory inherit from PetInven, the construction of Animal and Accessory will not prompt the construction of PetInven. Instead, Sale must construct PetInven as well as Animal and Accessory.

S U M M A R Y

- A constructor may be implemented in the declaration section for a class in the form `constructor name (variables) {assignments};`.
- Alternatively, you can replace the assignment statements within a constructor body with a constructor initialization list.
- A constructor initialization list is inserted after the argument list for the constructor function, preceded by a colon.
- The difference between assignment and initialization is subtle. Constructor initialization lists initialize class members upon construction, rather than assigning values to them at a later time.

- Reference variables and constant class members cannot be assigned values; they must be initialized.
- When you create a derived class and instantiate an object, a parent class object must be constructed first with a constructor initialization list. The derived class constructor is called subsequently.
- If a base class constructor is not the default—that is, if it requires arguments—then you must provide a constructor for the derived class.
- When you construct a derived class object, the base class constructor is called first. When a derived class object is destroyed, the child class destructor is called first and the base class destructor is called last.
- A base class may be initialized in a constructor initialization list.
- You may override the class access specifier for any specific class members in a derived class.
- A derived class may have more than one base class; the derived class then includes all members of both base classes.
- With multiple inheritance, any function name conflict can be resolved using the scope resolution operator.
- A derived class with more than one parent must provide for the constructors of all parents.
- If a class inherits from two classes that have a common ancestor, you can avoid duplicate inheritance by using the keyword virtual, which indicates that the base class should be used only once.
- If a class inherits from two classes that have a common ancestor, the derived class must handle the construction needs for all of its ancestor classes.

QUESTIONS

1. The most common operation used in constructors is _____.
   a. addition
   b. overloading
   c. assignment
   d. polymorphism

2. Which constructor function prototype would be correct in the declaration section of a class named Product that contains one data member, prodNum?
   a. Product(int n);
   b. Product(int n) {prodNum = n;};
   c. Product(int n) : prodNum(n) {};
   d. all of the above

3. A constructor initialization list produces similar results to _____.
   a. overriding
   b. assignment
   c. redeclaring
   d. output

4. A constructor initialization list is preceded by _____.
   a. a semicolon
   b. a colon
   c. two colons
   d. a space

5. The statement `double total = 0.0;` performs _____.
   a. assignment
   b. initialization
   c. rationalization
   d. polymorphism

6. Reference variables and const class members _____.
   a. must be assigned values in any derived class
   b. must never be initialized in a base class
   c. must be initialized, rather than assigned values
   d. must not exist if a class is to be a base class

7. When you create a derived class and instantiate an object, _____.
   a. the parent class object must be constructed first
   b. the child class object must be constructed first
   c. the parent class object must not be constructed
   d. the child class object must not be constructed

8. When you instantiate a derived class object, a constructor for the derived class _____.
   a. is not called
   b. is called prior to the base class constructor
   c. is called simultaneously with the base class constructor
   d. none of the above

9. You must provide a constructor for a derived class _____.
   a. always
   b. if the base class constructor requires arguments
   c. if the base class constructor does not require arguments
   d. never

10. The prototype for a derived class constructor may include arguments for _____.
   a. data members of the derived class
   b. data members of the base class
   c. both (a) and (b)
   d. neither (a) nor (b)

11. A child class _____ exist if there is no parent class.
   a. must
   b. may
   c. cannot
   d. can

12. You may override the class access specifier for _____.
   a. public members
   b. public and protected members
   c. any specific class members you choose
   d. no class members

13. If class P is a parent to child class C, and C inherits with public access, P's function F() can be made private with which statements?
   a. private:
     P::F();
   b. private:
     P::F;
   c. private:
     C::F();
   d. private:
     C::F;

14. You can override a class's inherited access to make an individual member's access more _____.

    a. liberal

    b. conservative

    c. either (a) or (b)

    d. neither (a) nor (b)

15. Which is true?

    a. A derived class may have more than one base class.

    b. A base class may have more than one derived class.

    c. both (a) and (b)

    d. neither (a) nor (b)

16. Which is a correct class definition for class Child, which inherits from Mother and Father classes?

    a. class Child::Mother, Father

    b. class Child : Mother; Father

    c. class Child:: public Mother, public Father

    d. class Child : public Mother, public Father

17. The keyword virtual indicates that _____.

    a. a derived class has public access to a base class

    b. more than one base class exists

    c. a base class should be used only once in inheritance

    d. a derived class should have more than one base class constructed

18. The code `class Descendant : virtual  public Ancestor` indicates that _____.

    a. the members of Ancestor will be included more than once in Descendant

    b. the members of Ancestor will be included only once in Descendant

    c. the members of Descendant will be included more than once in Ancestor

    d. the members of Descendant will be included only once in Ancestor

E X E R C I S E S

1. Create a class named Account for a bank. Data members include an account number and a balance. Functions include a constructor that requires the account number and balance parameters, as well as a display function. Derive two classes from Account: Savings, which includes an interest rate, and Checking, which includes a monthly fee. Write a main() program to demonstrate the classes.

2. Create two classes named Account and Customer for a bank. Select appropriate data members and functions. Derive a class, CustomerAccount, that inherits from both base classes. Write a main() program to demonstrate the classes.

debugging ▶ **3.** Each of the following files in the TUT07 folder contains syntax and/or logical errors. Determine the problem in each case, and fix the program.

    a. DEBUG7-1.CPP

    b. DEBUG7-2.CPP

    c. DEBUG7-3.CPP

TUTORIAL 8

Advanced Input and Output

case ▶ The Fraction class you've been developing for Teacher's Pet Software is almost complete, and you've learned a lot about object-oriented programming. Lately, you've noticed that other programmers refer to cout and cin as objects.

"If cout and cin are objects," you ask Audrey Burns, your supervisor, "does that mean they have member functions, inheritance, and polymorphism like other objects?"

"Yes, they do," replies Audrey. "You can use their function members just as you do with other objects. This feature also makes it easy to read to and write from a disk."

"I'd like to save my Fraction class objects to a disk file," you say. "Show me how!"

Previewing the FILEOUT and FILEIN Programs

1 Open the **FILEOUT.CPP** file in the TUT08 folder. This program prompts a user for his or her name, allows the user to enter a series of numerators and denominators, and then displays those figures as reduced fractions. In addition, it creates an output file of the fractions created.

2 This program will write a file named **STUFRAC.DAT** to the default drive. If you need to change the output location for this file, you may add a path to the filename in the fourth line of the main() function.

3 Run the program, entering any five values for numerators and denominators.

4 Load the **FILEIN.CPP** program, which is located in the TUT08 folder.

5 If you changed the path for the **STUFRAC.DAT** file in step 2, then change the file path in the third line of the main() function in this program as well.

6 Run the program. The fractions you entered during the execution of the FILEOUT.CPP program should display.

7 Examine the code for both **FILEOUT.CPP** and **FILEIN.CPP**. You will be creating similar programs in this tutorial.

In this lesson you will learn:

- How cin and cout act as objects
- How to use istream member functions
- How to use ostream member functions
- How to use and create your own manipulator functions

Using cin and cout Objects

The Input and Output Objects

From the first day you wrote a line of code in C++, you have probably used cout to display data; shortly thereafter, you may have started to use cin for input. You were able to use the objects cin and cout long before you knew anything about object-oriented programming, in part because cout and cin resemble real-world objects (your screen and your keyboard), and real-world objects are easy to understand. Now you can apply what you have learned about object-oriented programming to gain a deeper understanding of input and output.

You can think of cout and cin as real-world objects because they are C++ objects and therefore members of a class. Their class is derived from another class (which is derived from yet another class), so they use inheritance. The cout and cin objects can take advantage of overloaded operators, such as << and >> (which are also used for shifting bits). These objects also use polymorphism—generating different machine instructions when put together with different types of variables (with integers versus with characters, for example). In other words, cout and cin are every bit as much class objects as any you have created throughout this book.

When you include iostream.h in a program, you are including a file that contains the definition for a derived class named **iostream**. The grandparent base class from which iostream is derived is named **ios**. The istream and ostream classes are both derived from ios. The **istream** class handles input and includes a definition of the extraction operator >>. The **ostream** class handles output and includes a definition of the insertion operator <<. The iostream class is derived from both istream and ostream, so it inherits all the properties of both its parent classes, including the >> and << operators. The iostream class provides a working example of multiple inheritance. Figure 8-1 illustrates the relationships among ios, istream, ostream, and iostream.

tip

You don't have to understand objects or classes to use cin or cout. That's part of the appeal of object-oriented programming. Just as you can use a microwave oven without knowing how it works, you can use well-designed C++ objects without delving into the implementation details.

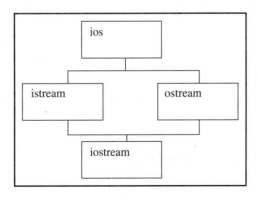

Figure 8-1: iostream's family tree

istream Member Functions

In C++, the easiest way to read in a character is to use cin with the extraction operator:

```
char letter;
cin>>letter;
```

The extraction operator is actually an overloaded function named operator>>(). Another member function of the istream class is get(). This function takes a character argument and returns a reference to the object that invoked it, so that more than one get() function can be included in a statement. Its prototype has the following form:

```
istream& get(char &c);
```

For example, the following code segment accepts three characters from the keyboard in two statements.

```
char first, middle, last;
cin.get(first);
cin.get(middle).get(last);
```

Most compilers overload get() so that, in addition to taking a character reference as an argument, it also can take no argument. This version of the get() function returns the character being read in as an integer. Its prototype is

```
int get();
```

This form of the function often is used when it doesn't matter which character is extracted and you do not need to store the character, as in

```
cout<<"Press any key to continue";
cin.get();
```

The get() function is also overloaded so that it can take two or three arguments. The prototype is as follows:

```
istream &get(char *str, int len, char c = '\n');
```

This form of get() allows you to input a string of characters. The first argument consists of the address of the string. The second argument comprises the number of characters that will be stored. The third argument is the character that terminates the entry. The default value, as you can see from the prototype, is the enter key; if you don't supply an alternative third argument, the enter key will automatically become the signal to end data entry.

The second argument of the get() function—the number of characters to be stored—is very important. Without it, a user could destroy memory by entering a string of characters that was longer than the area prepared to receive it. In the following example, a 10-character array is set up for userName. Because the length of the string is limited to 10 in the cin.get() statement, if a user enters a name longer than nine characters, only the first nine characters, plus a string-ending null character, will be stored. If no provision was made to limit the user's entry, a long entry could be stored starting at the address of the userName array, but it would continue past the end of the array and wipe out other values stored in memory.

```cpp
#include<iostream.h>
void main()
  {
    char userName[10];
    cout<<"Enter your name ";
    cin.get(userName,10);
    cout<<"Hello, "<<userName<<endl;
  }
```

One unfortunate side effect of the get() function is that it leaves the '\n' character in the input stream. A subsequent call to get() retrieves this '\n' character, whether or not that retrieval was intended. For example, when you run the following program, you are allowed to enter only one initial. The first cin.get() statement accepts your first initial from the keyboard, and the second cin.get() statement accepts the enter key you press after entering your first initial. The program doesn't stop to obtain your last initial.

```cpp
char first,last;
cout<<"Enter your first initial ";
cin>>first;
cout<<"Enter your last initial ";
cin>>last;
cout<<"Your initials are "<<first<<last;
```

The output from the program above includes your first initial and a newline. To allow the user to enter a last initial, you could add a third cin.get() statement to the program:

```
char first,last;
cout<<"Enter your first initial ";
cin.get(first);
cin.get();      // this is simply for the Enter key
cout<<"Enter your last initial ";
cin.get(last);
cout<<"Your initials are "<<first<<last;
```

This program accepts a user's first initial after the prompt, and then uses the cin.get() statement to read the newline character, but not store it. The second prompt and the entry of the user's last initial follow.

As an alternative to using an extra call to get(), you can include another istream member, getline(). Its prototype is

```
istream &getline(char * str, int len, char  c = '\n');
```

The getline() function reads a line of text until it reaches either the length used as the second argument or the character used as the third argument. (If you don't supply a third argument, the line-ending character becomes '\n' by default.) Additionally, getline() discards the newline character, so any following data entry begins fresh. The following program segment correctly accepts initials into two strings.

```
char first[2], last[2];
char first,last;
cout<<"Enter your first initial ";
cin.getline(first,2);
cout<<"Enter your last initial ";
cin.getline(last,2);
cout<<"Your initials are "<<first<<last;
```

Most compilers support other istream member functions; you could also write your own. The istream class is not mysterious. It is just a class, and cin is just an object. As an object, cin has member functions like objects of any other class.

In the following steps, you will create the beginning of a program that will become an exercise using fractions. The program will provide a friendly greeting and prompt the user for a name.

1   Open a new file.
2   Begin the program with an include statement, the main() function header, and the opening curly bracket.

```
#include<iostream.h>
void main()
  {
```

3   Declare a character array to hold the name of the student who will use the program:

```
char studentName[30];
```

4   Create a prompt, an input statement, and a thank you:

```
cout<<"Welcome to the fraction drill.  Enter your name. ";
cin.get(studentName,30);
cout<<"Thank you "<<studentName<<endl;
}
```

5   Compile and test the program. Your output should resemble Figure 8-2.

```
Welcome to the fraction drill. Enter your name. Andrea
Thank you Andrea.
```

Figure 8-2: Output from FRACFILE.CPP

6   Save the program as **FRACFILE.CPP**.

tip
• • • • • • • • • • • • • • • • •
You will probably prefer using manipulators to using ostream member functions. Nevertheless, it's important to understand how ostream member functions work so that you can write your own manipulators. Manipulators are discussed in the next section.

ostream Member Functions

What you have learned about the cin object applies to the cout object as well. It is a member of the ostream class, which supports member functions and overloaded operators just like the istream class—or any other class, for that matter. (You already know how to use one overloaded ostream class operator function—the operator<<() function.) Like other class instantiations, the cout object has data members, or states.

Many of the states of the cout object are contained in a single long integer field, in which each bit represents some condition of the cout object. For example, the bit that represents "show positive sign" may be on. If so, any positive value subsequently sent through the output stream will be preceded by a plus sign (+) when it is displayed.

The arguments that determine the state of the cout object are called **format flags** or **state flags.** All of the format flags begin with **ios::.** As you know from your work with classes, :: is the scope resolution operator, and its use indicates that the format flags are members of the ios base class. Some of the commonly used format flags are

- ios::left—left-justifies output within the field size, which may be set by the width() function, as described below

- ios::right—right-justifies output within the field size

- ios::dec—formats numbers in decimal (base 10)

- ios::hex—formats numbers in hexadecimal (base 16)

- ios::oct—formats numbers in octal (base 8)

- ios::showpos—inserts a + before positive numbers

- ios::showpoint—causes the decimal point and six decimal positions to display for all floating-point numbers

One member function of the ios class, the **setf()** function, takes arguments to set the bits of cout. Like any member function, setf() is called by using an object's name, followed by a dot, followed by the function name. The statement `cout.setf(ios::showpos);` causes the bit that forces the display of the plus sign with positive numbers to be turned on. Subsequent output will show a + with positive values. Another member function, **unsetf(),** can be used to deselect the bit:

```
cout.unsetf(ios::showpos);
```

You may also combine format flags using the bitwise OR operator (|). The statements

```
cout.setf(ios::showpos | ios::dec | ios::showpoint);
cout<<4.0;
```

produce output that is signed, in base 10 format, and with six decimal places. The output is +4.000000.

You can change the output field width with the **width()** member function.

```
cout.width(5);
cout<<13;
```

The preceding code produces three blanks followed by 13, for a total output of five characters. The width() function applies only to the first subsequent field to be output. As a result, you must call it each time you want a width specification to take effect. For example,

```
int x;
cout.width(10);
for(x = 0; x <3; ++x)
   cout<<20<<endl;
for(x = 0; x<3; ++x)
   {
      cout.width(10);
      cout<<33<<endl;
   }
```

produces the output shown in Figure 8-3. The first 20 is displayed in a field of size 10, but the next two 20s are not, because width() was not called again. The 33s are all displayed in fields of 10 because the width() function is called prior to each output.

Figure 8-3: Demonstration of width() function

One problem you may encounter when using cout with floating-point numbers relates to the loss of desired decimal positions. For example, when a C++ program executes a statement like cout<<12.5432;, the output appears as 12.5432. Of course, that format is absolutely correct mathematically, but you may want output to appear differently. The **precision**() member function allows you to control the number of positions displayed. For example,

```
cout.precision(4);
cout<<12.5432;
```

produces 12.54 for output. No more than four positions are displayed (though fewer may be if that is all that is required to represent the value). Unlike the width() function, the precision() function applies to all subsequent output fields until the precision is reset.

Manipulator Functions

The code to produce output in the desired format using the ostream member functions can become quite tedious to write. For example, if you need to produce a list of figures in currency format (with a dollar sign, in base 10), in a field of size eight, you could code the following before outputting the actual dollar figure that you wish to display:

```
cout<<'$';
cout.setf(ios::dec | ios::showpoint);
cout.width(8);
cout<<amountMoney<<endl; // the figure is finally output
```

You can code manipulators for cin as well as cout, but the need is not as great.

The amountMoney variable would display with a dollar sign in base 10 in a field of eight. At least the first statement, `cout<<'$';`, and the last statement, `cout.width(8);`, would have to be executed again before the next dollar figure was displayed using the same format.

Not only are a lot of statements needed to obtain the correct format, but nothing in the final cout statement indicates that amountMoney will display in any particular format. If the program is revised and new statements are added between the several cout calls, it will become difficult to see just how amountMoney will look on output.

If you create a manipulator function, the desired results become much clearer. A **manipulator function** is used to manipulate, or change, the state of the cout object. Any output manipulator function you create should take as an argument an instance of ostream as a reference. It should return the same input argument. This approach allows manipulators to be chained or stacked with other calls to the cout insertion operator.

For example, a manipulator to format output as currency might be written as follows:

The manipulator function currency is not a member function of the ostream class. It is a separate global function.

```
ostream& currency(ostream &s)
  {
     cout<<'$';
     cout.setf(ios::dec |ios::showpoint);
     cout.width(8);
     return s;
  }
```

Once this function has been written, the statement

```
cout<<currency<<amountMoney;
```

displays amountMoney with a dollar sign in base 10 in a field of size eight. The new code is cleaner and clearer; the display format is part of the cout statement that contains the data variable.

Some manipulators are so useful that they are already coded and placed in libraries included with your C++ compiler. You have already used endl to output a newline character and flush the output stream. In addition, C++ provides you with a **flush** operator to flush the stream without sending a newline character, and an **ends** operator to send a null (or space) character rather than a newline.

The **setprecision()** manipulator allows you to specify the number of decimals that will print. To use setprecision(), you must include the IOMANIP.H file in your program. For example, the following code segment,

```
#include<iostream.h>
#include<iomanip.h>
void main()
  {
     cout<<setprecision(2)<<0.888<<endl;
     cout<<setprecision(5)<<34.65479<<endl:
  }
```

produces the figures 0.89 and 34.655 as output. The figures are rounded to two and three decimal places respectively. The setprecision() manipulator doesn't perform any functions that the cout.precision() member function can't accomplish, but the statement that actually outputs the data includes the precision, and the code is clearer.

The **setw()** function allows you to set the width of a field for output. Use of this function also requires the inclusion of the iomanip.h file. The following code produces output consisting of four spaces and the digit 8, because 8 is printed in a field five positions wide and numbers are automatically right-justified within their field:

```
cout<<setw(5);
cout<<8;
```

Similarly, the following code produces the letter G preceded by nine spaces.

```
cout<<setw(10);
cout<<'G';
```

tip

C++ will print six decimal places if you do not explicitly set a precision for output.

tip

Any C++ manipulator that takes an argument requires the inclusion of the IOMANIP.H file.

tip

With many compilers, if you include the iomanip.h file, you don't have to include the iostream.h file because iomanip.h also includes iostream.h.

tip

The setprecision manipulator is not defined for all compilers.

tip

If the parameter sent to setw() is too small, as in cout<<setw(3)<<5467;, then the width is simply ignored. Instead, the entire correct value is output.

As you might guess, setw() actually uses the member function cout.width(). Just as with the width() function, after setw() is inserted into the stream, C++ resets the field size. You must repeat setw() for each new output, even if you are using only one cout object. For example, cout<<'X'<<setw(5)<<2<<13<<299; produces

```
X     213299
```

That is, the width of 5 remains in effect only for the first output value. On the other hand, cout<<'X'<<setw(5)<<2<<setw(5)<<13<<setw(5)<<299; produces

```
X     2    13   299
```

Two additional manipulators, **setiosflags()** and **resetiosflags()**, perform several manipulations each, depending on the flags they receive as arguments (such as ios::dec or ios::showpoint). The setiosflags() manipulator turns on bit codes for the attributes named as arguments; the resetiosflags() manipulator turns those bit codes off. As with other manipulators, the advantage of using setiosflags() and resetiosflags() relates to their ability to be placed in a cout statement chain as opposed to using a cout.setf() member function call prior to actual data output. As with setf(), the bitwise or operator (|) can be used with setiosflags() or resetiosflags(), as in

```
cout<<setw(7)<<setiosflags( ios::hex | ios::left)<<24;
```

This code displays output left-aligned in a field of size seven, in hexadecimal format.

Adults are used to reading and writing fractions as two integers separated by a slash—for example, 6/7. When children first learn about fractions, however, they usually write the fractions with the numerator directly above a horizontal line, which appears directly above the denominator. In the following steps, you will create a fracForm manipulator that formats numbers for display in this manner.

1   Open the **FRAC7.CPP** file that you created in Tutorial 7, or the similar **FRACTION.CPP** file found in the TUT08 folder. Each of these files contains a definition for the Fraction class, including the constructors that were subsequently removed in Tutorial 7 for demonstration purposes.

2   To the public declaration section of the Fraction class, add prototypes for two new member functions. These simple functions will be used only to access the private numerator and denominator:

```
int getNum(void);
int getDenom(void);
```

3   Add the functions to the implementation section. The only task of each function is to return the integer value.

```
int Fraction::getNum(void)
  {
    return(Fraction::numerator);
  }
int Fraction::getDenom(void)
  {
    return(Fraction::denominator);
  }
```

4   Save the file as **FRAC8.CPP**.
5   Open the **FRACFILE.CPP** program that currently greets the student.
6   After the **IOSTREAM.H** include statement, add

```
#include"frac8.cpp"
```

7   After the include statements, add a global manipulator function that will format either the numerator or the denominator of a fraction so it is right-aligned in a field of size 5:

```
ostream& fracForm(ostream &strm)
  {
   cout.setf(ios::right);
   cout.width(5);
   return strm;
  }
```

8   At the end of the main() program after the input of the student name, ask the user to input a numerator and denominator, and display the fraction in reduced form with the numerator directly over and right-aligned with the denominator:

```
Fraction aFrac;
cin>>aFrac;
cout<<endl<<endl;
cout<<fracForm<<aFrac.getNum()<<endl;
cout<<" ---"<<endl;  // two spaces and three dashes
cout<<fracForm<<aFrac.getDenom()<<endl;
```

9   Compile and test the program. Run it several times, confirming that fractions with numerators and denominators of varying sizes (such as 1/100) display correctly.

10   Modify the program so it can display several fractions in sequence by changing the single aFrac to an array of Fractions. Remove the `Fraction aFrac;` declaration and replace it with

```
const numFracs = 5;
Fraction frac[numFracs];
```

11   Immediately after the array declaration, begin a for loop:

```
for(int x = 0; x < numFracs; ++x)
{
```

12   Replace each instance of aFrac with `frac[x]`. Three such instances appear in the program—in the cin statement, with the getNum() function, and with the getDenom() function.

13   Add a final curly bracket to end the for loop just before the closing curly bracket of the program.

14   Compile and test the program. You are allowed to perform data entry for five fractions.

15   Save the program as **FRACFORM.CPP**.

tip

....

▶ **Older C++ compilers may not support the use of omanip.**

Creating your own manipulator involves writing a function. Creating one that takes an argument involves writing two functions. When you use a manipulator that requires no argument, such as endl or the currency manipulator developed above, the address of the output or input stream is passed to the function. With manipulators that take an argument, such as setw(), both the address of the stream and the argument itself must be passed to a function. This task is handled by **omanip**, which is defined in the file iomanip.h.

For example, to create a currency manipulator to which a variable field width may be passed, you may write the following code:

```
ostream& curren(ostream &s, int fieldSize)
{
    cout<<'$';
    cout.setf(ios::dec |ios::showpoint);
    cout.width(fieldSize);
    return s;
}
omanip<int> currency(int fieldSize)
{
    return omanip<int>(curren, fieldSize);
}
```

tip

The function omanip is actually a class template function. Template creation is the subject of Tutorial 9.

Once this function has been written, a statement such as

```
cout<<currency(7)<<12.45;
```

calls the currency function. This function actually overloads the insertion operator to take both the address of the curren() function and the passed field size. The result is output formatted with a dollar sign in a field of whatever size was passed to currency().

S U M M A R Y

- cout and cin are C++ objects, which means that they are members of a class.
- The iostream.h file contains the definition for a derived class named iostream. The grandparent base class from which iostream is derived is named ios. Two classes that are derived from ios are istream and ostream.
- The istream class handles input and includes a definition of the extraction operator >>. The extraction operator is actually an overloaded function named operator>>().
- The ostream class handles output and includes a definition of the insertion operator <<.
- The get() function is a member of the istream class. One prototype for this function takes the form `istream& get(char &c);`. (Other prototypes are available as well.)
- Most compilers overload get() so that, in addition to taking a character reference as an argument, it also can take no argument. This form of the function often is used when it doesn't matter which character is extracted and the character does not need to be stored.
- The get() function is also overloaded so that it can take two or three arguments. This form allows you to input a string of characters.

■ The getline() function reads a line of text at the address of its first argument until it reaches either the length used as the second argument or the character used as the third argument.

■ C++ instantiates three ostream objects. Besides cout, which is associated with the standard output device (usually a monitor), C++ includes cerr and clog, which are used for error conditions.

■ Many of the states of the cout object are contained in a single long integer field, in which each bit represents some condition of the cout object.

■ The arguments that determine the state of the cout object are called format flags; they begin with the ios:: operator. Some commonly used format flags are ios::left, ios::right, ios::dec, ios::hex, ios::oct, ios::showpos, and ios::showpoint.

■ The setf() function, a member of the ios class, takes arguments to set the bits of cout. Another member function, unsetf(), can be used to deselect bits.

■ You can combine format flags using the bitwise OR operator (|).

■ You can change output field width using the width() member function, which must be called prior to each output for which a width setting is desired.

■ The precision() member function allows you to control the number of digits of precision displayed.

■ A manipulator function is used to manipulate, or change, the state of the cout object.

■ Any output manipulator function you create should take as an argument an instance of ostream as a reference and should return the same input argument.

■ C++ provides you with endl, flush, and ends manipulators.

■ The setprecision() manipulator allows you to specify the number of decimals that should print. To use setprecision(), you must include the IOMANIP.H file in your program.

■ The setw() function allows you to set the width of a field for output. After setw() is inserted into the stream, C++ resets the field size; as a result, you must repeat setw() for each new output.

■ Two additional manipulators, setiosflags() and resetiosflags(), perform several manipulations each, turning bits on or off depending on the flags used as arguments with them (such as ios::dec or ios::showpoint).

Q U E S T I O N S

1. Which of the following is a C++ object?
   a. >>
   b. read()
   c. cin
   d. iostream

2. Which of the following is a C++ class?
   a. >>
   b. read()
   c. cin
   d. iostream

3. Which of the following is true?
   a. iostream is derived from istream.
   b. istream is derived from ostream.
   c. ostream is derived from iostream.
   d. ostream is derived from istream.

4. The extraction operator >> is a(n) _____.
   a. overloaded function
   b. C++ class
   c. C++ object
   d. static reference variable

5. The get() function returns _____.
   a. a character
   b. void
   c. a reference to the object that invoked it
   d. a copy of the object that invoked it

6. The statement `get();` _____.
   a. reads from a file
   b. accepts a keyboard character
   c. accepts a keyboard character and stores it
   d. is illegal

7. The statement `cin.get(itemName,20);` _____.
   a. will accept as many as 19 characters
   b. requires you to enter exactly 19 characters
   c. requires you to enter at least 19 characters
   d. requires you to enter "19"

8. The getline() function reads a line of text until _____.
   a. the length used as the second argument is reached
   b. the character used as the third argument is reached
   c. either (a) or (b)
   d. neither (a) nor (b)

9. If you don't supply a third argument to getline(), the line-ending character is _____.
   a. '\n'
   b. '\0'
   c. endl
   d. flush

10. The arguments that determine the state of the cout object are called _____.
   a. classes
   b. manipulators
   c. format flags
   d. state controllers

11. The function that takes arguments to set the bits of cout is _____.
   a. setf()
   b. bitset()
   c. ios()
   d. flag()

12. Format flags may be combined using _____.
   a. the bitwise OR operator (|)
   b. the logical OR operator (||)
   c. the bitwise AND operator (&)
   d. the logical AND operator (&&)

13. The code `cout<<'X'<<cout.width(5)<<3<<4;` produces _____.
   a. X3 4
   b. X 34
   c. X 3 4
   d. X34

14. The code cout<<setprecision(1)<<2.222<<3.333; produces _____.
    a. 2.2223.333
    b. 2.23.333
    c. 2.23.3
    d. 23

15. A function that changes the state of the cout object is called a(n) _____.
    a. member
    b. adjuster
    c. manipulator
    d. operator

16. Any output manipulator function you create _____.
    a. should take as an argument an instance of ostream as a reference
    b. should return void
    c. must be a member function of the ostream class
    d. must inherit ostream

17. The functions setw() and setprecision() are _____.
    a. member functions
    b. virtual functions
    c. manipulators
    d. overloaded

18. The biggest advantage of manipulators is _____.
    a. shorter code
    b. faster compile time
    c. all manipulaters are already coded
    d. clarity of intention

E X E R C I S E S

1. Write a program that allows you to input the names of 40 friends. Display the names 15 at a time, pausing to let the user press a key before the list continues.

2. Write a program that allows you to enter 10 floating-point values into an array, and then displays each of them to an accuracy of three positions.

3. Write a program that allows you to enter 10 floating-point values into an array. The program then prompts you for the desired precision. It subsequently displays each value to the correct precision.

4. Write a program that allows you to enter 10 item stock numbers, descriptions, and prices. Display all the data in report form—that is, aligned correctly in columns.

LESSON B
o b j e c t i v e s

In this lesson you will learn:

- How to create simple file output
- How to read in simple data from a file
- How to write objects to a file
- How to read in objects from a file

File Output and Input

Simple File Output

You have used a descendant of the ios class, ostream, and its descendant iostream to produce all sorts of screen output. In C++, when you write to a file rather than the screen, you use a class named **fstream**, which, like ostream, is ultimately derived from ios. Figure 8-4 shows the relationship between fstream and some other input and output classes.

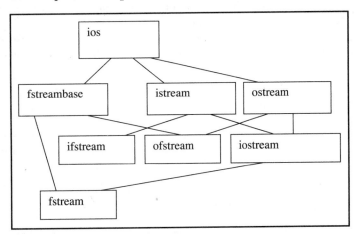

Figure 8-4: fstream's family tree

The fstream class is defined in the fstream.h file, which must be included in any C++ program that writes to or reads from a disk. Figure 8-4 shows that fstream inherits from iostream and its ancestors; therefore you can use the manipulators that work with screen output for file output as well.

When you want to perform standard screen output, you use cout, an object that is a member of the ostream class that has already been instantiated. To perform file output, you must instantiate your own member of the ofstream class. The reason an object has not already been instantiated for you is because programs use only one standard output device but often more than one output file. You will need to create an object with a unique name for each file.

You instantiate an ostream output file object as you do any other object—by calling its constructor. When you call an ofstream constructor, you can use a filename as an argument. The constructor will then open the file. For example,

When you write a program that has both file and screen output, just include fstream.h. As a subclass, it automatically includes iostream.h.

```
ofstream outFile("data.txt");
```

instantiates an object named outFile that is a member of the ofstream class.

tip

••••••••••••••••

▶ You may also use a complete path name in the outFile constructor or with the open function. As the backslash character is also the escape character, you should use two backslashes in any path names, such as

"c:\\newdata\\data.txt"

tip

••••••••••••••••

▶ Don't think your program's internal name for the file object, such as outFile, is stored on the disk. The disk file is recognized only by the filename passed to your object's constructor.

The filename "data.txt" is passed to the constructor, which opens the file on the disk; you do not need a special "open file" statement, as many other programming languages require. When the constructor is called, if the file does not exist, it is created. If the file already exists, it is overwritten. The name outFile is then used within the program in the same way as any other object.

If you don't provide a filename as an argument when you instantiate an ofstream object, then no file is opened. You can explicitly open the file later with the **open()** member function, as in

```
ofstream outFile;
outFile.open("data.txt");
```

Whether you open a file with the constructor or with an explicit open() call, you may add a second argument after the filename to indicate file modes. For example,

- ios::app means append the file (rather than recreate it)
- ios::ate means position the file pointer at the end of the file (rather than at the beginning)
- ios::nocreate means the file must exist, otherwise the open fails
- ios::noreplace means the file must not exist, otherwise the open fails

You can check whether either an explicit open() or a constructor open has failed in several ways. If, for example, you try to open a file named data.dat as nocreate,

```
ofstream out("data.dat",ios::nocreate);
```

you might choose to implement any of the following equivalent tests:

```
if(out)
  cout<<"File opened!";
if(out.good())
  cout<<"File opened!";
if(!out.fail())
  cout<<"File opened!";
```

In other words, the values of out and out.good() will both be non-zero (or true) if the file was opened successfully; the value of out.fail() will be non-zero if the file was not opened successfully. The opposite condition can be tested with any of the following:

```
if(!out)
  cout<<"Open didn't work.";
if(!out.good())
  cout<<"Open didn't work.";
if(out.fail())
  cout<<"Open didn't work.";
```

Because you can use the overloaded insertion operator within the ofstream class, once the file is open, you can write to it with a statement such as the following:

```
out<<"This is going to the disk";
```

After you have written to a file, you do not need to explicitly execute any sort of "close file" statement, as you do in many other languages. Instead, whenever your ofstream object goes out of scope, as with any other object, a destructor is called. In this case, ofstream's destructor closes the file for you. If you want to close a file before the file object goes out of scope, however, you may use the **close()** function. For example,

```
out.close();
```

In addition, you can explicitly call the file object's destructor, and the file will be closed.

```
out.~ofstream();
```

Simple File Input

To read a file from within a program, you can create an object that is an instantiation of the ifstream class. As with ofstream, when you declare an ifstream object, you pass a filename to the object's constructor and the file opens:

```
ifstream someData("data.txt");
```

tip

Many file modes, such as ios::ate, may be used as arguments to ifstream constructors or open() statements just as they are with ofstream objects. Tests such as if(someData.good())… are allowed as well.

The name of the ifstream object you instantiate can be any legal C++ identifier. It certainly does not have to be the same name as that of any ostream object employed to create the file. The file is identified by the filename used as a parameter to the ifstream object's constructor, *not* by the name of the ifstream object.

The ifstream class uses the get() member function to access file data. Therefore, if someData has been instantiated as an ifstream object, then a character may be read from a disk file with the following code:

```
char aChar;
someData.get(aChar);
```

tip

· · · · · · · · · · · · · · · · · ·

▶ The end of file condition
may also be determined
by testing the return values of someData.eof(),
someData.bad(),
someData.fail(), or
someData.good().

The ifstream class returns a 0 when it reaches the end of file, so an entire file can be read in and displayed on the screen, one character at a time, with the following code:

```
while(someData)
 {
  someData.get(aChar);  // read in a character
  cout<<aChar;  // display character on screen
 }
```

As with ofstream objects, when an ifstream object goes out of scope, the file is closed automatically.

If the input file you are using is organized so that records are separated by new-line characters, then you can use the getline() member function to read input data. This function reads in data until a newline is encountered, discarding the newline character. For example, if customer ID numbers and names have been stored on a file named PEOPLE.DAT, one record per line, 40 characters per record, the file might appear as in Figure 8-5 and be read in with the program that follows.

```
389Weiss      Janice
412Adamson    Richard
890Hernandez  Maria
```

Figure 8-5: Sample PEOPLE.DAT file

```
#include<fstream.h>
void main()
  {
    char recordIn[40];  // to hold record
    ifstream fileIn("people.dat");
      // instantiates and opens
    while(fileIn)           // while not end of file
      {
        fileIn.getline(recordIn,40);   // get an entire record
          // up to 40 characters or newline, whichever comes first
        cout<<recordIn<<endl;   // display record on screen
      }
  }
```

File Output with Objects

The use of the ofstream class's overloaded insertion operator to write characters and strings to files is simple and intuitive. It makes sense, however, that you should also be able to write objects to disk files in object-oriented programs. The **write**() function allows you to do just that.

Assume you have declared a Customer class as follows, with three data members and a data entry function:

```cpp
#include<fstream.h>
#include<iomanip.h>
class Customer
  {
    private:
      int idNum;
      char last[11];
      char first[11];
    public:
      void enterData(void);
      void displayData(void);
  };
void Customer::enterData(void)
  {
    cout<<"ID number ";
    cin>> Customer::idNum;
    cin.get();
    cout<<"Last name ";
    cin.getline(Customer::last,10);
    cout<<"First name ";
    cin.getline(Customer::first,10);
  }
void Customer::displayData(void)
  {
    cout<<setiosflags(ios::left)<<setw(5)<<Customer::idNum;
    cout<<Customer::last<<", "<<Customer::first<<endl;
  }
```

You can create an array of customer objects, perform the data entry required for the Customers, and write the output to a disk. The prototype for write() is

```cpp
ostream& write(char *c, int length);
```

You performed a cast in Tutorial 3 when you ensured that the integer numerator was converted to a double before determining the floating point value.

The arguments for write() consist of a pointer to a character and an integer. The character pointer points to the address of the argument being written to the disk. If this argument is not a character—for example, if it is a Customer object—then you must perform a cast on the address of the object to convert it to character. The second argument to write() represents the size of the object being written. Therefore, when you call write() to write an object to a file, the general format of the statement is

```
outputObject.write((char*)(&object), sizeof(object));
```

A main() program that performs data entry for five customers and writes the data to a disk file can be written as follows:

```
void main()
{
  const num = 5;
  Customer custs[num];   // declare five Customers
  ofstream dataFile("people.dat");
  for(int x = 0; x<num; ++x)
  {
    custs[x].enterData();
    dataFile.write((char*)(&custs[x]), sizeof(custs[x]));
  }
}
```

This program executes a for loop num times, performing data entry and writing to the file each time. Alternatively, you might fill the array with data, and then write the entire array to the file with a single write() call. To accomplish this goal, simply move the call to the write() function outside and after the for loop, and change the two references to custs objects (custs[x]) in the statement to references to the entire array (custs).

```
void main()
  {
    const num = 5;
    Customer custs[num];   // declare five Customers
    ofstream dataFile("people.dat");
    for(int x = 0; x<num; ++x)
      {
        custs[x].enterData();
      }
    dataFile.write((char*)(&custs), sizeof(custs));
      // use the array named custs
  }
```

You will now add some steps to the FRACFORM.CPP program you began to develop in Lesson A of this tutorial. In addition to greeting the student and allowing him or her to enter numerators and denominators, the program will now create a disk file containing the fractions that the student has created. This disk file could be used by the teacher to review what the student is doing or by the student at a later date within more sophisticated fraction applications.

1   Open the **FRACFORM.CPP** file.
2   Because this program will write to a disk file, change the statement `#include<iostream.h>` to `#include<fstream.h>`.
3   Within the main() function, prior to the beginning of the for loop, instantiate an output file object:

```
ofstream out("stufrac.dat");
  // you may add a file path if desired
```

4   Just after the Fraction display statements within the for loop and inside the closing bracket of the for loop, add the statement that will write each Fraction object to the file:

```
out.write((char*)(&frac[x]), sizeof(frac[x]));
```

5   Compile and test the program. The screen display should not be changed, but a disk file is created.
6   Save the program as **FRACOUT.CPP**.

File Input with Objects

You have used the getline() function with ifstream objects to read in a line of text. If the line of text actually represented a data record containing values such as customer ID numbers and names, it then would take several lines of code to distinguish the individual fields and place the data into appropriate variables. It would be more convenient to read a data file directly into an array of class objects. You can accomplish this goal with the **read**() function.

The read() function prototype is very similar to the prototype for the write() function:

```
istream &read(char *, int length);
```

The read() function requires a pointer to a character, so you must perform a cast when you read an object. It also requires the size of the object being read. To read a Customer class object named custs into an inFile ifstream object, you would write

```
inFile.read((char*)&custs, sizeof(custs));
```

The following program reads in Customer data from a file named PEOPLE.DAT and displays each record on the screen.

```
void main()
{
 const num = 5;
 Customer custs[num];   // declare five Customers
 ifstream dataFile("people.dat");
 for(int x = 0; x<num; ++x)
  {
    dataFile.read((char*)(&custs[x]), sizeof(custs[x]));
    custs[x].displayData();
  }
}
```

This program executes a for loop *num* times, reading and displaying one Customer object with each pass through the loop. Alternatively, you can perform one read for the entire array, and then loop to display the array elements.

```
void main()
  {
    const num = 5;
    Customer custs[num];  // declare five Customers
    ifstream dataFile("people.dat");
    dataFile.read((char*)(&custs), sizeof(custs));
      // use the array named custs
    for(int x = 0; x<num; ++x)
      {
        custs[x].displayData();
      }
  }
```

In the following steps, you will write a new program to display the fractions saved to the **STUFRAC.DAT** disk file in the **FRACOUT.CPP** program.

1 Open a new file and enter the following include statements:

```
#include<fstream.h>
#include"frac8.cpp"
```

2 Write a program that will read in the entire array of fractions from the **STUFRAC.DAT** file and display them.

```
void main()
  {
    const numFracs = 5;
    Fraction frac[numFracs];
    ifstream in("stufrac.dat");  // add a path if needed
    in.read((char*)(&frac), sizeof(frac));
    cout<<"The fractions this student created today are:"
      <<endl;
    for(int x = 0; x <numFracs; ++x)
      {
        cout<<frac[x]<<endl;
      }
  }
```

3 Compile and test the program. Output should be similar to Figure 8-6 although, of course, your actual fraction values may differ.

```
The fractions this student created today are:
1/2
3/4
7/8
1/3
2/9
```

Figure 8-6: Sample run of FRACOUT.CPP

4 Save the program as **FRACIN.CPP**.

S U M M A R Y

- In C++, when you write to a file rather than the screen, you use a class named fstream, whose base class is ios and is defined in the file fstream.h.
- To perform file output, you instantiate a member of the ofstream class.
- You instantiate an ostream output file object by calling its constructor, optionally using a filename as an argument. If you use a filename, the constructor opens the file.
- You can explicitly open a file with the open() member function.
- You may add a second argument after the filename in either a constructor or an open() function to indicate file modes. Possible modes include ios::app, ios::ate, ios::nocreate, and ios::noreplace.
- You can check whether either an explicit open() or a constructor open has failed by using the object name; alternatively, you can employ the good() or fail() member functions.
- You can close a file by letting the object go out of scope, using the close() function, or calling the object's destructor.
- To read a file from within a program, you can create an object that is an instantiation of the ifstream class.
- The ifstream class uses the get() member function to access file data.
- As with ofstream objects, an ifstream file object can be opened by calling its constructor or using the open() function. Likewise, an ifstream object file can be closed by using close(), letting it out of scope, or calling the destructor.
- The write() function can be used to write to a file; the read() function is called to read from a file. Arguments for each function consist of a pointer to a character and an integer. The character pointer points to the address of the argument being written to the disk. The integer represents the size of the object being written.
- With either a read() or a write() function, either a single object or an array of objects may be manipulated with a single function call.

Q U E S T I O N S

1. When you write to a file rather than the screen, you use the C++ class _____.
   a. iostream   c. fstream
   b. filed.   d. diskclass

2. When you want to perform file output, you use _____.
   a. an object that has already been instantiated
   b. an object you instantiate
   c. either (a) or (b)
   d. neither (a) nor (b)

3. When you instantiate an ofstream output file object, you _____.
   a. call its constructor   c. must give the filename an extension
   b. must give the file a name   d. must not give the file a name

4. If you use a filename as an argument when calling an ofstream constructor, _____.
   a. the file opens
   b. the file is appended
   c. a prompt asks if you want to open the file for input or output
   d. you receive an error message

5. If you don't provide a filename as an argument when you instantiate an ofstream object, then _____.
   a. the file can never be opened   c. no file opens at the time
   b. the file can never be opened for output   d. you receive an error message

6. You can explicitly open a file with _____.
   a. the open manipulator
   b. the open() member function
   c. the operator open
   d. you cannot explicitly open a file in C++

7. Which of the following is NOT a mode in which you can open a file?
   a. ios::app   c. ios::close
   b. ios::noreplace   d. ios::nocreate

8. In the statement `if(X) cout<<"File opened!";`, X must be a _____.
   a. filename   c. stream object
   b. stream manipulator   d. class

9. Which statement is equivalent to out.good()?
   a. out   c. !out
   b. out.fail()   d. out.open()

10. Which statement is NOT equivalent to out.good()?
    a. out   c. out.fail()
    b. !out.good()   d. none of the above

11. You can close a file object _____.
    a. with the close() function   c. by calling its destructor
    b. by letting it go out of scope   d. all of the above

12. If you instantiate an object with the statement `ifstream items("c:inven.txt");`, then the file on the disk is identified by the name _____.

a. items
c. either (a) or (b)

b. inven.txt
d. neither (a) nor (b)

13. The getline() function reads until _____.

a. whitespace is encountered

b. end of file is encountered

c. a newline is encountered, discarding the newline character

d. a newline is encountered, retaining the newline character

14. To write an object to a disk file, you can use _____.

a. get()
c. out()

b. write()
d. getline()

15. When you use the read() or write() functions with objects, you usually must _____.

a. use both in the same program

b. not use both in the same program

c. ensure that the same program does not include screen output or keyboard input

d. perform a cast on the address of the object to be input or output

16. The arguments needed by read() and write() are _____.

a. a pointer and an integer

b. a character and a float

c. a pointer, a string, and an object reference

d. a stream reference

17. If you create an array of objects, the write() function can work with _____.

a. one object at a time
c. either (a) or (b)

b. the entire array of objects at once
d. neither (a) nor (b)

18. If you create an array of objects, the read() function can work with _____.

a. one object at a time
c. either (a) or (b)

b. the entire array of objects at once
d. neither (a) nor (b)

E X E R C I S E S

1. Write a program that lets you enter a five-line limerick and save it in a file. Write another program that reads the file and displays the limerick on the screen.

debugging ▶

2. Create a class for books. Data members include the book's title, author, price, and number of pages. Member functions include data entry and display functions. Create an array of 10 book objects. Write data about all of the books to a disk file.

3. Write a program that reads the disk file created in exercise 2 and displays book data to the screen.

4. Modify exercise 3 to prompt the user for a minimum page number. Display only books with that number of pages or greater.

5. Each of the following files in the TUT08 folder has syntax and/or logical errors. Determine the problem in each case, and fix the program.

a. DEBUG8-1.CPP

b. DEBUG8-2.CPP

c. DEBUG8-3.CPP

d. DEBUG8-4.CPP

Templates

case ▶ "Since I've been working at Teacher's Pet Educational Software," you tell your supervisor, Audrey Burns, "I've been reading a few books on educational theory. They all seem to agree that positive reinforcement is important."

"Why don't you include some positive messages in the programs you're working on?" Audrey asks. "When the student gets a problem right, you could display a message of congratulations on the screen."

"Good idea," you say. "I think I'll create a function to display the right answer and a message. But some problems have answers that are fractions, and some have answers that are floating-point numbers. We may even develop a multiple-choice test where the answers are letters. I don't have time to write separate functions for all those tasks."

"What you need," Audrey says, "are template functions."

Previewing the TEMPFUNC.CPP Program

1 Load the **TEMPFUNC.CPP** program that is located in the TUT09 folder. You may wish to change the path in the #include "frac9.cpp" statement. You may also be required to comment out the sleep(1) statement if your compiler does not recognize it.

2 Compile and run the program. You will be asked for the answers to three simple arithmetic problems. For each one you solve correctly, you will receive 20 congratulatory messages.

3 Examine the code. Notice that the same function displays the answer, whether it is an integer, a double, or a Fraction object. You will be creating similar code in this tutorial.

In this lesson you will learn:

- How to create template functions
- How to use multiple parameters in a template function
- How to overload template functions
- How to use more than one type in a template function
- How to explicitly specify the type in a template function
- How to use template functions with class objects

Template Functions

Creating Template Functions

The concepts involved in the use of variables are basic to all programming languages. In all cases, it is the use of variable names that make programming worthwhile. When you label a computer memory location with a variable name like employeeSalary, you are aware that employeeSalary may contain hundreds or thousands of unique values during each execution of the program that declares it.

Similarly, creating functions within programs is helpful because functions can operate on any values passed to them (as long as the values are of the correct type). A function that is prototyped as `void compute(int num);` may receive any integer value—whether it is a constant (like 15) or a value stored in another integer variable in the calling function (which could also be called num, though it need not have this name). The compute() function may be called dozens of times from various locations in a program, and it may receive dozens of different integer values. Each integer value, however, will have the name num within the compute() function.

In previous tutorials, you have created many functions that included a wide variety of types in their argument lists. Not only have you used scalar types like int, double, and char in function argument lists, but you have also passed programmer-created class objects to functions. In each case, the function's argument types have been determined at the time that the function was created and compiled. Once the function was created, the argument types remained fixed.

You have also learned that you can overload a function so that it accepts different argument lists. Overloading involves writing two or more functions with the same name but different argument lists. It allows you to employ polymorphism, using a consistent message that acts appropriately with different objects. For example, you might want to create several functions named reverse(). A reverse() function might change the sign of a number if a numeric variable is passed to it, reverse the order of characters in a string if a string is passed to it, set a code for a collect call if a PhoneCall class object is passed to it, or issue a refund to a customer if a Customer class object is passed to it. Because "reverse" makes sense in each of these instances, and because such diverse tasks are needed for the four cases of reverse(), overloading is a useful and appropriate tool.

Sometimes the tasks required are not so diverse, however, and overloading requires a lot of unnecessary, tedious coding. For example, assume you need a very simple function named reverse() that reverses the sign of a number. You might write several overloaded functions with different argument lists so that the function could work with integers, doubles, or floats:

```
int reverse(int x)
  {
    return (-x);
  }
double reverse(double x)
  {
    return (-x);
  }
float reverse(float x)
  {
    return (-x);
  }
```

The function bodies are identical. Because these functions differ only in the type involved, you could write just one function with a variable name standing in for the type, as in the following:

```
// it would be nice if it was this simple,
// if variableType could stand in for any type
// but it won't work like this -- it's not a template yet
variableType reverse(variableType x)
  {
    return (-x);
  }
```

A group of functions that is generated from the same template is often called a **family** of functions.

C++ also allows you to define **macros**, which permit generic substitution. Macros are seldom recommended, however, because no type checking is performed (unlike with a template). Object-oriented C++ programmers rarely use macros.

C++ lets you create functions that use variable types, called template functions. **Template functions** allow you to write a single function that serves as an outline, or template, for a group of functions that differ in the types of parameters they use.

In a template function, at least one argument is **generic,** or **parameterized.** If you write a template function for reverse(), for example, a user can invoke the function using any type for the parameter, as long as negating the value with a unary minus makes sense and is defined for that type. Thus, if an integer argument is passed to reverse(), it will return a negative integer; if a double argument is passed, the function will return a negative double.

Before coding a template function, you must include a **template definition** with the following information:

■ the keyword `template`
■ a left angle bracket (<)
■ a list of generic types, separated with commas if more than one type is needed
■ a right angle bracket (>)

Each generic type in the list of generic types has two parts:

- the keyword `class`
- an identifier that represents the generic type

For example, the template definition for the reverse() function can be written

```
template <class T>
 // T stands for any type -- simple or programmer-defined
```

tip

Although any legal C++ identifier may be used for the type in the template function, many programmers prefer T (for Template).

The entire function is

```
template<class T>
// T stands for any type -- simple or programmer-defined
T reverse(T x)
   {
     return(-x);
   }
```

tip

For clarity, some newer C++ compilers (like Borland 5.0) also allow you to replace class with typename in the template definition. This substitution makes sense because the template is creating a new typename.

The template keyword `class` does not necessarily mean that T will stand for a programmer-created class type, but it may. Despite the `class` keyword, T can represent a simple scalar type like int. T is simply a placeholder for the type that will be used at each location in the function definition where T appears.

When you call a template function, as in

```
double amount = -9.86;
reverse(amount);
```

tip

You can't place the function definition and the function code in separate files because the function can't be compiled into object format without knowing the types, and the function won't "know" that it needs to recognize the types without the template definition.

the compiler determines the type of the actual argument passed to the function (in this case, a double). It then substitutes that type for the generic type in the template function, creating or instantiating a **generated function** that uses the appropriate type. The compiler generates code for as many different functions as it needs, depending on the function calls made.

In this case, the generated function is

```
double reverse(double x)
   {
     return(-x);
   }
```

Function templates are placed at the start of a program, in the global area above the main() function. Alternatively, you may place them in a separate file, which is included in your program with `#include` placed at the top of the program. In either case, the definition of the template function and the template function itself must reside in the same source file.

In the following steps, you will create a template function that will display a correct answer and a congratulatory message when a student guesses the correct answer to a problem. The function will be used whether the problem needs an integer, float, double, or character answer.

1 Open a new file. Enter the needed include statements for this program:

```
#include<iostream.h>
#include<iomanip.h>
#include<dos.h>  // this one is optional -- see step 3
```

2 Create the template function that will fill a screen with 20 messages. The function will accept an answer and display it in a field size that increases by a size of two with each new line. The result will be a series of cascading messages, each one appearing further to the right as the congratulations proceed down the screen.

```
template<class T>
void fillScreen(T answer)
  {
    int width = 5;      // initial width
    for(int t = 0; t < 20; ++t)   // repeat 20 times
      {
        cout<<setw(width)<<answer;
        cout<<"  Another Teacher's Pet Success"<<endl;
        width = width + 2;
        // increase width by 2 for each successive line
      }
  }
```

The use of setw() was discussed in Tutorial 8.

3 Depending on your processor, this function may operate too quickly for you to truly appreciate the cascading of the messages. You have several ways to slow the output. For example, you can include the DOS.H file at the top of the program and add

```
sleep(1);
```

If your compiler does not support the sleep() function, you will have to use the for loop.

as the last statement inside the for loop. This code will cause a one-second delay between executions of the loop. Alternatively, you might code a do-nothing loop as the last statement inside the for loop:

```
for(int a = 0; a< 1000; ++a)
  for(int b = 0; b<1000; ++b);
```

These statements cause the compiler to loop 1,000,000 times (1000 x 1000) before executing the next cout. You can adjust the number of loops up or down if the time lag seems inappropriate.

4 Write a short main() program to test the function. First, create an integer variable to hold a user's answer. Then ask the user to solve an integer addition problem. If the answer is correct, call the fillScreen() function with an integer argument.

```
void main()
  {
    int iUserAns, iCorrectAns = 11;
    cout<<"What is 4 + 7? ";
    cin>>iUserAns;
    if(iUserAns==iCorrectAns)
      fillScreen(iUserAns);
```

5 Now add code for a floating-point problem.

```
    double dUserAns, dCorrectAns = 5.3;
    cout<<"What is 3.3 + 2? ";
    cin>>dUserAns;
    if(dUserAns == dCorrectAns)
      fillScreen(dUserAns);
  }
```

6 Compile and test the program. When you enter the correct answer to the arithmetic problems, the screen should fill with the congratulatory message whether the answer is an integer or a floating-point number.

7 Save the program as **TEMPLATE.CPP**.

Using Multiple Parameters and Overloading Function Templates

Function templates may have more than one parameter. You might, for example, write a function that compares two arguments and returns the larger of the two. The following template function named larger() accomplishes this task:

```
template<class T>
T larger(T x, T y)
 {
   T big;
   if (x>y)
      big = x;
   else
      big = y;
   return(big);
 }
```

Two parameters are passed to larger(). Within this function, a temporary variable named big is declared. If the first parameter passed to larger(), x, is larger than the second parameter, y, then x is assigned to big; otherwise y is assigned to big. Finally, the value of big is returned. The variables x, y, and big may be of any type, but must all be of the *same* type. The larger() function takes two arguments of type T (whatever type T is). The compiler can create object code for larger(int,int) and larger(double,double), but it will not compile larger(int,double) or larger(double,int).

The following program segment uses the larger() template function to produce the commented results.

```
int a = 7, b = 12;
double  c = 4.5; d = 1.3;
cout<<larger(a,b);  //output is 12
cout<<larger(c,d);  //output is 4.5
cout<<larger(a,c);  //produces an error -- different types
```

You also may overload function templates, as long as each version of the function takes different arguments, allowing the compiler to distinguish between them. For example, you can create an invert() function template that swaps the values of its parameters if it receives two parameters, but reverses the sign if it receives only one parameter:

Different versions of over-loaded template functions do not need to use the same identifier to stand in for the variable type or class. For example, one function could use T while the other might use U.

```
template<class T>
void invert(T &x, T &y)
  {
   T temp;
   temp = x;
   x = y;
   y = temp;
  }
template<class T>
void invert(T &x)
  {
   x = -x;
  }
```

The first invert() function will be generated if invert() is called with two parameters; the second invert() function will be generated if the call includes only one parameter. Note in the code above that the definition `template<class T>` must be repeated before each parameterized function. With the two overloaded functions, this program segment produces the commented results:

```
double d1 = 3.4, d2 = 5.6;
invert(d1);     // d1 becomes -3.4
invert(d1,d2);  // values of d1 and d2 are swapped
```

The option of using multiple types in a template function may not be available on some older C++ compilers.

Using More Than One Type in a Template Function

Of course, many functions use more than one type. To create a template function that employs multiple types, you simply use a unique type identifier for each type.

For example, suppose you wanted to create a firstIsLarger() function that compares values of various types and then prints a message.

The template function in this situation is

It is perfectly legal to include some non-parameterized types in the function argument list, along with the parameterized ones.

```
template <class T, class U>
void firstIsLarger(T val1, U val2)
  {
    if (val1  > val2)
       cout<<"First is larger"<<endl;
    else
       cout<<"First is NOT larger"<<endl;
  }
```

The following program segment produces the commented results:

```
firstIsLarger(2.1,9);      //First is NOT larger
firstIsLarger('A',12);     //First is larger
firstIsLarger('B',88.8);   //First is NOT larger
firstIsLarger(3,-9);       //First is larger
firstIsLarger('y','z');    //First is NOT larger
```

In each case, the function works correctly in recognizing the types of the two parameters, whether or not they are the same. The only requirement is that T and U are types for which the greater than comparison (>) is valid.

Explicitly Specifying the Type in a Template Function

When you call a template function, the arguments to the function dictate the types to be used. To override deduced types, you can explicitly code types within angle brackets immediately following the function name in the function call. For example, if reverse() is defined as

```
template<class T>
T reverse(T x)
  {
    return(-x);
  }
```

the following program segment produces two different results for reverse(). In the first call to reverse(), the template function correctly perceives that it is receiving a double. In the second call to reverse(), the double is received as an integer, and the function returns an integer.

```
double amount = 45.66;
cout<<reverse(amount); // result is -45.66
cout<<reverse<int>(amount);  // result is -45; int is explicit
```

Explicitly specifying a type is particularly useful when at least one of the types you need to parameterize or generate within the function is not an argument to the function. The compiler can deduce template function types only by using the values passed to the function. For example, if the return type of a function must vary independently from the arguments, the compiler cannot deduce this requirement. In this case, you must specify the type within angle brackets.

As an example, suppose you want the reverse of a value to be of the same type as the value in some cases, but on other occasions you want the reverse of a value to be an integer, no matter what type is passed to reverse(). The template is

```
template <class T, class U>
T reverse(U x)
  {
   return(-x);
  }
```

This template requires two types, named T and U. Type U can be deduced from the reverse() function's parameter argument; type T must be explicitly coded.

```
double amount = -8.8;
cout<<reverse(amount);
 // error -- type U is double but type T is unknown
cout <<reverse<int>(amount);
 // type U is double and T is integer; output is 8, an integer
cout<<reverse<double>(amount);
 // type U is double and T is double; output is 8.8, a double
cout<<reverse<int,double>(amount);
 // type U is double and T is integer; output is 8, an integer
```

Using Template Functions with Class Objects

When programming in an object-oriented environment, you naturally want your template functions to work with class objects as well as with scalar variables. The good news is that template functions work just as well with classes as they do with simple data types. Your only additional responsibility is to ensure that any operations used within the template function have been defined for the class objects passed to the template functions.

As an example, recall the reverse() template function:

```
template<class T>
 // T stands for any type -- simple or programmer-defined
T reverse(T x)
  {
   return(-x);
  }
```

Let's say you have a class named PhoneCall. Its data members include an integer to hold the length of the call in minutes, and a character to hold a code that indicates how the phone call is billed. When you use the reverse() function with a PhoneCall object, it should signal that you are "reversing" the billing, or changing the billing code to a C for "Collect." The reverse() template function can easily accomplish this task. You still need to ensure that the unary minus has meaning with a PhoneCall object. That is, when a PhoneCall object is passed to reverse() and becomes known as x, -x must have some meaning. This step requires overloading the minus, so that it sets the billing code to 'C' when used with a PhoneCall.

The PhoneCall class can be coded with two data members, a constructor, a display function, and an overloaded minus.

```cpp
class PhoneCall
   {
     private:
       int lengthOfCall;
       char billCode;
     public:
       PhoneCall(const int l, const char b);  // constructor
       PhoneCall PhoneCall::operator-(void);  // unary minus
       void showCall(void);
   };
```

The constructor and showCall() functions are straightforward:

```cpp
PhoneCall::PhoneCall(const int len = 0, const char b = ' ')
   {
     PhoneCall::lengthOfCall = len;
     PhoneCall::billCode = b;
   }
void PhoneCall::showCall(void)
   {
     cout<<"The code is "<<PhoneCall::billCode<<endl;
   }
```

The operator- (minus) is overloaded to change the PhoneCall's billCode to 'C'.

```
PhoneCall PhoneCall::operator-(void)
  {
    PhoneCall::billCode = 'C';
    return(*this);
  }
```

The operator-() function changes the billCode of the object that invokes it. It returns the newly coded PhoneCall via the this pointer. Therefore, when the following program is executed, it has the effect noted in the comments.

```
void main()
  {
    PhoneCall aCall(10,'S');
    // aCall lasts 10 minutes, Standard billing
    aCall.showCall();    // displays 'S'
    aCall = reverse(aCall); // aCall becomes a Collect call
    aCall.showCall(); // displays 'C'
  }
```

This example demonstrates that the reverse() template function can operate correctly on a class object as well as any simple data type—as long as all operations within the template function are defined for the class objects passed to it. Whether the unary minus is overloaded for such diverse purposes in various classes as to issue a credit on a Customer bill, fire an Employee, or reformat a Disk, the template function class that uses the minus can handle each call successfully.

In the following steps, you will allow the displayScreen() function you created in the TEMPLATE.CPP program to work on Fractions.

1 If you wish to use the Fraction file you have been developing throughout these tutorials, open **FRAC8.CPP** and immediately save it as **FRAC9.CPP**. Alternatively, you can use the **FRAC9.CPP** file included in the TUT09 folder. Open the **TEMPLATE.CPP** program and add the following include statement at the top of the program:

```
#include"frac9.cpp"
```

2 Add declarations for a fraction problem. You will have two Fractions that are part of the problem, a user's answer, and a correct answer.

```
Fraction f1(3,5), f2(1,5), fUserAns, fCorrectAns;
    // fCorrectAns will be 4/5
```

3 The Fraction class has cin defined, so prompts for numerator and denominator are already included. In addition, operator<< and operator+ have been defined. Thus, the creation of the actual program code is brief and intuitive. Add the following statements at the end of the main() program, just before the closing curly bracket.

```
cout<<"What is "<<f1<<" + "<<f2<<"?";
cin>>fUserAns;
fCorrectAns = f1 + f2;
if(fUserAns == fCorrectAns)
    fillScreen(fUserAns);
```

4 Compile and test the program. When you answer the arithmetic problems correctly, the fillScreen() function displays the correct answer along with the Teacher's Pet message 20 times for each problem, whether the answer is an integer, a double, or a Fraction. A partial listing of the output to the Fraction portion of the program appears in Figure 9-1.

```
4/5 Another Teacher's Pet Success
 4/5 Another Teacher's Pet Success
  4/5 Another Teacher's Pet Success
   4/5 Another Teacher's Pet Success
    4/5 Another Teacher's Pet Success
     4/5 Another Teacher's Pet Success
      4/5 Another Teacher's Pet Success
       4/5 Another Teacher's Pet Success
```

Figure 9-1: Partial output of TEMPLATE.CPP

5 Save the program.

SUMMARY

- Functions are useful because they work with varied values.
- Once a standard function is created, its argument types remain fixed.
- Functions with the same name that accept different argument lists are overloaded.
- If the tasks to be carried out are similar, overloading requires a lot of unnecessary, tedious coding.
- C++ lets you create a function that uses variable types, called a template function. Template functions enable you to write a single function that serves as an outline, or template, for a group of functions that differ in the types of parameters they use.
- In a template function, at least one argument is generic, or parameterized.
- Before you code a template function, you must include a template definition.

- A template definition contains the keyword `template`, a left angle bracket (<), a list of generic types (separated with commas if more than one type is needed), and a right angle bracket (>).
- Each generic type in the list of generic types has two parts: the keyword `class`, and an identifier that represents the generic type.
- The template keyword `class` does not necessarily mean that the identifier will stand for a programmer-created class type, but it may.
- When you call a template function, the compiler determines the type of the actual argument passed to the function and substitutes it for the generic type in the template function.
- When you call a template function, a generated function that uses the appropriate type is created or instantiated.
- The compiler generates code for as many different functions as it needs, depending on the function calls made.
- Function templates are placed at the start of a program in the global area above main() or in a separate file, which is then included in the program.
- Function templates may have more than one parameter.
- You can overload function templates, as long as each version of the function has different arguments, enabling the compiler to distinguish between them.
- A template function can have arguments of more than one type; you simply use a unique type identifier for each type.
- Template functions work with classes in the same way that they work with simple data types as long as operations used within a template function have been defined for the class objects passed to them.

Q U E S T I O N S

1. A function that is prototyped as `double calculate(int num);` may _____.
   a. receive an integer constant such as 5
   b. receive an integer variable
   c. either (a) or (b)
   d. neither (a) nor (b)

2. A function that is prototyped as `double calculate(int num);` may _____.
   a. receive a double constant such as 3.9
   b. receive a double variable
   c. either (a) or (b)
   d. neither (a) nor (b)

3. A function that is prototyped as `int calculate(int num);` may _____.
   a. receive an integer variable named num from the main() program
   b. receive any integer variable from the main() program
   c. either (a) or (b)
   d. neither (a) nor (b)

4. Overloading involves writing two or more functions with _____.
   a. different names and different argument lists
   b. different names and the same argument list
   c. the same name and different argument lists
   d. the same name and the same argument list

5. A function that uses variable types is called _____.
   a. overloaded
   b. a template function
   c. a variable function
   d. a virtual function

6. In a template function, _____ argument is generic.
   a. no
   b. exactly one
   c. at least one
   d. more than one

7. A C++ term meaning "generic" is _____.
   a. argument
   b. parameterized
   c. universal
   d. global

8. Before you code a template function, you include a _____.
   a. template definition
   b. class header
   c. function resolution
   d. pound sign

9. Each generic type in a template function definition is preceded by the keyword _____.
   a. template
   b. function
   c. type
   d. class

10. The generic type in a template function _____.
    a. must be T
    b. can be T
    c. cannot be T for functions you create, but may be for C++'s built-in functions
    d. cannot be T

11. In the statement `template<class T>`, _____.
    a. T is a class
    b. T is a scalar variable
    c. either (a) or (b)
    d. neither (a) nor (b)

12. The compiler determines the type used in a template function via _____.
    a. the name of the function
    b. the first variable declared within the function
    c. the type of the argument passed to the function
    d. the type of the value returned from the function

13. The function that is actually created from a call to a template function is said to be _____.
    a. generated
    b. inherited
    c. spawned
    d. declassified

14. You can place function templates _____.
    a. at the end of main()
    b. at the start of a program above main()
    c. in two files—one for the definition and one for the function
    d. any of the above

15. Function templates _____.
   a. must have exactly one parameter
   b. may have more than one parameter as long as they are of the same type
   c. may have more than one parameter of any type
   d. may not have parameters

16. You ___ overload function templates.
   a. may, as long as each version has the same arguments,
   b. may, as long as each version has different arguments,
   c. must
   d. must not

17. When two types are used in a function template and one is labeled T, the other _____.
   a. must also be named T
   b. must be named U
   c. can be any legal C++ identifier
   d. It is illegal to have two types.

18. If template functions are to work with class objects, _____.
   a. the functions must be members of the class
   b. the functions must be friends of the class
   c. the class must define any operations used in the functions
   d. the template must have friend operators that are defined in the class

E X E R C I S E S

1. Create a function template to display a value that is both preceded and followed by 10 asterisks on a line. Write a main program that tests the function with character, integer, double, and Fraction objects.

2. Create a function template that adds two values, returning their sum. Write a main program that tests the function with integer, double, and Fraction objects.

3. Overload the >operator to work with your Fraction class. Create a generic function that determines the smaller of two values. Write a main program that tests the function with character, integer, double, and Fraction objects.

In this lesson you will learn:

- The advantages of using template classes
- How to create a complete class template
- How to create container classes

Template Classes

Template Classes

Template functions allow you to create generic functions that have the same bodies but can take different data types as parameters. Similarly, in some situations classes are similar and you wish to perform very similar operations with those classes. If you find it necessary to create several similar classes, you might consider developing a template class. A **template class** is a class in which at least one type is generic or parameterized. It provides the outline for a family of similar classes.

To create a template class, you begin with the template definition, just as you do with a template function. Then you write the class definition using the generic type or types in each instance for which a substitution should take place.

For example, consider a very simple Number class that has one data member that can hold any number, a constructor that takes an argument, and a display() function. The template class is

```cpp
template<class T>
class Number
  {
    private:
      T theNumber;
        // note the type of theNumber is variable
        // or parameterized
    public:
      Number(const T n);
      void display(void);
  };
```

The class is named Number. Its private data member, theNumber, may be of any type. If it becomes a double, for example, then the Number() constructor takes a constant double argument. If the private member is an integer, then Number() takes an integer.

Within a program, you can instantiate objects that have the class template type. You add the desired type to the current class instantiation by placing its name between angle brackets following the generic class name. For example, if you want an object named myValue to be of type Number, and you want myValue to hold an integer, your declaration is

```
Number<int> myValue;
```

Alternatively, to pass a value of 77 to the myValue object's constructor, your declaration is

```
Number<int> myValue(77);
```

To use the Number class member display() function with myValue, add the dot operator, just as you would with an instantiation of any other class:

```
myValue.display();
```

If you instantiate another Number object with a double, the display() function is called in exactly the same way:

```
Number<double> yourValue(3.46);
yourValue.display();
```

tip

Some C++ programmers reserve the term "class template" to indicate the source code they write, using "template class" to refer to the actual generated class that exists for a specific type after C++ determines what type applies.

Creating a Complete Class Template

Assume you want to create a very simple generic class to handle any object that takes one argument of variable type for construction. You create the class template to have one private member, an instance of the class. You also create two public functions: a constructor and a display function.

```
template<class T>
class Generic
  {
    private:
      T instance;
    public:
      Generic(T n);
      void print(void);
  };
```

The generic class name is Generic. It has one private member of any type T, named instance. The Generic() constructor takes one argument, an object of the class T. In other words, if instance becomes an integer, then an integer is required to construct a Generic object. If instance is a character, then a character is required to construct a Generic object. In addition, a print() function takes and returns no arguments.

The Generic constructor code is

```
template<class T>
Generic<T>::Generic(T i = 0)
  {
    Generic::instance = i;
  }
```

The code `template<classT>` must appear immediately before the constructor function code, so that the constructor recognizes T.

The header for the constructor indicates that the Generic constructor belongs to the Generic<T> class (whatever T turns out to be), and that its name is Generic(). Thus, like all other constructors, the Generic constructor shares its class name.

```
Generic<T>::Generic(T i = 0)
```

The constructor header also indicates that the Generic constructor takes one argument. That argument will be of type T. Within the Generic constructor the argument will be known as i. If no value is provided for i, it will default to 0.

The body of the function simply sets Generic's data member to the value of i, which was passed to the constructor, or to 0, if no value was passed.

```
  {
    Generic::instance = i;
  }
```

The Generic<T> print() function takes and returns void:

```
template<class T>
void Generic<T>::print(void)
  {
    cout<<"Generic printing: "<<endl;
    cout<<Generic<T>::instance<<endl;
  }
```

tip

▶ **In the last line of code,** cout<<Generic<T> **may also be written as** cout<<Generic.

This function belongs to the Generic<T> class, its name is print(), and it displays two lines—the label "Generic printing," followed by the instance of the object. For the print() function to work properly, the insertion operator << must be defined for T. In other words, if you use print() with a char or an int, C++ automatically knows how to insert those values into the output stream; nothing special is required on your part. If you will use print() with a class of your own creation, however, then the insertion operator must be defined for that class with an operator<< function.

Assume you have created a simple Employee class containing an idNum and salary, along with a constructor and an overloaded insertion operator:

```
class Employee
  {
    private:
      int idNum;
      double salary;
    public:
      Employee(int id);
      friend ostream& operator<<(ostream& out, const Employee &e);
  };
```

The constructor initializes the data members to a passed employee ID number and a company minimum wage:

```
Employee::Employee(int id = 0)
  {
    Employee::idNum = id;
    Employee::salary = 4.95;
  }
```

The insertion operator is overloaded for the Employee class to print the Employee data in readable format:

```
ostream& operator<<(ostream& out, const emp &emp)
  {
    out<<"Employee number "<<emp.idNum;
    out<<"  Salary "<<Employee.salary;
    return(out);
  }
```

Because the Generic class works with the print() message "Generic printing:," the following main() program produces the output shown in Figure 9-2:

```
void main()
  {
    Generic<int> anInt(7);
    Generic<double> someMoney(6.65);
    Generic<Employee>  aWorker(333);
    anInt.print();
    someMoney.print();
    aWorker.print();
  }
```

```
Generic printing:


7


Generic printing:


6.65


Generic printing:


Employee number 333 Salary 4.95
```

Figure 9-2: Output using Generic class

In this program, anInt is constructed as a simple integer with a value of 7. When the integer is printed using the Generic print() function, the "Generic printing" message and a 7 display. Similarly, someMoney is a scalar double with a value of 6.65, and the print() function produces the message and this value. Upon construction of the Employee named aWorker, aWorker's idNum is set to 333 because the Employee constructor sets idNum equal to any integer passed to it. When the Employee name aWorker is printed with Generic::print(), the "Generic printing:" message displays, but all print formatting assigned to each Employee object via Employee's insertion operator function applies. As a result, text appears along with the idNum and salary.

This example represents a stretch of the intended use of class templates. If you simply want to construct and print integers, doubles, and even Employees, a Generic class is unnecessary, and it is too much trouble to create it. After all, each operation (construction and printing) is already defined for these types, and the generic class merely adds a layer of complexity.

If extensive print formatting was applied prior to any object's individual print formatting, however, then creating a class template might be worth the effort.

Imagine, for example, that a company name and address, followed by a logo, always need to be printed before data, whether the data belong to the class used for Employees, Customers, or Suppliers. In such as case, it might make sense to create a template class that handled the formatted printing for each of the different type objects. Programmers commonly use template classes for even more generic applications, such as linked lists, stacks, and queues. Such generic classes are called container classes.

Container Classes

> In Smalltalk, all objects derive from the same container class, called Object. This consistently ensures that every object will have at least some standard functionality.

> Many linked lists provide more than a pointer to the next logical object. For example, they contain another pointer to the previous object, enabling the list to be traversed backward as well as forward. Providing this extra link adds complexity to the programming task, but adds functionality to the linked list.

Many C++ compilers come with class libraries called container classes. **Container classes** are simply template classes that have already been written to perform common class tasks; the purpose of container classes is to manage groups of other classes. Of course, you can always write your own container classes, but the creators of C++ have already done much of the work for you.

A common programming task is to create a linked list. A **linked list** is a chain of objects, each of which consists of at least two parts—an object and a pointer to another object. For example, a school might want to place students in a linked list based on their registration dates. The first student in the list would be the first student to register. When a second student registers, perhaps additional memory is allocated, and this new memory address is stored in the pointer that belongs to the first student. The second student object will hold a pointer to the address of a third student, and so on. The last student's pointer typically holds a dummy value, such as a null character, to indicate the end of the list.

The same school might want to link employees by Social Security number, inventory supplies by item number, and alumni by a combination of major, year of graduation, and student ID number. Although each of these diverse objects has a different size and different data members, the procedures involved with linked lists are basically the same.

No matter what types of objects are linked, procedures must be developed to establish links between objects and to insert new member objects into appropriate spots within the linked list, including assigning the correct links to the new list members. Common procedures also include deleting a member from the list, making sure that the object pointing to that member ID is adjusted to point to the next member, and retrieving and displaying the objects in a particular order. You might also want functions that count the number of items in a list or search through a list for a certain object and pinpoint its position. Each of these functions may prove useful in a linked list regardless of what type of object is being linked.

A generic class that holds an object and a link, plus all linked list functions that handle the list's chores, is a useful tool when working with lists, whether they link Students, Employees, Supplies, or Alumni. As such a class may be used with a number of other class objects, the developers of C++ have already created such a container class. Its name is List, and it contains functions like add(), detach(), and getItems(). The List container class is a template class because the programmers who designed your compiler could not have predicted the exact characteristic of all classes you might create. Even if they could, it would be pointless to develop an Employee linked list class, a Student linked List class, and a Supply linked list class when the "linking" aspects are identical in each case. If you use the List container class, you never have to write your own linked list class, and you can use this tool with any class you create.

Different compilers include different built-in container classes. Indeed, some compilers may not offer any container classes. The more container classes your compiler supplies, the less you may find it necessary to write your own template classes. Nevertheless, it is still beneficial to understand how it's done.

As a simple example, consider developing an Array class. You must perform many standard operations on array data, no matter what type is involved. For example, whether you are working with integers, characters, or Employees, you often want to perform such generic tasks as storing them in an array, printing the array, and printing only the first element of the array. Class templates offer the perfect way to accomplish this goal.

A generic Array class might have two data members: a pointer to the beginning of the array, and an integer representing the size of the array.

```
template<class T>
class Array
  {
    private:
      T *data;    // T is the type of the array
      int size;
```

The only variable in the private data section of the class declaration is the type that the Array will eventually hold.

Continuing the class definition, you include a constructor and two member functions: one to print the entire array, and one to print the first element only.

```
    public:
      Array(T *d, int s);
      void showList(void);
      void showFirst(void);
  };
```

The constructor assigns the array address to the generic array address, and assigns the array size to the generic integer size:

```
template<class T>
Array<T>::Array(T *d, int s)
  {
    Array<T>::data = d;
    Array<T>::size = s;
  }
```

The showList() function displays each element of the Array, from element 0 through size-1:

```
template<class T>
void Array<T>::showList()
  {
    int sz = Array<T>::size;
    cout<<"Entire list:"<<endl;
    for(int x = 0; x< sz; ++x)
    cout<<Array<T>::data[x]<<endl;
  }
```

The showFirst() function is even simpler—it simply shows element 0 of the array:

```
template<class T>
void Array<T>::showFirst()
  {
    cout<<"First element is ";
    cout<<Array<T>::data[0]<<endl;
  }
```

When creating an Array object, you must supply the beginning address of the array and the size of the array. Assuming you have an array such as

```
int nums[4];
```

you can call the constructor for an arrayOfIntegers with

```
Array<int> arrayOfIntegers(nums,4);
```

Instead of hard-coding the size of the array, with a number such as 4, an even more flexible method for calling the constructor involves calculating the array size. The size of the entire array is divided by the size of each element in the array, giving the number of elements in the array.

```
int ArraySize = sizeof(nums)/sizeof(nums[0]);
Array<int> arrayOfIntegers(nums,ArraySize);
```

Either way, the array address (nums) and an integer size are passed to the generic constructor.

Assuming an Employee class has been created with a properly overloaded insertion operator, you can write the following program:

```
void main()
  {
    int vals[4] = {22,33,44,55};
    Array<int> val(vals,sizeof(vals)/sizeof(vals[0]));
      // that is, size is 4
    Employee workers[6] = {110,220,330,440,550,660};
    Array<Employee> worker(workers, sizeof(workers)/sizeof(workers[0]));
      // that is, size is 6
    val.showList();
    val.showFirst();
    worker.showList();
    worker.showFirst();
  }
```

Output appears as shown in Figure 9-3.

```
Entire list:
22
33
44
55
First element is 22
Entire list:
Employee number 110 Salary 4.95
Employee number 220 Salary 4.95
Employee number 330 Salary 4.95
Employee number 440 Salary 4.95
Employee number 550 Salary 4.95
Employee number 660 Salary 4.95
First element is Employee number 110 Salary 4.95
```

Figure 9-3: Output using Array container class

If the Array class is carefully constructed, and new member functions are added as needed by various applications, this strategy enables you to handle arrays that are not type-specific. In future programs, whether you create arrays of people, equipment, college courses, or any other items, you will have tried-and-true methods for working with the arrays. The program development process will go more smoothly and be less error-prone.

S U M M A R Y

- A template class is a class that provides an outline for a family of similar classes by parameterizing at least one type.
- To create a template class, you begin with the template definition, followed by the class definition using the generic type or types in each instance for which a substitution should take place.
- Within a program, you instantiate objects that have the class template type by adding the desired type between angle brackets following the generic class name.
- To use a template class member function, you use the dot operator with an instantiation of the class.
- Programmers commonly use template container classes for generic applications, such as linked lists, stacks, and queues. These generic classes are called container classes.
- Container classes are employed to manage groups of other classes.
- A linked list is a chain of objects, each of which consists of at least two parts—an object and a pointer to another object.
- Different compilers come with different built-in container classes.
- If a container class is carefully constructed, and new member functions are added as needed by applications, you develop ways to handle classes that are not type-specific.

Q U E S T I O N S

1. With a template class, _____ type is generic.
   a. no
   b. at least one
   c. exactly one
   d. at most one

2. To create a template class, you begin with _____.
   a. the template definition
   b. the keyword class
   c. the function definitions
   d. the keyword definition

3. Within a program, you can instantiate _____ that have a class template type.
   a. classes
   b. functions
   c. parameters
   d. objects

4. You add the desired type to a specific template class instantiation by placing the type's name _____.
   a. between angle brackets
   b. in parentheses
   c. on a line by itself
   d. immediately prior to the class name

5. The type to be used in an instantiation of a class template follows _____.
   a. the generic class name
   b. the keyword template
   c. the keyword class
   d. the template definition

6. To use a template class member function, use the _____ with the instantiation.
   a. scope resolution operator
   b. dot operator
   c. class definition
   d. keyword template

7. If you create an instantiation of a class template with an int, and then create a second instantiation with a double, then _____.
   a. you must precede each function call with the word int or double
   b. once a function is used as one type, it becomes unavailable for use with the other type
   c. there is no difference in the procedure to call a member function
   d. you cannot perform this operation in C++

8. To use a class template with a class object, you must ensure that _____.
   a. the template and the object have the same name
   b. the template and the object are of the same type
   c. all operators used in the class functions have been defined for your class
   d. your class object has no functions with the same name as the class template's functions

9. Template classes that have already been written to perform common class tasks are called _____.
   a. container classes   c. repository classes
   b. receptacle classes   d. alembic classes

10. A programming structure that contains data and a pointer to the next object is a _____.
    a. template   c. pointer class
    b. class   d. linked list

11. You _____ write your own container classes.
    a. must   c. should not
    b. may   d. must not

12. If container classes are carefully constructed, then these tools are available to work with structures that are not _____.
    a. valid without container classes   c. type-specific
    b. programmer-defined   d. public

E X E R C I S E S

1. Create a class template for a class that holds an object. It should provide a standard data input function that begins with a generic warning message to enter data carefully, as well as a standard output function that includes a generic "Here's the data you requested" message. Write a main() program that tests your template class with an integer and two programmer-designed classes.

2. Create a class template for a class that holds an object and the number of data elements in the object. For example, if an Employee class had 2 data elements, an id number and a salary, then the class template would hold the number 2 as well as an employee object. Code a standard input function for the object that displays a message on the screen—"You will be asked to enter X items"—where X is the number of data elements. Write a main() program that tests your template class with an integer and two programmer-designed classes.

debugging ▶ 3. Each of the following files in the TUT09 folder has overloaded operators, and contains syntax and/or logical errors. Determine the problem, and fix the program.
   a. DEBUG9-1.CPP
   b. DEBUG9-2.CPP
   c. DEBUG9-3.CPP
   d. DEBUG9-4.CPP

Exception Handling

case ▶ You've come a long way at Teacher's Pet Software. You can create classes and objects, and you now understand polymorphism and inheritance. You are truly an object-oriented programmer.

"One thing still bothers me about my programs," you tell Audrey Burns, your supervisor. "No matter how well I write my code, the user can mess everything up by inputting bad data. Even if my code is perfect, the user can enter mistakes."

"Then your code isn't perfect yet," Audrey says. "Besides taking care of ordinary situations, your programs must be able to handle exceptions."

Previewing the EXCEPT Program

1 Load the **EXCEPT.CPP** program and execute it. (Change the path for the include file if necessary.)

2 When prompted, enter values for the numerator and denominator of a fraction. Run the program once with valid values, and then a second time with 0 for the denominator.

3 Examine the code to observe how the program handles the invalid denominator value. You will be creating similar code in this tutorial.

In this lesson you will learn:

■ What exceptions are
■ How to throw exceptions
■ How to use try blocks
■ How to catch exceptions

Exceptions

> **tip**
>
> • • • • • • • • • • • • • • •
>
> ▶ To use the exit() function, you must include the file that defines it, STDLIB.H.

Exceptions

Most beginning programmers assume that their programs will work as expected. Experienced programmers, on the other hand, know that things often go awry. If you issue a command to read a file from a disk, the file may not exist. If you want to write to a disk, the disk may be full or unformatted. If the program asks for user input, users may enter invalid data. Such errors are called **exceptions**—so-named because, presumably, they are not usual occurrences. The object-oriented techniques to manage such errors comprise the group of methods known as **exception handling.**

Programmers had to deal with error conditions long before object-oriented methods emerged. Probably the most popular error-handling method was to terminate the program. For example, many C++ programs contain code similar to the following:

```
if(userEntry < 0)
    exit(1);
// rest of program goes here
```

In this example, if the userEntry is a negative value, the function in which the code appears would be terminated. If the program is a spreadsheet or a game, the user might become annoyed that the function has stopped working and that an early exit has been made. If the program monitors a patient's blood pressure during surgery, the results could be far more serious.

A better alternative has the function that discovers the error return a value to the calling program. For example, the following code returns a 1 if the function isEntryNegative() detects an error and a 0 if it does not:

```
int isEntryNegative(void)
  {
    int userEntry;
    cout<<"Enter a positive value ";
    cin>>userEntry;
    if(userEntry<0)
      return(1);
    else
      return(0);
  }
```

The calling function can check the return value of the function and take appropriate action. This error-handling technique has at least two drawbacks, however. First, because a function can return only one value, the function can return only the value indicating the error status. If userEntry must be returned, no method for making this happen exists, because the error code is returned. In this particular case, the function could be rewritten to return the userEntry unless it is negative, in which case an arbitrary value such as -1 could be returned. If you wanted to return the value of userEntry even if it was invalid, however, you would have no value for the error code.

Second, any error code returned by a function must be of the same type as the function's return type. It may be natural to think of an error code as a simple integer, but if the function return type is double, then any error code returned must be a double. Of course, the error code could be stored globally, avoiding the return issue. In that case, however, any function could change the error code, and the "feel" of encapsulation and object-orientedness would be lost.

C++'s exception-handling techniques circumvent these problems. A function can contain code to check for errors, sending a message when it detects an error. In object-oriented terminology, an exception is a message (an object) that is passed from the place where a problem occurs to another place that will handle the problem. This object can be of any type, including a scalar or class type, and a variety of error messages of different types can be sent from the same function regardless of its return type. In addition, true to object-oriented style, exception handling acknowledges inheritance and can be overridden by the programmer.

Throwing Exceptions

The general principle underlying object-oriented error handling is that any function that is called should check for errors but should not be required to handle an error if one is found. The error may need to be handled differently depending on the purpose of the calling function. For example, one program that uses a data entry function may need to terminate if the user enters a negative value. Another program may simply want the user to reenter the data. The calling function should have the responsibility of handling the error detected by the function.

When an object-oriented program detects an error within a function, the function is said to **throw an exception**. A throw resembles a return statement in a function, except that the execution of the program does not continue at the location from which the function was called.

You throw an exception by using the keyword `throw` followed by any C++ object, including an object that is a built-in scalar type, a nonscalar type such as a string or numeric array, or even a programmer-defined object. For example, if a negative userEntry is an error condition, then the following code throws an error message:

```
int dataEntry(void)

  {

    int userEntry;

    cout<<"Enter a positive value ";

    cin>>userEntry;

    if(userEntry<0)

      throw("Invalid entry");

    return(userEntry);

  }
```

In this example, if userEntry is invalid, then a string is thrown and the execution of the function is finished. Therefore, only valid (that is, non-negative) entries cause the program to execute all the way to the return statement. The string that is thrown is not "returned" from the dataEntry() function; the function can return only an int. Either the error message string is thrown or the userEntry integer is returned.

A function can make more than one throw. Assume, for example, that you need one error message if a value is negative, but a different error message if a value is greater than 12. The following function throws two different error messages, based on a userEntry:

```
int dataEntry(void)

  {

    int userEntry;

    cout<<"Enter a positive value less than 13 ";

    cin>>userEntry;

    if(userEntry<0)

      throw("Value is negative");

    if(userEntry>12)

      throw("Value is too high");

    return(userEntry);

  }
```

In addition to making multiple throws, a function can make throws of different types. Assume you need a function that throws an error message if userEntry is negative, but throws the actual value entered if the user inputs a number greater than 12. The following function accomplishes this goal:

```
int dataEntry(void)
  {
    int userEntry;
    cout<<"Enter a positive value less than 13 ");
    cin>>userEntry;
    if(userEntry<0)
      throw("Negative number");
    if (userEntry>12)
      throw(userEntry);
    return(userEntry);
  }
```

tip

In Tutorials 3 and 6, you developed code for preventing zero denominators. Even though those methods work, throwing exceptions is a more truly object-oriented technique.

With this dataEntry() function, if the user enters a value greater than 12, the actual number entered is thrown. This statement does not mean that the number is returned to the calling function. Only values between 0 and 13 are returned to the calling function, which presumably continues processing using the value. Instead, the thrown value is sent to a different function where it can be caught.

In the previous tutorials, you have created a Fraction class that has a wide variety of member functions. One of these functions is an overloaded extraction operator (>>) to be used with cin. You can now add code to the Fraction operator>> function to throw an error message if the user enters a zero denominator for a fraction object.

1 Open the Fraction class file you have been creating named **FRAC9.CPP** and immediately save it as **FRAC10.CPP**. Alternatively, you can open the **FRAC10.CPP** file in the TUT10 folder. The file contains a definition for the Fraction class, including member functions to overload the operators >> and <<. The operator >> function currently has the following form:

```
istream& operator>>(istream &in, Fraction &frac)
  {
    cout<<endl;
    cout<<"Enter a numerator for a fraction"<<endl;
    in>>frac.numerator;
    cout<<"Enter a denominator"<<endl;
    in>>frac.denominator;
    frac.reduceFraction();
    return(in);
  }
```

2 Immediately after the line `in>>frac.denominator;`, add an if statement to throw an error message if 0 is entered as the fraction denominator:

```
if(frac.denominator == 0)
   throw("Denominator cannot be zero!!");
```

3 Compile the program and correct any syntax errors. Save the file.

4 Open a new file. Write a short main() program to demonstrate that the cin object works correctly with the overloaded >> operator:

```
#include<iostream.h>
#include"frac10.cpp"
void main()
  {
   Fraction aFrac;   // declare one fraction
   cin>>aFrac;
   cout<<aFrac<<endl;
  }
```

5 Compile and run the program, entering valid values for both the numerator and denominator (that is, not 0). The program should work as expected, allowing data entry and displaying a fraction. If you enter a 0 for the denominator, the program will not work correctly, because the call to the operator >> function that includes the `throw` statement has not yet been properly included in a `try` block.

6 Save the main() demonstration program as **THROW.CPP**.

Try Blocks

When a function may cause an exception, and therefore includes a throw statement to handle errors, the call to the potentially offending function should be placed within a try block. A **try block** includes the following components:

- the keyword **try**
- an opening curly bracket
- the code that is to be tried
- a closing curly bracket

For example, a main() program that calls any of the dataEntry() functions created so far in this lesson would place the call to dataEntry() within a try block.

```
void main()
 {
  int value;
  int dataEntry(void);  // function prototype
  try
     {
        value = dataEntry();
     }
// rest of the program that uses this value
```

When this program is executed, if no exception is thrown—that is, if the userEntry is valid—then the program continues using the valid value returned from the dataEntry() function. The dataEntry() function may be called without a try block, and if all entered data are valid, no ill effects will ensue. If the dataEntry() function is called without a try block, however, then any exception encountered within dataEntry() will cause the program to terminate. If the dataEntry() function is called from a try block, as in this example, then whatever the function throws can be caught.

Catching Exceptions

To handle a thrown object, you include one or more **catch blocks** in your program immediately following a try block. A catch block includes the following components:

- the keyword **catch**
- a one-entry argument list in parentheses
- an opening curly bracket
- one or more statements describing the exception action to be taken
- a closing curly bracket

For example, assume you have written a dataEntry() function that throws an error message:

```
int dataEntry(void)
  {
    int userEntry;
    cout<<"Enter a positive value ";
    cin>>userEntry;
    if(userEntry<0)
      throw("Invalid entry");
    return(userEntry);
  }
```

You might write a main() function that can catch and display the thrown message.

```
void main()
  {
    int value;
    int dataEntry(void);   // function prototype
    try
      {
        value = dataEntry();
      }
    catch(const char* msg)
      {
        cout<<msg<<endl;
      }
// rest of the program that uses the valid value
```

When this program executes, if no exception is thrown—that is, if the userEntry is valid—then the program bypasses the catch block and continues after this block, using the valid value returned from the dataEntry() function. The message "Invalid entry" that is thrown from the dataEntry() function is a constant string. It can be caught by the catch block, as this block takes a constant character pointer as its argument.

In the following steps, you will change the main() program named THROW.CPP that you created in the first part of this tutorial so that it properly uses try and catch blocks with the thrown message.

1   Open **THROW.CPP** if necessary. It is repeated here for your convenience:

```
#include<iostream.h>
#include"frac10.cpp"
void main()
  {
   Fraction aFrac;   // declare one fraction
   cin>>aFrac;
   cout<<aFrac<<endl;
  }
```

2 Surround the statement `cin>>aFrac;` with a try block so that it becomes

```
try
  {
    cin>>aFrac;
  }
```

3 Immediately following the try block, add a catch block that displays the message that may be thrown by the operator >> function.

```
catch(const char *errorMessage)
  {
   cout<<errorMessage<<endl;
  }
```

4 Compile and run the program several times. When you enter a nonzero value for the denominator, the fraction displays normally. When you enter a 0 for the denominator, the message "Denominator cannot be zero!!" appears prior to the display of the offending fraction. A typical run is shown in Figure 10-1.

```
Enter a numerator for a fraction
3
Enter a denominator
0
Denominator cannot be zero!!
3/0
```

Figure 10-1: Program using try and catch

5 Save the program. It does not yet correct the problems caused by a zero denominator, but rather simply notifies the user that a problem exists. You might wish to add a member function to the Fraction class that forces a denominator to become 1. This function can subsequently be called when the user enters a zero denominator.

6 Open the **FRAC10.CPP** file that contains the Fraction class definition.

7 In the public section of the class declarations, add a prototype for a function that will force a denominator to 1.

```
void forceDenom(void);
```

8   To the implementation section, add the following function:

```
void Fraction::forceDenom(void)
  {
    Fraction::denominator = 1;
  }
```

9   Save the **FRAC10.CPP** file.

10   Open the **THROW.CPP** program. Add the statement a `Frac.forceDenom();`
     as the last statement in the catch block. Run the program several times. If you
     enter a valid denominator for a fraction, the fraction should display normally.
     If you enter a 0, the error message displays, and the fraction is converted to a
     fraction with a denominator of 1. A typical run is shown in Figure 10-2.

```
Enter a numerator for a fraction
3
Enter a denominator
0
Denominator cannot be zero!!
3/1
```

Figure 10-2: Typical run of THROW.CPP

tip

A catch block is not
required to display or
manipulate the thrown
value. This value simply
determines which catch
block executes. The block
itself may contain any
valid C++ statements.

Recall the previously developed dataEntry() function that throws an exception
if the user enters a negative value. Depending upon the application, other types of
entries may be invalid as well. For example, it might be the case that the
userEntry value must not be negative, but also must not exceed 12. The
dataEntry() function in this situation should throw multiple types of exceptions:

```
int dataEntry(void)
  {
    int userEntry;
    cout<<"Enter a positive value less than 13");
    cin>>userEntry;
    if(userEntry<0)
      throw("Value is negative");
    if (userEntry>12)
      throw(userEntry);
    return(userEntry);
  }
```

When a function throws more than one type of exception, then multiple catch blocks can be written:

```
void main()
  {
    int value;
    int dataEntry(void);  // function prototype
    try
      {
        value = dataEntry();
      }
    catch(const char* msg)
      {
        cout<<msg<<endl;
      }
    catch(const int badValue)
      {
        cout<<"The number you entered, "<<badValue<<" is greater than 12."<<endl;
      }
// rest of program that uses valid value
```

In this case, if no exception is thrown, the program bypasses both catch blocks. If a string is thrown, the first catch block executes and the second catch block is bypassed. If an integer is thrown, the first catch block is bypassed and the second catch block executes.

If an exception is thrown, and no catch block matches the type of the thrown parameter, then the program terminates.

In the following steps, you will add a second `throw` condition to the overloaded operator >> for the Fraction class. This throw will occur when the user enters a negative denominator. Because a fraction such as 4/-5 would look awkward when displayed, the throw will reverse the sign for the numerator, giving -4/5.

1 Open the **FRAC10.CPP** file that contains the Fraction class definition.

2 After the if statement in the operator >> function that checks for a 0 denominator, add an if statement that checks for a negative denominator.

```
if(frac.denominator < 0)
  throw(frac.denominator);
```

The operator >> function now throws two separate types of exception: a character string and an integer.

3   Add a function prototype to the public section of the declarations for the Fraction class. The function will switch the sign of a numerator.

```
void switchSigns(void);
```

4   To the implementation section of the Fraction class definition, add the following function:

```
void Fraction::switchSigns(void)
  {
    Fraction::numerator = -Fraction::numerator;
    Fraction::denominator = -Fraction::denominator;
  }
```

5   Save the **FRAC10.CPP** file.

6   Open the **THROW.CPP** program file and add a new `catch` block immediately after the existing one.

```
catch(const int neg)
  {
    aFrac.switchSigns();
  }
```

> **tip**
> ....
> Depending on your compiler, you may receive a warning that the variable neg is unreferenced. Because the value of neg is not intended to be used, you may safely ignore the warning.

7   Run the program several times, confirming that each throw is caught correctly. When a 0 denominator is entered, it is converted to 1; when a negative denominator is entered, the signs of the numerator and denominator are reversed.

8   Save the program.

S U M M A R Y

- Unexpected errors that occur during the run of a program are called exceptions.
- The object-oriented techniques to manage unexpected errors comprise the group of methods known as exception handling.
- Probably the most popular error-handling method has been to terminate the program using an exit() call.
- A function can return a value based on an error. This is limiting because a function can return only one value. It can't return anything other than the value indicating error status, and any error code returned by a function must be of the same type as the function's return type.
- C++'s exception-handling techniques include sending an exception message from the place where a problem occurs to another place that will handle the problem.

- The general principle underlying object-oriented error handling is that a called function should check for errors but should not be required to handle any errors detected. The calling function should handle the errors instead.
- When an object-oriented program detects an error within a function, the function is said to throw an exception.
- A throw resembles a return statement in a function, except that the execution of the program does not continue at the location from which the function was called.
- You throw an exception by using the keyword `throw` followed by any C++ object.
- A function can make more than one throw.
- In addition to making multiple throws, a function can make throws of different types.
- When a function may cause an exception and therefore includes a throw statement for errors, the call to the potentially offending function should be placed within a try block.
- A try block consists of the keyword try, an opening curly bracket, the code to be tried, and a closing curly bracket.
- To handle a thrown object, you include one or more catch blocks in your program immediately after a try block.
- A catch block consists of the keyword catch, a one-entry argument list in parentheses, an opening curly bracket, one or more statements describing the exception action to be taken, and a closing curly bracket.
- When a function called from a try block does not throw an exception, the program bypasses any catch blocks.
- When a function throws more than one type of exception, then multiple catch blocks can be written.
- If an exception is thrown and no catch block matches the type of the thrown parameter, the program terminates.

Q U E S T I O N S

1. The generic name used for unexpected errors that occur during the execution of a program is _____.
   a. infractions
   b. exceptions
   c. deviations
   d. anomalies

2. Before object-oriented exception handling was practiced, _____.
   a. no run-time errors occurred
   b. programmers could not deal with run-time errors
   c. the most popular error-handling method was to terminate the program
   d. the most popular error-handling method was to throw an exception

3. One drawback to returning an error code from a function is _____.
   a. functions cannot return error codes
   b. error codes must be integers, and some functions can't return an integer
   c. a function can return only one value, so it can return only the error code
   d. a function that returns an error code will identify all returns as errors

4. Another drawback to returning an error code from a function is that any error code returned by the function _____.
   a. must be of the same type as return type of the function
   b. must not be a character
   c. cannot be checked in a main() program
   d. can have multiple meanings

5. In object-oriented terms, an exception may be considered a(n) _____.
   a. child
   b. encapsulation
   c. message
   d. scalar type

6. The general principle underlying object-oriented error handling is that a called function should _____.
   a. neither check for, nor handle errors
   b. check for errors but not be required to handle any detected
   c. handle errors, but not check for them
   d. both check for and handle errors

7. When an object-oriented program detects an error within a function, the function _____.
   a. throws an exception
   b. throws a fit
   c. catches a message
   d. catches an exception

8. The difference between a return and a throw is that _____.
   a. with a throw, no value can be sent
   b. with a return, no value can be sent
   c. with a throw, execution takes place at the location from which the function was called
   d. with a return, execution takes place at the location from which the function was called

9. You can throw _____.
   a. a scalar variable
   b. a constant
   c. a programmer-defined class object
   d. any of these

10. A function can make _____.
    a. one throw
    b. one throw of each scalar type
    c. one throw of each programmer-defined type
    d. as many throws of as many types as necessary

11. When a function includes a throw statement for errors, the call to the potentially offending function should be placed within a _____ block.
    a. throw
    b. try
    c. catch
    d. scope

12. Catch blocks must _____.
    a. appear in every object-oriented program
    b. appear within try blocks
    c. appear immediately after throw statements
    d. appear immediately after try blocks

13. Within parentheses, catch blocks can have _____.
    a. no arguments
    b. one argument
    c. two arguments
    d. as many arguments as necessary

14. If two types of errors may be thrown, you should write _____.
   a. no catch blocks
   b. one catch block with two arguments
   c. two catch blocks—one with an argument, and one without
   d. two catch blocks with one argument each

15. If no exception is thrown, _____.
   a. a catch block will cause an error
   b. the first catch block coded will execute
   c. the last catch block coded will execute
   d. any catch blocks coded will be bypassed

16. If an exception is thrown and no catch block matches the type of the thrown parameter, then _____.
   a. the program terminates
   b. the first catch block is executed
   c. the last catch block is executed
   d. the program proceeds with the code following the catch blocks

E X E R C I S E S

1. Create a class named RealEstate that has data members to hold the price of a house, the number of bedrooms, and the number of baths. Member functions include overloaded data entry and display functions. Write a main( ) program that instantiates a RealEstate object, allows the user to enter data, and displays the data members entered. The user should receive an appropriate error message if negative values are entered for any of the data members.

2. Modify the program created in Exercise 1 so that if negative values are entered for any of the data members of a RealEstate object, they are replaced with a zero.

3. Create an Inventory class with data members for stock number, quantity, and price, and overloaded data entry and output functions. The data entry functions should throw:
   ■ an error message, if the stock number is negative or higher than 999
   ■ the quantity, if it is less than 0
   ■ an error message, if the price is negative
   ■ the price, if it is over 100.00

LESSON B
objectives

In this lesson you will learn:

■ How to throw objects
■ How to use the default handler
■ About exception specifications
■ How to handle constructor failure

Advanced Exceptions

tip

● ● ● ● ● ● ● ● ● ● ● ● ● ● ●

▶ Programmers often give names that begin with a lowercase x (for exception) to classes that are created specifically to handle exceptions.

Throwing Objects

Just as simple variables such as doubles, integers, and strings can be thrown via exception-handling techniques, so can programmer-defined class objects. This approach is particularly useful in two types of situations:

■ If a class object such as an Employee, Item, or Fraction contains errors, you may want to throw the entire object, rather than just one data member.
■ Whenever two or more values must be thrown, you can encapsulate them into a class object so that they can be thrown together.

You can create a class that represents the actual exception. For instance, you might create a class that contains bad data and a message concerning that data. The class is instantiated only when an exception occurs.

For example, if a class is defined to hold Employee objects as follows, then the member function getData() can be designed to throw the Employee object if either the idNum or the salary is less than or equal to 0.

tip

• • • • • • • • • • • • • • • • •

▶ When creating a class to
hold an exception, make
sure that the instantiation
of your exception class
does not cause the same
problem as the original
error did. For example, if
the original error was
caused by insufficient
memory, it's probably a
poor idea to have the
exception class constructor
allocate more memory.

```cpp
class Employee
  {
    private:
      int idNum;
      double salary;
    public:
      void getData(const int id, const double sal);
      void showData(void);
  };
void Employee::getData(const int id, const double sal)
  {
    Employee::idNum = id;
    Employee::salary=sal;
    if (Employee::idNum <= 0  || Employee::salary <= 0.0)
      throw(*this);
    return;
  }
void Employee::showData(void)
  {
    cout<<"Employee: "<<Employee::idNum
      <<" Salary "<<Employee::salary<<endl;
  }
```

A main() program could then try the getData() function and catch any error:

```cpp
void main()
  {
    Employee Laura;
    try
      {
        Laura.getData(277, -10.00);
      }
    catch(Employee emp)
      {
        cout<<"Invalid data for ";
        emp.showData();
      }
  }
```

The fraction operator>> function currently throws a message when the denominator is 0. In the following steps, you will change it to throw a Fraction object.

1 Open the **FRAC10.CPP** fraction class file.

2 Change the statement that currently throws the message "Denominator cannot be zero!!" when the denominator is 0 to the following:

```
if(frac.denominator == 0)
    throw(frac);
```

3 Save the file.

4 Write a new main() program to test throwing the object. Open a new file.

5 Enter the following program:

```
#include<iostream.h>
#include"frac10.cpp"
void main()
  {
    Fraction aFrac;
    try
      {
        cin>>aFrac;
      }
    catch(Fraction badFrac)
      {
        cout<<"Invalid fraction."<<endl;
        badFrac.forceDenom();  // forces denominator to 1
        aFrac = badFrac;  // aFrac now has a valid denominator
      }
    cout<<aFrac;
  }
```

6 Compile and test the program. When you enter a valid fraction, it simply displays that value. When you enter a fraction with a zero denominator, you receive the error message, followed by a valid fraction with the numerator you entered and a denominator of 1.

7 Save the file as **CATCH.CPP.**

If you need to throw both a base and a derived class from the same function and then carry out different operations when they are caught, code the catch for the derived object first. The derived object throw will match the base class catch if it encounters that catch first.

The Default Handler

If any object is thrown with a `throw` statement, then a subsequent catch block has a usable match if

- the type of the thrown object and the type of the catch argument are identical (for example, int and int)
- the catch argument contains the const qualifier, a reference qualifier, or both (for example, int can be caught by const int, int&, or const int&)
- the catch argument type is a parent class of the thrown argument

You can code a **default exception handler** by creating a catch block with an ellipsis (...) as its argument. If you use a default catch block, it must be the last catch block listed after a try. The default catch block will catch any type of thrown object that has not been caught by an earlier catch block.

Exception Specifications

You may explicitly indicate the exceptions that a function may possibly throw by writing an **exception specification** in the function header immediately after the list of function arguments. Simply write the keyword `throw` followed by a list of argument types in parentheses. For example, for a dataEntry() function that might throw a character pointer or an integer, you could code the function header as follows:

```
int dataEntry(void) throw(char*, int)
```

Besides throwing an Employee, the function `int dataEntry(void) throw(Employee)` could also throw any object derived from the Employee class.

A dataEntry() function that might throw an Employee object is coded as follows:

```
int dataEntry(void) throw(Employee)
```

A function with empty parentheses following `throw` will not throw any exceptions:

```
int dataEntry(void) throw()
```

Be careful when writing an exception specification using a function template because any type may eventually be instantiated. You can't predict what type the function may throw.

Of course, a function that does not refer to `throw` works just like all the other functions you have written to this point: it may throw an object of any type, or it may not throw anything. In other words, if you do not specify the exception, then any type exception might be thrown.

```
int dataEntry(void)   // nothing about a throw is mentioned
                      // anything may be thrown
```

Creating an exception specification provides documentation for later users of the function by indicating what types of errors may possibly be thrown. The user can then plan appropriate catch blocks. If a function throws an error whose type was not listed in its exception specification, then it will produce a run-time error.

In the following steps, you will add exception specifications to the operator>> function in the Fraction class.

1 Open the **FRAC10.CPP** file, which contains the Fraction class definition.
2 Add the exception specifications to the operator>> function prototype and header. The function currently may throw an integer or a Fraction object, so the new prototype is

```
friend istream& operator>>(istream &in, Fraction &frac) throw(int, Fraction);
```

and the new header is

```
istream& operator>>(istream &in, Fraction &frac) throw(int, Fraction);
```

3 Save the file.
4 Open the **CATCH.CPP** file and run the program. It should run as before.

Constructor Exceptions

Recall that you can use the operator new to allocate new memory. A common place to allocate memory is within a constructor. For example, a program used in a music store might contain a CD class that holds information about each compact disk for sale:

```
class CD
  {
    private:
      char *title;
      double price;
    public:
      CD(const char *name,const double p);//constructor
      ~CD();  // destructor
      void showCD(void);
  };
```

Because titles of CDs vary widely in length, you might want to allocate memory dynamically when you construct a CD object.

```
CD::CD(const char *name = '\0',const double p = 0.0)
  {
    CD::title = new char[strlen(name)+1];
      // include string.h to use strlen function
      // this allocates enough memory to hold the title,
      // plus one more character for a NULL
    strcpy(CD::title,name);      // copy name to CD title
    CD::price = p;
  }
```

There may not be enough memory for the new title, however.

```
CD::CD(const char name = '\0',const double p = 0.0)  throw(char*)
  {
    CD::title = new char[strlen(name)+1];
      // include string.h to use strlen function
      // this allocates enough memory to hold the title,
      // plus one more character for a NULL
    if(CD::title ==0)    // if title is NULL or not assigned
      throw("Not enough memory!");
    strcpy(CD::title,name);      // copy name to CD title
    CD::price = p;
  }
```

When a CD object is instantiated, the instantiation can be placed within a try block so that the error can be handled:

```
try
  {
    CD oneDiskOfMine("Bridge Over Troubled Waters",8.99);
  }
catch (const char *message)
  {
    cout<<message<<endl;
  }
// rest of program
```

As an out-of-memory condition would cause a problem in any application, the creators of C++ have created an out-of-memory exception handler for you. The **set_new_handler()** function is defined in the new.h library. You use set_new_handler by creating a function to handle the error, then passing a pointer to that function to the set_new_handler() function. The function you create to handle the error must be type void. Once you have created your error-handling function and your main() program, you must call set_new_handler within your program.

```
set_new_handler(nameOfYourFunction);
```

Assume, for example, that you create a program that attempts to create 30,001 Fraction class objects. Further assume that only enough memory is available for 30,000 Fraction objects. If you want to exit the program when memory runs out, you can code the following:

```
#include<iostream.h>  // for input and output

#include<new.h> // for set_new_handler

#include<stdlib.h> // for exit()

#include"frac10.cpp" // for the Fraction class

extern void (*set_new_handler(void(*outOfMemory) () )) ();

void outOfMemory()

  {

    cout<<"Out of memory!!"<<endl;

    exit(1);

  }
```

A subsequent main() program would contain two pointers. The first points to the 30,000 newly created Fractions. The second pointer points to one more newly created Fraction:

```
void main()

  {

    set_new_handler(outOfMemory);

    Fraction *pt1 = new Fraction [30000];

    cout<<"First allocation of 30000 is successful";

    Fraction *pt2 = new Fraction;

    cout<<"Second allocation of one more is successful"<<endl;

  }
```

The output from this program is shown in Figure 10-3. The first 30,000 Fraction objects are successfully allocated. The second success message never prints.

```
First allocation of 30000 is successful
Out of memory!!
```

Figure 10-3: Unsuccessful memory allocation

You can attempt to create your own out-of-memory situation.

1 Open a new file.

2 Create a class definition for a very large class. This class has no purpose other than using a lot of memory.

```cpp
#include<iostream.h>
#include<new.h>
#include<stdlib.h>
class BigClass
  {
    private:
      double someStuff[3000];
      double someMoreStuff[3000];
  };
```

3 Write the noMem() function:

```cpp
void noMem()
  {
    cout<<"No more memory"<<endl;
    exit(1);
  }
```

4 Create a main() that attempts to instantiate many instances of this class.

```
void main()
  {
    set_new_handler(noMem);
    BigClass *pt1 = new BigClass[30];
    cout<<"First allocation works"<<endl;
    BigClass *pt2 = new BigClass[30000];
    cout<<"Second allocation works"<<endl;
  }
```

You may receive a warning that pt1 and pt2 are assigned values that are never used. Such warnings may be ignored.

5   Compile the program, and then run it. Depending on your computer, you may receive two, one, or no success messages. If you do not receive any success messages but instead receive an out of memory error, lower the numbers in the new BigClass array allocation statements until the first allocation succeeds. If you receive two success messages, try adding a third or fourth pointer to new arrays of BigClass items until memory allocation fails.

6   Save the program as **MEMORY.CPP**.

SUMMARY

■ Programmer-defined class objects can be thrown using exception-handling techniques.

■ You can create a class that represents the actual exception and is instantiated only when an exception occurs.

■ If any object is thrown with a throw statement, then a subsequent catch block has a usable match if the types of the thrown object and the catch argument are identical; the catch argument contains the const qualifier, a reference qualifier, or both; or the catch argument type is a parent class of the thrown argument.

■ You can code a default exception handler by creating a catch block with an ellipsis (...) as its argument.

■ A default catch block must be the last catch block listed after a try.

■ The default catch block will catch any type of thrown object that has not been caught by an earlier catch block.

■ You may explicitly indicate the exceptions that a function may throw by including an exception specification in the function header immediately after the list of function arguments.

■ An exception specification includes the keyword throw in the function header, followed by a list of argument types in parentheses.

■ A function that does not refer to throw may throw an object of any type or nothing at all.

■ Creating an exception specification documents the working of a function by indicating what types of errors may possibly be thrown. Later users can then plan for appropriate catch blocks.

■ If a function throws an error whose type was not listed in its exception specification, then it will produce a run-time error.

■ A common place to allocate memory is within a constructor. You can instantiate an object in a try block so that a potential error can be handled.

- As an out-of-memory condition would cause a problem in any application, the creators of C++ have created an out-of-memory exception handler called set_new_handler.
- You use set_new_handler by creating a function to handle the error, then passing a pointer to that function to the set_new_handler() function.

QUESTIONS

1. In a C++ program, which of the following can be thrown?
   a. scalar variables
   b. programmer-defined objects
   c. both (a) and (b)
   d. neither (a) nor (b)

2. If an integer object is thrown with a `throw` statement, then a subsequent catch block has a usable match if the type of the catch argument is _____.
   a. int
   b. double
   c. either (a) or (b)
   d. neither (a) nor (b)

3. If an integer object is thrown with a `throw` statement, then a subsequent catch block has a usable match if the type of the catch argument is _____.
   a. const int &
   b. int &
   c. either (a) or (b)
   d. neither (a) nor (b)

4. If a class object is thrown with a `throw` statement, then a subsequent catch block has a usable match if the type of the catch argument is _____.
   a. a parent class of the thrown class
   b. a child class of the thrown class
   c. either (a) or (b)
   d. neither (a) nor (b)

5. You can code a default exception handler by creating a catch block _____.
   a. with no arguments
   b. with a void argument
   c. with an ellipsis as its argument
   d. with an argument identical to that thrown

6. A default exception block must be placed _____.
   a. first among the catch blocks
   b. last among the catch blocks
   c. globally, at the top of the file
   d. at the end of all code in the program

7. A default catch block catches _____.
   a. all thrown objects
   b. no thrown objects
   c. any thrown object that has not been caught by an earlier catch block
   d. all thrown objects that have been caught by an earlier catch block

8. You may explicitly indicate the exceptions that a function may throw by writing an exception _____.
   a. specification
   b. header
   c. template
   d. statement

9. Any exception specification appears in _____.
   a. the main() program
   b. a catch block
   c. a try block
   d. the header of a function that throws an exception

10. An exception specification begins with the keyword _____.
   a. exception
   b. try
   c. throw
   d. catch

11. When the function `void someFunction(int x) throw(char)` is executed, _____.
   a. it will throw nothing
   b. it may throw an integer
   c. it may throw a character
   d. it may not throw anything

12. When the function `int someFunction(char c) throw()` is executed, _____.
   a. it can throw anything
   b. it may throw an integer
   c. it may throw a character
   d. it may not throw anything

13. When the function `char someFunction(int x)` is executed, _____.
   a. it will throw nothing
   b. it will throw an integer
   c. it will throw a character
   d. it may or may not throw anything

14. The primary purpose of exception specification is _____.
   a. documentation
   b. object-orientedness
   c. structure
   d. reduction of code

15. The C++ operator used to allocate memory is _____.
   a. mem
   b. allocate
   c. new
   d. create

16. A predefined function that may be used to handle memory allocation errors is _____.
   a. handle_error
   b. set_new_handler
   c. new_fix
   d. memory_error

E X E R C I S E S

debugging ▶

1. Create a class named Student that holds a student ID and a grade point average, and contains functions for construction and display. The constructor function should throw a Student object if the ID is larger than 4 digits or the grade point average is negative or greater than 4.0. Write a main( ) program to try to instantiate a student and catch any error.

2. Add a first, last, and middle name to the Student class created in Exercise 1. Use a character pointer for each name, and allocate new memory based on the size of each of the student's three names. In a main ( ) demonstration program, include code to handle any memory allocation errors that occur.

3. Each of the following files in the TUT10 folder has syntax and/or logical errors. Determine the problem in each case, and fix the program.
   a. DBUG10-1.CPP
   b. DBUG10-2.CPP
   c. DBUG10-3.CPP
   d. DBUG10-4.CPP

Index

F

I

P